Stephen Vincent Benét

Stephen Vincent Benét

Essays on His Life and Work

Edited by DAVID GARRETT IZZO
and LINCOLN KONKLE

McFarland & Company, Inc., Publishers
Jefferson, North Carolina, and London

Frontispiece: Stephen Vincent Benét circa 1930.

Library of Congress Cataloguing-in-Publication Data

Stephen Vincent Benét : essays on his life and work / edited by David Garrett Izzo and Lincoln Konkle.
    p.   cm.
    Includes index.
    "Stephen Vincent Benét bibliography": p.

    ISBN 0-7864-1364-6 (softcover : 50# alkaline paper) ∞

    1. Benét, Stephen Vincent, 1898–1943. 2. Authors, American—20th century—Biography. I. Benét, Stephen Vincent, 1898–1943.
II. Izzo, David Garrett. III. Konkle, Lincoln.

PS3503.E5325 Z75 2003
818'.5209—dc21
[B]
                            2002035857

British Library cataloguing data are available

On the cover: Stephen Vincent Benét. Portrait by Ruth Bobbs, Paris, 1926.

Manufactured in the United States of America

McFarland & Company, Inc., Publishers
  Box 611, Jefferson, North Carolina 28640
   www.mcfarlandpub.com

To Carol Ann Corrody (my Rosemary),
and Thomas Carr Benét, a faithful son.
—DGI

For Bridget, Matt, and Brooke,
who, along with God, are the light in my life.
—LK

Acknowledgments

I thank Michael Perry, who saw the drama in Benét's life; my T. Wilder expert and great friend, Martin Blank; and our contributors, who have allowed us the honor of being their editors.

—DGI

I want to thank Karissa D'Ambrosio and Bridget Konkle for research assistance and Paulette LaBar and Tanja Howard for typing or formatting of some manuscripts.

—LK

Contents

To strive at last, against an alien proof
And by the changes of an alien moon,
To build again that blue, American roof
Over a half-forgotten battle-tune.

—Invocation to
John Brown's Body

Introduction

David Garrett Izzo and Lincoln Konkle

Though his work is not widely known today, when Stephen Vincent Benét died in 1943 at the age of 44, the loss was felt by an entire country to whom Benét was a national hero. Author of the epic poem *John Brown's Body* and the short story "The Devil and Daniel Webster," he was one of the best known poets of the first half of the twentieth century and the only American poet who was read with enthusiastic admiration by a national audience. As a writer of fiction he had an even larger audience with his tales that presciently fused fantasy, myths, and the American past into a versatile repertoire of themes and genres. What might he have accomplished had he lived for a normal span of another thirty years that could have been the fulfillment of an artistic maturity? Still, he did more than enough in the time given him.

July 22, 1998, was the one hundredth anniversary of Benét's birth, and years of teaching Benét to the widest range of high school, college, and adult readers verify that his writing endures with the only audience that matters—the people who actually read him. Yet reading or teaching Benét was often no easy feat, since until the 1999 Penguin anthology, all his work except for *John Brown's Body* was out of print.

Being a fan of Benét sometimes feels like being a member of a secret cult. Even Benét's son, Tom, 73, wrote of his frustration in a letter after he'd read an article written about his father: "It is always pleasing, too, to hear from someone who is an enthusiast. It has been depressing in recent years to meet so many people who don't know my father's stories and poems.... I particularly like the fact that you [Izzo] emphasize the effect that my father's work had on a later, post–Second World War generation—from the Kennedys to country music to the sci-fi world, even though he died in 1943" (letter to Izzo, 4 October 1997).

1

Exactly what effect was that, both before and after World War II? Margaret Mitchell wrote *Gone with the Wind*, in part, because she loved *John Brown's Body*; later Jackie Kennedy said that JFK also loved it. Benét's short story "The Sobbin' Women," a parody of the Sabine women, became the basis for the film musical *Seven Brides for Seven Brothers* (1954). Charlie Daniels' hit record about a fiddle-playing devil who meets his match was inspired mainly by Benét's poem "The Mountain Whippoorwill" with a hint of "The Devil and Daniel Webster" as well. Dee Brown's book *Bury My Heart at Wounded Knee*, which records the tragic history of Native Americans, took its title from the last line of Benét's 1930 poem "American Names," in which the poem's speaker, while acknowledging his European heritage, declares America to be his true home even though it has faults that should be recognized:

> I shall not rest quiet in Montparnasse
> I shall not lie easy in Winchelsea.
> You may bury my body in Sussex grass
> You may bury my tongue at Champmedy,
> I shall not be there. I shall rise and pass.
> Bury my heart at Wounded Knee [*SWSVB* 368].

And whether or not one knows Benét's name, everyone knows the science-fiction genre he created with his 1937 story "By the Waters of Babylon." This story about a future world reduced to rubble and few survivors after an apocalyptic war first established traits of a sci-fi subgenre that has been continually imitated (*Science Fiction Encyclopedia* 66, 291).

"Babylon" is only one of many compact classics by Benét. How good are his short stories? A Hawthorne expert, Professor Nancy Bunge, once said to Izzo, "Don't ask me to compare anyone to Hawthorne"—but she has now read Benét and favorably compares him to Hawthorne in her essay in this book. Some of the other writers in this collection also started skeptically, not having read Benét, but have since joined the "secret club" of fans.

Why has Stephen Vincent Benét been in eclipse? For one thing, he had the decency to be decent. He was not involved in any scandals, salacious or otherwise; he was married once only, to Rosemary Carr, in a perfect marriage of mutual devotion that produced three loved children. He was an FDR New Deal liberal Democrat who didn't hesitate to take on the rich and defend the unemployed during the Depression. Benét said of his liberalism, "If you're a liberal, that means you're always out on a limb. It isn't very comfortable out on the limb, but then God never intended liberals to be comfortable. If he had, he'd have made them conservatives" (qtd. in Fenton 279). Indeed, Benét was a liberal. As was Archibald MacLeish, Yale, 1917, and Thornton Wilder, Benét's classmate, Yale, 1919. All three were friends who exemplified the liberal humanist as public activist and patriot. Their patriotism was not of the *My country, right or wrong* variety, but rather, *My country, let's get it right*—and that meant equally right for everybody. Benét wrote during the Depression, "It is horrible to see the nervous violence of the comfortable ones once they get the idea that one cent of their precious money is being touched.... What a sorry class of rich we have here—their only redeeming feature is their stupidity" (qtd. In Fenton 282).

Later, when fascism became a reality too ugly to be ignored, Benét and MacLeish engaged in what MacLeish called "Public Speech." This meant the artist should respond to the events of his time before those events prevented the artist from being able to respond. Benét wrote, "If the artist believes, I think he should state his belief.... He ought to think and think hard. For neither his freedom of speech nor his liberty of action will automatically preserve themselves. They are part of civilization and they will fail if it fails. And he has a responsibility to his own art and that is to make it great. I doubt if he can do so by blacking himself out" (*Letters* 378).

Benét didn't black himself out. After the war began, he went to work for the United States of America, writing radio scripts like *We Stand United* and *Listen to the People*, doing whatever he could to rally his fellow citizens. He never took a fee directly, asking that the money be given to the USO. He knew that writing for his country against the fascist threat might be held against him someday, and he wrote, "If what I am writing today will hurt my eventual reputation as a writer, very well, then let it" (Fenton 357). His country came first. If a country is not free, neither are its artists. Artistic integrity is a gift of freedom.

During his life and for a decade or more after, Benét was held in high esteem as a major American writer. His initial success was as a poet, as evidenced not only by the Pulitzer Prize for *John Brown's Body* and the posthumous Pulitzer for *Western Star*, but also by the prizes for individual poems, such as "King David." Subsequently, Benét evolved into a short story writer of high regard as well, winning three O. Henry prizes. Why did Benét fall out of "the canon"? It might be more accurate to consider whether Benét ever really belonged. A search of the *Modern Language Association International Bibliography* for works on Benét results in approximately a dozen articles published in scholarly journals.[1] Parry Stroud's comprehensive but thin 1962 volume in Twayne's United States Author Series, *Stephen Vincent Benét*, is the only book-length study. Charles Fenton published the only biography of Benét in 1958 and edited a collection of his letters in 1960. It appears unlikely that the academy ever appreciated Benét as much as magazine editors, publishing house editors, or the reading public did. In fact, it may well be that a cynical mistrust of his popularity disqualified Benét as a subject of academic literary criticism.

Inspired by centennial events in Bethlehem, Pennsylvania, Frank Keegan, in an editorial for the Easton (PA) *Express-Times*, addressed why Benét has been neglected by scholars. Keegan asks, if "the right brands him a liberal, why is he not embraced by the left? Because in a time when the radical chic of our academic left requires a sneering hostility against America, a primal self-loathing of our native land, Benét loves it unabashedly with all his being." Keegan calls for a revival of the idea that one can be an artist *and* a patriot—an idea that he says can be perpetuated by reading and teaching the works of Benét.

Stephen Vincent Benét was born in Bethlehem, Pennsylvania, to Colonel James Walker and Frances Neill Benét. Contrary to the contemporary stereotype of a military man, his father was an expert in the appreciation of poetry. Stephen was the youngest of three children. His brother, William Rose, and sister, Laura, also became poets and writers. Benét published his first book of verse, *Five Men and Pompey* (1915), at age seventeen; it featured dramatic monologues by classical Roman figures. A penchant for the dramatic became a Benét standard.

Benét attended Yale and was recognized as a rising star by such future literary luminaries as Thornton Wilder (his Yale classmate and friend), Malcolm Cowley, John Peale Bishop, and F. Scott Fitzgerald.[2] While at Yale Benét published two more volumes of verse: *Young Adventure* (1918) and *Heavens and Earth* (1920). Both feature youthful exuberance and sonorous lyrical fluidity in a manner more nineteenth century than twentieth. A strong influence on Benét's verse at this time was the poet Vachel Lindsay, whom Benét met twice at Yale. Lindsay was the first poet as performance artist and his recitals were electrifying theatrical events.

With a master's degree earned from Yale in 1921, Benét ventured to Paris like so many of his contemporaries whom Gertrude Stein dubbed "the Lost Generation." Unlike those expatriate writers and artists, Benét never lost his allegiance to America, but he did have to go to Paris to find something as dear: Rosemary Carr, his future wife, who was working there as a journalist for the *Chicago Tribune*. His courtship featured cleverly playful love poems, many of which were collected in *Tiger Joy* (1925). Stephen and Rosemary married in 1921; she became his muse and moral compass. They would have three children, and their marriage was the great love story behind the rest of his life and work.

Back in New York City, Benét set out to make a living as a writer. In 1922 he published the two long poems that marked the beginning of his poetic maturity: *The Ballad of William Sycamore*, appearing in the *New Republic*, and *King David*, in the *Nation*. These poems were a blend of style and substance that foreshadowed the landmark Civil War epic still to come.

In the 1920s, Benét struggled to earn money from his writing. Although the poems in *Tiger Joy* received critical praise and comparisons to Thomas Hardy, Benét turned to fiction and the theatre for an income. The theatrical venture was an utter failure; Benét cowrote with John Farrar, his friend from Yale, two plays, *Nerves* and *That Awful Mrs. Eaton*, that opened and closed almost simultaneously in September of 1924. Benét would not again attempt any form of dramatic writing until 1930 when he worked on the screenplay for the D. W. Griffith film *Abraham Lincoln*; in the late thirties he wrote two opera libretti.

Motivated by his determination to earn a living as a writer, Benét wrote four novels in five years: *The Beginning of Wisdom* (1921), *Young People's Pride* (1922), *Jean Huguenot* (1923), and *Spanish Bayonet* (1926). A fifth novel, *James Shore's Daughter*—and his best with a theme of an America corrupted by money—was published in 1934. Taking these five novels as a group, one can best characterize them as sentimental, sometimes melodramatic, and not quite up to the achievement of *John Brown's Body*.[3] In fact, one could argue that Benét's best novel *is John Brown's Body* and his second best novel *Western Star*, despite their being epic poems. The fictional characters and action Benét invents to help tell the story of America's colonialization and Civil War are superior to those in the novels in terms of realism and subtlety except perhaps for *James Shore's Daughter*, written after the Civil War epic. As Stroud says, "Benét's talents as a novelist did not develop at the same pace as his gift for poetry or his hard-won ability for short fiction. His intermittently interesting early novels show flashes of expertness; but their interest, chiefly biographical and historical, is limited to the student of Benét or of the 1920s" (81).

Nonetheless, his first novel, *The Beginning of Wisdom*, published by Holt in 1921, earned immediate recognition. John Peale Bishop praised it in a tripartite review in *Vanity Fair* titled "Three Brilliant Young Novelists (*The Beautiful and the Damned* by F. Scott Fitzgerald; *The Beginning of Wisdom* by Stephen Vincent Benét; *Three Soldiers* by John Dos Passos)":

> Stephen Vincent Benét has already published three volumes of verse, *Five Men and Pompey*, *Young Adventure*, and *Heavens and Earth*. If *The Beginning of Wisdom* is his first novel, it is certainly

not his last, for *Jean Huguenot* is already completed and a third
novel is in preparation—all this at twenty-three. *The Beginning of
Wisdom* is a picaresque novel of a young man who successively
encounters God, country and Yale.... [Benét] has so rare a skill
with color, so unlimited an invention of metaphor, such humorous delight ... so brave a fantasy...." [Bishop 231].

The novels show the influence of other American novelists on Benét.
Both *The Beginning of Wisdom* and *Young People's Pride*, though heavily
autobiographical, also resemble F. Scott Fitzgerald's early novels, especially
his first, *This Side of Paradise*.[4] Telling the stories of female American protagonists abroad in *Jean Huguenot* and *James Shore's Daughter*, Benét follows in the footsteps of Henry James. Benét may have been emulating
James Fenimore Cooper with *Spanish Bayonet*, a historical novel set in
colonial times. Finally, the episode of the incarceration and deportation
of striking miners belonging to the IWW, the strongest section of *The
Beginning of Wisdom*, may have been influenced by Stephen Crane, Frank
Norris, or Theodore Dreiser.[5] As with his poetry and short stories, Benét
employed a variety of American settings in his novels: Yale, Arizona, and
Hollywood in *The Beginning of Wisdom*; Manhattan, Long Island, and St.
Louis in *Young People's Pride*; the South and New England in *Jean
Huguenot*[6]; Florida and New York in *Spanish Bayonet*; and Manhattan and
Colorado in *James Shore's Daughter*. Though Benét could not serve in the
military due to his eyesight, World War I figures in all four of his contemporary novels, usually in the death of a friend or lover of the protagonist, or in a summational statement of the war's effect, such as the
following sentence from *The Beginning of Wisdom*: "Meanwhile the war
fell over the world like rain" (241). In addition to such flashes of a poetic
prose style, one can find moments of insight in the novels, as in this one
from *Jean Huguenot*: "She lay awake for a long while, but this time without terror, unless all thought is terror" (122); or the following from *James
Shore's Daughter*: "Then I found myself laughing at my own grandiosity
and the little man in all of us who shakes his fist at the skies" (250). Thus
did Benét leave his stamp upon the American novel, forced as he was to
write primarily for money, first through serialization and then book publication.[7]

Reading Benét's novels in their order of composition, rather than
their publication, one might have predicted good things for Benét as a novelist based upon the quality and potential evident in *The Beginning of Wisdom* and *Jean Huguenot*. However, *Young People's Pride*, written third but
published second, represents an unfortunate step backward from which

Benét as novelist did not recover until *James Shore's Daughter*.[8] Nevertheless, Benét's novels are of interest for how they relate to the rest of his *oeuvre* regarding the American theme and for their role in Benét's career. Had he lived longer, he might have returned to the novel with the benefit of more wisdom and a writing proficiency that *James Shore's Daughter* seemed to signify.

The turning point for Benét as poet—indeed for his career overall— was his winning a Guggenheim fellowship in 1926, which meant he would receive a stipend just to write and not have to worry about writing to support himself and his family. The Benéts returned to Paris where the grant money would stretch further. Benét spent the next two years researching and writing *John Brown's Body*.

John Brown's Body was perhaps the first truly American verse epic and certainly the first of the twentieth century. The fifteen thousand lines chronicle the five years of the Civil War with extended and well-defined portrayals of Brown, Lincoln, Lee, Davis, Grant, Jackson, and many more, as well as fictional creations exemplifying composites of slaves, farmers, soldiers, and their families. While this epic has the classic structure of Homer and Virgil, the story is unabashedly American.

The poem's release was highly anticipated. It made the front page of literary reviews and won the Pulitzer Prize for Poetry. *John Brown's Body* became a best seller, not just in the poetry category, but of all books of any type, and it has never been out of print. A major part of its appeal was that in dramatizing the Civil War Benét showed both the Northern and the Southern points of view, rather than casting them in the respective roles of heroes and villains. The success of *John Brown's Body* encouraged contemporaries to write their own poetic epics, novels in verse, and verse plays for the next twenty years, ranging from MacLeish's *Conquistador* (1931) to W. H. Auden's *The Age of Anxiety* (1947), also Pulitzer winners.

Financial success was brief as Benét lost almost all of his earnings to the stock market crash. After *John Brown's Body* Benét did not publish new verse again until collaborating with Rosemary on *American Songs* (1933), a collection of children's poems about American themes and personas. In 1933 he became editor of the prestigious Yale Younger Poets series (his successor was W. H. Auden), and many of his choices became poets of international standing, such as Margaret Walker, Norman Rosten, Muriel Rukeyser, and Jeremy Ingalls.

In 1936 he returned to writing adult verse with fury in *Burning City*. The Depression had motivated Benét to side with Franklin Roosevelt and against special interests. Poems such as "Ode to Walt Whitman" are written in declamatory and very modern free verse. Benét also voices early concern about fascism a year before the Spanish Civil War directed everyone's attention to the fascist threat. In more than one review of *Burning City* Benét was referred to as a "national poet" (Fenton 288).[9]

Although he was already respected and popular, when his story "The Devil and Daniel Webster" appeared in 1936, Benét became an influential public figure and a literary advocate for democracy. In 1940, the antifascist poem "Nightmare at Noon" was published in *Life* magazine and became a national sensation. Subsequently, Benét wrote radio scripts affirming the United States' war effort that were heard by millions of Americans every week. Having been in poor health for years, Benét, only forty-four, died in March 1943 from a heart attack.

Western Star, a planned verse epic about the settling of America, was not completed; nonetheless, the book-length opening sections were published posthumously and won Benét a second Pulitzer Prize in 1944. In *Western Star* Benét further chronicled the destiny of America. Like *John Brown's Body*, *Western Star* intermingles historical figures (for example, Columbus, William Bradford, John Smith) with fictional characters (early settlers from England who sailed west for fortune or freedom from religious persecution). Just as he alternated between North and South in *John Brown's Body*, in *Western Star* Benét alternates between Plymouth and Virginia. There are fewer historical characters here than in Benét's earlier epic and no central figure like John Brown to unify the poem, but both Fenton and Stroud praise *Western Star* for its realism and greater technical consistency if also less ambitious poetic form than *John Brown's Body*. Also as in his first great work, Benét affirms America, here in its "elusive godhead of national soul" (Stroud 146), but does not neglect to mention its original sins: breaking treaties with the Indians, slavery, persecution of the Quakers, and the Salem witch trials. As Fenton notes, taken together, *John Brown's Body* and *Western Star* constitute "a twinhood of American epic…, the *Iliad* and *Odyssey* of America" (344).

Finally, *Western Star*, with the rest of Benét's *oeuvre*, forms a metanarrative of American history. From the colonial period as exposition, dramatized in *Western Star* and *Spanish Bayonet*, to the rising action of pre–Civil War days, as developed in stories such as "Jacob and the Indians" and "The Devil and Daniel Webster"; from the turning point of the war in *John Brown's Body*, the denouement of the South in "The Die Hard" and *Jean Huguenot*, and the resumption of the westward progression of the frontier ("O'Halloran's Luck" and "The Sobbin' Women"), to the second act climax of World War I (*The Beginning of Wisdom*) and *komos* of the Roaring Twenties (*Young People's Pride*); from the subplot of the stock market crash and the Great Depression alluded to in *James Shore's Daughter*, to the third-act rising action of the threat of fascism and World War II in *Burning City* and the patriotic pieces for radio: the plot of American history is sung with jubilation informed by folk wisdom and humor as well as a cautionary note not to remain passive in responding to the enemies of democracy. It is a great story, and no other American writer had told it with such gusto and such diversity of modes as Benét.

From 1928 with the publication of *John Brown's Body* until his untimely passing in 1943, Stephen Vincent Benét was one of the most popular and widely read authors in America. The commercial success of *John Brown's Body* was unprecedented and propelled Benét into the forefront of literary recognition, a position he sustained with poetry, fiction, libretti, and radio scripts that tackled social issues such as the Great Depression, the rise of fascism, support for the Allied Forces at the outset of World War II, and then for the United States after Pearl Harbor.[10] In addition, Benét's short story "The Devil and Daniel Webster" appeared in the *Saturday Evening Post* in 1936 and became an American legend. (The actor Alec Baldwin recently directed an updated film version starring Anthony Hopkins as Webster.) If Benét's good friend Archibald MacLeish could be described as an American Stoic, then Stephen Vincent Benét was an American Romantic who wore his heart on his pen.

This volume reconsiders Benét for appreciation by discerning readers of poetry, fiction, and drama, as well as by scholars who have otherwise neglected Benét.

To this end there are essays both informal and formal. There is a reminiscence from Benét's son Thomas Carr Benét who remembers his father, mother, relatives, and friends of the Benét family. Patricia McAndrew uncovers through never-before-seen letters the endearing love story of "Stephen and Rosemary." Izzo then considers the writer's role in America. Unlike today, when most artists fear to appear more than apolitical in the public eye, the artist of the 1930s and 1940s could be a writer, humanist, public activist, and patriot. Benét, Archibald MacLeish, and Thornton Wilder were such writers. Laura Shea looks at Benét and some of his Yale classmates who also entered the world of theater: Philip Barry, Jed Harris, and Wilder again.

Next come articles that appraise Benét's art. Jared Lobdell examines the influence of Yale on the young Benét and Benét's historical verse. Gary Grieve-Carlson looks at *John Brown's Body* and how well it holds up as a history of the Civil War. Many of Benét's short stories also have historical contexts, and Nancy Bunge compares them to the works of another

American short fiction master, Nathaniel Hawthorne. Benét's most famous short story, "The Devil and Daniel Webster," had incarnations in theatre, opera and cinema, and Lincoln Konkle looks at how Benét met the challenges of rewriting his story for these diverse media. Science-fiction novelist Toby Johnson summarizes Benét's contributions to sci-fi and to fantasy. Finally, Izzo and Konkle cover Benét as a dramatist for the stage, film, and radio.

This volume's purpose is to reintroduce Stephen Vincent Benét as man and artist to new generations who can learn to appreciate his life and also his art for the viscerally appealing works they still are.

NOTES

1. Searching the *Modern Language Association International Bibliography* on CD-ROM, which indexes primarily scholarly journals, books, and dissertations from 1963 to the present, results in 24 hits for Benét. Of these, 10 are articles in scholarly journals, four are articles in books, four are dissertations, and the remaining six are foreign language publications (three), a memoir by Laura Benét, a critical edition of *John Brown's Body*, and a piece by Benét on writing. Furthermore, only half of the 24 hits are on Benét alone; the other 12 are on Benét and another author or a genre.

2. Fitzgerald even paid tribute to Benét's early notoriety when he referred to him in his first novel, *This Side of Paradise* (1920).

3. Especially the two written to be serialized in magazines, *Young People's Pride* and *Spanish Bayonet*, which are pure plot machines, the former farcical and the latter adventure, with almost no depth of characterization or any literary quality. *Young People's Pride* might have worked as a screwball comedy for the movies since its best scenes employ slapstick humor. Similarly, *Spanish Bayonet*'s cliffhanger-chapter endings and melodramatic characters might have entertained an undiscriminating movie audience. Its main appeal, as Stroud says, is its generic status as a "costume romance" (100).

4. In *Young People's Pride*, Benét alludes to Fitzgerald by having his protagonist observe a high society ball and say, "The beautiful and the damned" (quoted in Stroud 89). Stroud notes about *Young People's Pride*, "As in Fitzgerald's stories, the East appears as the glittering region of wealth and high culture" (87).

5. Interestingly, as the strikers march from the railroad car they were deported in, they shout "John Brown's body" (203).

6. Stroud suggests that in *Jean Huguenot* Benét anticipated Faulkner and his great theme of the decay and decadence of the South. Indeed, Benét's heroine, Jean, reads like a Caddy Compson sans siblings and parents. Also like Faulkner Benét depicts a lynching, but the incident is used only as a plot device, foiling the tryst of Jean and her first love, rather than as social commentary.

7. Fenton explains, "The primary influence on *Young People's Pride*, of course, was that of [his agent] Carl Brandt" (114). In other words, Brandt directed Benét to write formula fiction that he could sell to be published in slick magazines.

8. Fenton, Stroud, and Izzo all agree that Benét's best novel was his last, *James Shore's Daughter*. Konkle, however, prefers the literary texture of the third-person narration of *Jean Huguenot* [which Fenton admits entails "a complex characterization" (106)] over the first-person narration that runs toward the sentimental in *James Shore's Daughter*.

9. On the other hand, Morton Dauwen Zabel's review of *Burning City* in the magazine *Poetry* attacked Benét as an example of what Zabel called "bardic romantics" (see Stroud 38–45). It may have been this biting criticism that initiated the plunge of Benét's reputation among the American literati.

10. As Stroud says, "Benét's extraordinary ability to master one genre after another makes him one of the most versatile of American writers" (154).

Chronology of Benét's Life

1898   Born on July 22 in Bethlehem, Pa., the third child and second son of Captain James Walker Benét and Frances Neill Rose Benét. Laura and William are his brother and sister.

1899   Family moves to Watervliet, N.Y., Arsenal.

1904   Major Benét and family at Rock Island, Ill., Arsenal.

1905   Family moves to Benecia, Cal., Arsenal.
        Stephen attends military academy in San Rafael, Cal.

1911   Family moves to Augusta, Ga., Arsenal.

1911–15 Stephen attends coeducational academy in Augusta.

1915   First sale of a poem to the *New Republic*. Enters Yale. Publishes first volume of verse, *Five Men and Pompey*.
        Elected to editorial board of *Yale Literary Magazine*.

1918   Elected Chair of *Yale Literary Magazine*. After junior year at Yale enlists in the Army. Discharged due to poor eyesight. *Young Adventure* (verse) published. Works briefly for State Department in Washington.

1920   Graduates from Yale in June. Enters Yale graduate school in fall. Begins a novel in Henry Seidel Canby's writing class. Awarded M.A. from Yale and receives traveling fellowship; visits Paris; meets Rosemary Carr; completes first novel, *The Beginning of Wisdom*.

1921   Proposes to Rosemary; they marry in Chicago, then return to Europe.

1922   Back to New York City. *New Republic* publishes "The Ballad of William Sycamore." Second novel, *Young People's Pride*, published.

1923   Poem "King David" awarded *Nation*'s Poetry Prize. Third novel, *Jean Huguenot*, published.

1924   Birth of daughter, Stephanie Jane.

1925   Poem "The Mountain Whippoorwill" appears in *Century Magazine*. Volume of poems, *Tiger Joy*, published.

1926   *Spanish Bayonet*, novel, published. Awarded Guggenheim Fellowship to work on *John Brown's Body*. Benét and family live in Paris for duration. Son, Thomas Carr, born in Paris.

1927   Guggenheim Fellowship extended for six months.

1928   Benét's father dies. *John Brown's Body* published.

1929–30 Receives Pulitzer Prize for *John Brown's Body*. Returns to New York. Elected to National Institute of Arts and Letters. Goes to Hollywood to write screenplay for D. W. Griffith's film *Abraham Lincoln*.

1931   Daughter Rachel born.

1933   With Rosemary publishes *A Book of Americans*. Becomes editor of Yale Younger Poets series.

1934   Last novel, *James Shore's Daughter*, published.

1935   Regular reviewer for New York *Herald Tribune* and *Saturday Review of Literature*. First two "Nightmare" poems published in *New Yorker*. "Ode to Walt Whitman" in *SRL*. These poems begin a series by Benét that deals with the depression and the rise of Fascism in Europe.

1936   "Notes to be Left in a Cornerstone" (poem) appears in *New Yorker*. *Burning City*, a volume of verse in the mode of "public speech" addressing social and political issues, published. Story "The Devil and Daniel Webster" in *Saturday Evening Post* becomes a sensation and is awarded O. Henry Prize for best short story of the year.

1937   "Daniel Webster and the Sea Serpent" and "Johnny Pie and the Fool Killer" (stories) published; the latter reprinted as O. Henry Memorial Prize story. *Thirteen O' Clock* (volume of stories) published.

1938   "Into Egypt" and "Jacob and the Indians" (stories) appear in *Saturday Evening Post*. Elected to American Academy of Arts and Letters.

1939   Operetta of *The Devil and Daniel Webster* with music by Douglas Moore and libretto by Benét produced in New York. Benét hospitalized for nervous exhaustion caused by overwork. *Tales Before Midnight* (volume of stories) published.

1940   "Freedom's a Hard Bought Thing" receives O. Henry Prize for year's best short story. Radio speech "We Stand United" read by Raymond Massey at Carnegie Hall rally against fascism.

1941   "Listen to the People" (poetic radio script) published by *Life* magazine and read over national radio prior to address by President Roosevelt.

1942   *Selected Works* (2 volumes: prose, poetry) named Book of the Month Club selection. *A Child is Born, Dear Adolf, They Burned the Books* (radio scripts) performed. *All That Money Can Buy*, film version of "The Devil and Daniel Webster," released. Benét's "Prayer" read by Roosevelt at United Nations ceremonies.

1943   Dies of heart attack on 13 March in Rosemary's arms.

1944   Awarded Pulitzer Prize for verse, for *Western Star*.

Invocation

David Garrett Izzo

On 3 April 1998, when I was living in Chapel Hill, North Carolina, I attended an event in celebration of Margaret Walker, pioneering African-American poet (*For My People*) and novelist (*Jubilee*). She was very old and very frail. At the end of a daylong appreciation, she sat, having listened to much praise. She was quiet and tired, her shoulders a bit slumped, her head a bit southward with the chin tilted down and in as though she might sleep. Yet, her eyes were bravely open in respect for those who had organized this day—a special day, as it would be her last public appearance and poetry recital before she passed away a few months later.

When the final speaker's last words emerged, to be followed by applause, I guiltily approached the venerated senior citizen who needed rest more than she needed me asking her another question.

"Mrs. Walker."

She turned her eyes upward rather than her head to look at me.

"Mrs. Walker, I would like to ask you about Stephen Vincent Benét."

At his name, her enervation changed to energy; her shoulders arched up, the head now high, and she turned her whole body to face me. She told me that no one had mentioned his name to her in years. We talked a little more. Then her assistant reminded her (and me) that she needed her nap before her poetry recital that evening, which would also be followed by a discussion.

I arrived early to sit close. She transformed her frail self into a marvelous orator—warm, funny, vibrant. She finished with selections from her first volume of poems, *For My People*. The questions began. Mine was third: "Could you tell us how your career got started?" She replied,

I was twenty years old when I wrote *For My People*. [Later], when I was two years out of college, I carried it to *Poetry* magazine and [the editor] George Dillon liked it so much that he published it that fall. They paid me $14, which was the first money I had gotten for any poem, and I was very proud to have made $14. I had learned at Northwestern [University] about poetry and somewhat the Yale younger poets competition. I tried five years before I won the Yale younger poets competition. I tried when I was 21, 22, 23, right from one year to the other. Finally, they decided they wanted to publish it and they asked me for it in the year 1942 when I had *not* sent it in. Mr. Benét remembered the poem and he said the best way to know a good poem is the one you remember and he remembered "Delta" which is to me the best poem in the book. Everybody thinks "For My People" is the best poem, but "Delta" is a better poem. Stephen Vincent Benét was told, I guess, that they weren't going to publish a black woman and he was so disturbed by it he told them either they decided to publish me or no more from him, and they decided to publish me. [Spontaneous applause from the audience]

My book of poetry was the last book that [Benét] published. He had been editor of the series for ten years and that was the last one he judged. He died in '43 and they had to get someone else [W. H. Auden].

I went to see Benét once in his house on the upper 70s of New York [East side of Manhattan]. I was amazed to go in and see he had rooms full of books, nothing but books from the floor to ceiling, and he told me they had moved into that house so they could have a place to keep all their books.

I owe my whole career to Mr. Benét. He was a wonderful man.

Editor's note: The evening's program was recorded and her remarks transcribed.

LIFE, TIMES, PEOPLE

1. A Son Remembers

Thomas Carr Benét

This flesh was seeded from no foreign grain
But Pennsylvania and Kentucky wheat
And it has soaked in California rain
And five years tempered in New England sleet

That was my father's self-definition in the invocation he wrote to *John Brown's Body*—and it was all perfectly true. The son and grandson of erudite Army officers, he had, indeed, lived all over the country—in Bethlehem, Pennsylvania; Benicia, California; Watervliet, New York; Augusta, Georgia; Highlands, North Carolina—the names roll out as a roster of military stations and off-duty way points of a growing country as it entered the twentieth century.

It is also interesting that, in a brief curriculum vitae dashed off early in his career for his literary agent, Carl Brandt, my father said, "If I had to live in America permanently, would prefer California." This was the voice of a man just back from a number of years living in Paris expressing a gut sense of what might be the most agreeable life. [*Editor's note:* Tom Benét, perhaps in his father's stead, made San Francisco his home in 1949.]

Such a future was not to be. New York was the Mecca, in the thirties and forties, as it is now, of the commercial literary world—of publishing houses, radio stations, and, most particularly, of those now-forgotten magazines like the *Saturday Evening Post, Colliers,* and the *Delineator;* magazines that were read avidly by a public not yet tuned in to the siren song of television.

So we lived in New York, in a rented four-story brownstone typical of the Manhattan of the time—first at 220 East 69th Street between Third

19

Stephen Vincent Benét. Portrait by Ruth Bobbs, Paris, 1926.

and Second Avenues, and then, one loop around the corner, at 215 East 68th. It was a New York that has now pretty well devoured itself, as is the habit of the city. The entire block of brownstones—mostly rented and inhabited by middle-class Americans; doctors and lawyers and the like, and one struggling poet—was torn down long ago; 215 is now the address of a rather elegant apartment house. The fronting block on Third Avenue is now beetled over by an enormous Trump structure.

Rosemary Benét and Tom. Portrait by Ruth Bobbs, Paris, 1926.

The Second Avenue elevated train tracks were being torn down when we moved in during the 1930s, but the Third Avenue el continued to rumble and roar in the distance all during the time we lived in those roomy, hospitable brownstones. It was a sign of minor maturity when I was finally allowed to navigate my own way on foot to the Buckley School on 74th, and to cross Third Avenue with its massive iron el stanchions and swirling traffic. Once across the street—and heading toward Lexington Avenue—I

Stephen Vincent Benét and Thomas Carr Benét in Central Park, circa 1940.

would, occasionally, on winter mornings, be enveloped by steam emanating from pipes on the side of the New York Foundling Hospital. I'd stamp my knickerbockered legs and think of the sad, but warm, foundlings.

New York then was a city of neighborhoods. The people who ran the drugstore on the corner knew us all. The news vendor on the corner— there were at least seven or eight dailies at that time, including the *Herald-*

Tribune, the *Sun* and the *World-Telegram*—knew my father by sight and reputation. Mrs. Tavanne, who occupied a small apartment down on Second Avenue, was the official Tammany Hall representative. She was just "there" to be of help; to remind the indolent about what was politically important; to get out the vote. I remember she once offered to take us—myself and my sisters, Stephanie and Rachel—out to Central Park to see the new British monarch King George VI and Queen Elizabeth, as they rode by on their visit. But I think we were going anyway—so no obligation was incurred.

It was a New York where one generally ate dinner at home, in which our coal furnace was stoked every morning by a furnace man named Dominic, in which visitors often dropped by in the evening after dinner without prior notice. A favorite dropper-in was Basil Davenport, an editor of the Book-of-the-Month Club whose rich Kentucky/Yale/Oxford accents often resounded in the hallways as he spouted phrases in the original Greek from the Euripides he loved.

Ours was unmistakably the house of a literary man and his equally literary and supportive wife, my mother Rosemary Carr Benét. Books lined the walls. In my father's study—downstairs near the front door in one house, and on the top floor in the other—there were more books, on tables and chairs and spilling onto the carpet, and always stacks of the plain, yellow paper on which he made his first pencil drafts.

In line with this, probably the most notable family ritual when we were very young entailed my father reading aloud to us in the evening. My older sister, Stephanie, and I would have finished dinner, my parents were yet to have theirs, when the two of us would gather hard by my father's easy chair and he would launch into the current book. (Rachel, five years younger than I, would eventually become an individual and much favored audience of one as Steph and I turned to reading on our own.) The fare was high on adventure and fantasy. Tales of King Arthur and his pugnacious group went on and on. I remember my father wearying of the protracted individual sword duels, with their repeated "smotes" and cleavings and hackings. But it was not fair diluting the flow; we had to have every word.

Kipling—all of the Jungle Books and "Puck of Pook's Hill"—was very popular, as were the "Oz" books that had so far come out. A. Conan Doyle's "Brigadier Gerard" stories went over splendidly with me, although I think they had poor Stephanie yawning. Occasionally, there would be a general downer. We got deep into "The Rose and the Book," before it became clear that Thackeray's subtleties were beyond us—and produced sleep rather than sensible attention.

Poetry was part of it, too. My father once told me he'd give me a dollar if I would memorize Thomas Gray's "Elegy in a Country Churchyard." Such a fabulous amount of money was not to be missed—and those stately, sonorous iambs still echo in my mind.

My father was an omnivorous reader. Aside from the books on history—he always seemed in the middle of some study of the Massachusetts Bay Colony or a reminiscence of the Old South—and the articles and volumes he had to keep up with for various projects, he loved relaxing with the pulps of the time. *Black Mask*, pioneer of the new look in detective fiction of the era, was a regular presence in the house as was *Astounding* science-fiction magazine.

What was it like living with a poet and short-story writer working at the peak of his powers? I've thought about this many times since my father died (I was 15 at the time, really just beginning to get a sense of myself and the way the world worked) and my main recollection is of a kindly, gentle person, a benign and good-humored spirit who generally had something of a twinkle behind those wire-framed glasses. I was a shy and unsure little boy perhaps because of, rather than in spite of, a rather worldly background. I had had a devoted French governess, Françoise. But little "Tommy" didn't lack for parental support; he was cosseted to a certain degree, but also encouraged to do things on his own.

One summer, when I think I was about 10, we were occupying Henry Seidel Canby's[1] house in Killingworth, Connecticut, and my father would go into New Haven to pick up books at Yale's Sterling Library. I would trudge alongside him, lugging a tome or two myself, proud to be associated with this lively parent who was stopped so often as we crossed the campus by teachers and acquaintances who had known him during undergraduate days.

Yale was certainly important to him, and he regarded the institution with a warm loyalty. But he hardly fit in with the cookie-cutter image that many had of the neatly-dressed, conservative Yalie of the day. During the Hoover-Roosevelt election of the early thirties, we had "Torch Party" kerchiefs in the house, and in the little Lenox Hill kindergarten I went to, I was the only child in our class to cast a ballot for Norman Thomas.[2]

Once FDR was elected, however, SVB became a devoted supporter and even did some writing for him, contributing to the Freedom from Fear section of the Four Freedoms speech. His admiration of FDR is clearly reflected in a privately printed poem entitled "Tuesday, November 5th, 1940." It begins, "We remember, F.D.R. / We remember the bitter faces of the apple-sellers / And their red, cracked hands. We remember the grey, cold wind of '32 / When the jobs stopped, / and the merry-go-round broke down. And, finally, / Everything seemed to stop. The whole big works of America / Bogged down with a creeping panic / And nobody knew how to fix it...."[3]

But he was also far from being an unquestioning New Dealer. One of his close friends was an impressive— and staunchly Republican— lawyer named John Marshall Harlan, who was later to sit on the U.S. Supreme Court. My parents had many pals, too, among those who referred to FDR as "that man," and turned out to hiss him at the Trans-Lux newsreel theaters so popular then.

At this point, I'll try to call up a few people and places that may cast a little more light on the man and his time.

Rosemary Carr Benét with dramatist Philip Barry (late 1940s).

The Barrys: Phil Barry, the witty, elegant and fiery playwright [*Editor's Note:* See Shea in this volume], and his wife, Ellen, were great friends. I think my father had known Phil a little at Yale where they were both undergraduates at about the same time, but the bond grew into a close one as they shared creative and family experiences in New York. The relationship was an easy, often jocular one, with both men taking evident pleasure in each other's company. But they also supported one another during times of family misfortune (the Barrys had a daughter who died in infancy) and occasional poundings of critics.

One memory remains with me particularly. I had come down, stunned, from boarding school at the news of my father's sudden death on March 13, 1943, and on the day of my arrival, went over to Frank W. Campbell's then pretty dismal funeral parlor with my mother, Phil Barry and my father's friend and doctor, Dana W. Atchely. As we looked at the figure there, Phil leaned over and whispered in my ear: "Spirit departed, spirit departed." It was all he needed to say.

Stephen Vincent Benét (left) and Dick Myers, circa 1940.

Benét family friend Alice Lee Myers. Portrait by Czedekowski, circa 1926.

The Myerses: Dick and Alice Lee Myers from Chicago were also close. Alice Lee had been a friend of my mother's at the University of Chicago; they were both members of a ladies' group there known as the "Esoterics." When they each went to Paris after graduation, the connection deepened. My parents' early flirtation was fostered, so the family story went, when they both baby-sat for the Myers' newly arrived daughter, Fanny.

Dick Myers was a large, ebullient man with a truly invigorating warmth of spirit. In Paris, he was the representative for the *Ladies' Home Journal*; in New York he was a wine salesman. He was also a skilled musician and knew pretty much everybody in the cultural/social swim of the day. His letters, written in a direct, staccato style that would please today's "new" journalists, make for a vivid record of the mores and varied actors of those times. But, most of all, the generosity of his personality was a gift. As my father said: "I always feel better after seeing Dick."

Both the Myerses and the Barrys were part of the circle that swirled around the Gerald Murphys in Paris, the Riviera and New York. My parents knew and were fond of the Murphys but couldn't be considered part of the inner group, the Hemingway-Fitzgerald crowd that became so celebrated.[4]

After my father died, Gerald and Sara were certainly thoughtful about including my mother in their gatherings of old friends. When I was at Yale, my mother, perhaps concerned about certain rough edges, took me to dinner with Gerald, I think to have him check my manners and general sophistication. Just Gerald and the two of us. The occasion was a delight: good talk as well as an after-dinner brandy and a special cigar. With a smile, Gerald indicated to my mother that I was passable. Perhaps I received a gentlemanly "C."

The McVeys: Uncle Harry and Aunt Jo McVey were our Rebel connection. She was the sister of my mother's mother, Dr. Rachel H. Carr, and they lived in Richmond, Virginia, a world away, it seemed. Christmases were spent with them, and the overnight train trip taken several days before the holiday down to Richmond added to a sense of adventure in the occasion.

These relatives were very much of the South, and we basked in their hospitality and generous table: fried fish for breakfast; black-eyed peas (unheard of in the pinched North) with almost anything—enormous portions. There was considerable joshing about my "Yankee voice," and I always came home several pounds heavier. One summer, when my parents decided to stay in humid New York and work, my sister Stephanie and I spent a month with the McVeys at their cabin just south of Yorktown. Their daughter, cousin Margaret, was a games mistress at Sweet Briar College and wonderful with children. Driving out there, Uncle Harry gave us a partisan rundown on the Peninsular campaign battle sites—Seven Days, Seven Pines, etc.—through which we were passing. We came home to a cooling New York sunburned and happily relaxed.

Bill Benét: William Rose Benét, my "Uncle Bill," was tall and lanky, and as a well-known poet himself and an editor of the *Saturday Review* with a monthly column called the "Phoenix Nest," was very much a part

Tom Benét (standing) with (left to right) Stephen Vincent Benét's sister, Laura
Benét, mother, Frances Rose, and Tom's sisters, Stephanie and Rachel.

of the New York literary establishment.[5] He was a good deal older than
Stephen [twelve years], but the bond between brothers was strong. After
my father died, Uncle Bill used to take me, in benign, avuncular fashion,
around to art galleries to see his literary friends and to the theater. He had
a certain magnetism that attracted women. I knew him best when he was
happily married to his fourth wife, children's book author and illustrator
Marjorie Flack, and can recall poetry readings at their Greenwich Village
flat during which lady versifiers would fix glittering eyes on his imposing
frame as they declaimed their heartfelt stanzas.[6]

Since his first wife, Teresa Thompson, who died during the post–
World War I flu epidemic, was the sister of popular novelist Kathleen
Norris, he also became my connection to the wide-ranging Norris-
Thompson clan in the San Francisco Bay area. When I came out to work
for the *San Francisco Chronicle*, they cordially welcomed me as a cousin
even though my claim to such legitimacy was somewhat remote.[7]

Laura Benét: Aunt Laura was fated to be the prototypical "maiden
aunt" so prevalent—and accorded so little regard—in the post–Victorian
era. Absolutely devoted to her parents, she was a brimming repository of
family tales and myths, and often frankly boring to the children that we
were then with her endless and narrowly focussed stories of Benét doings.
But children aren't noted for their understanding. I discovered later in
my life, that here was a woman of rare independence and strength. The
family tales continued—now *my* children were the squirming listeners—

Tom Benét as editor at the *San Francisco Chronicle*, circa 1970. (Photograph by Bob Campbell.)

but I discovered a doughty, realistic lady who had carved out a life on terms that demanded respect.

   She lived alone, in Greenwich Village, at the Hotel Van Rensselaer and then at the Marlton. She supported herself, writing poetry and books for teens, like *The Boy Shelley*. She was ferocious in her refusal of financial assistance: "No, no, Tom, you need that for *your* family." The last time my wife, Joan, and I visited her hotel, it was clear that the neighborhood had gone downhill. There were a couple of burly transvestites in the lobby, and I had a sense some dope dealing was going on, too. But I also had the feeling that living anywhere else—most especially a nursing home—would kill her. This was *her* place; *her* part of the Village. The hotel's manager and the thuggish denizens of that patched and peeling lobby looked after "the little old lady." The unworldly "maiden aunt" had carved out a life very much on her own terms.[8]

Uncle Larry: Laurence Vincent Benét was one of the longer-lived Benéts; he died in 1948 at the age of 85, and he spent most of his long career as a director of the Hotchkiss company while living in France. He was something of an elegant boulevardier and a force in the American Chamber of Commerce in Paris. He and his wife, the former Margaret Cox of Washington, D.C., did considerable entertaining of the "gratin" at their apartment on the Avenue de Camoens overlooking the Trocadero.

The Hotchkiss company made a graceful motorcar and a handsome motorboat, but it also made a machine gun, and that line of endeavor led to a hostile piece by Westbrook Pegler[9] taking on the "grand, old man of the American Colony in Paris" as a merchant of death. The column cut to the quick. When interviewed on his return to the U.S., my white-goateed uncle remarked, "I suppose you will describe my slow, thin-lipped smile. Reporters always do. It would be much better to use the quotation, 'The mildest-mannered man that ever scuttled ship or cut a throat!' You might use that in a subhead."

No matter that he had been the major force behind founding of the American Ambulance Service, precursor to the American Field Service, during World War I.

Uncle Larry was the family genealogist and exceedingly proud of his Minorcan ancestry. The Benéts all came originally from that island to settle in Florida and eventually prospered in St. Augustine. Thanks to him, I have a riveting account of a naval action fought by Captain Don Pedro Benét in his launch *Our Lady of Carmen* against two British frigates off the coast of Cuba. Plagued by wet gunpowder, Don Pedro's vessel burned to the waterline after inflicting considerable damage on his adversaries. Nonetheless, his courage against odds earned unusual praise from the British naval officers.

Other Friends:—John Farrar and Christopher LaFarge. John Farrar, who after serving as editor for the *Bookman* became a partner in the publishing firm of Farrar & Rinehart and later gave his name to Farrar, Straus & Giroux, was an old friend from Yale days and a strong anchor. His counsel was sought, and listened to, by my father and our two families were easy companions.[10] "Kipper" LaFarge was a tall man of patrician demeanor who was also a successful, published poet.[11] He had a working farm in Rhode Island, called the River Farm, and I recall going there during the summer to learn how to handle a shotgun. The angular LaFarge had a resonant timbre to his voice, and I can recall the two men reading verse to each other in our New York house: first a set of booming, musical sounds (LaFarge), then a rejoinder, somewhat high-pitched and nasal (my father).

Places—Peacedale, Rhode Island: We spent a number of summers in the thirties at the Homestead in Peacedale, one of a number of houses connected to the Hazard family of Rhode Island. Other house names, as I remember it, were "Hollyhocks" and "The Acorns." My father's main friend, Thomas Pierrepont "Pier" Hazard, took his family just a couple of miles away to another enclave called "Crowfield" hard by the rocky Saunderstown shore, so the comfortable Homestead was ours for that period. And a congenial, artistic group it was. Douglas Moore, another Yale contemporary as well as a noted composer (he did the score for the operetta *The Devil and Daniel Webster*, and was to gain a considerable reputation for *The Ballad of Baby Doe*) was often there. Leonard Bacon, the scholar, poet and essayist, often occupied "The Acorns."[12] High-minded conversation was encouraged when the various children gathered together. Sometimes, a "topic" for table discourse was pronounced, but a descent into general silliness was not only understood— it was expected.

West Point: The grey-walled military academy just up the Hudson from New York had a special place in my father's heart. His grandfather General Stephen Vincent Benét had gone there and become chief of ordnance for the U.S. Army. His father, Colonel James Walker Benét, had also attended. The museum at West Point holds a rare working model of the Benét-Mercier machine gun as well as a pair of Napoleon's dueling pistols donated by Uncle Larry. We children, Stephanie, Rachel and I, were baptized somewhat late in life (I think I was about 10) at the West Point Chapel by the then corps chaplain, a Colonel Wheat, who was also an instructor in English at the academy. Our reward for not too much fidgeting was to watch the Corps of Cadets march in dazzling review that fall afternoon. [*Editor's Note:* See Fenton biography.]

Stonington: The house we purchased during the very early forties in this quiet town on the Connecticut coast was to be the first we would actually own, and the last my father would live in as a summer residence. There was, and is, considerable charm about the borough: old New England houses, handsome in the severity of their clean lines, face each other in quiet dignity along Main Street.

When we were first there, the resident population was a congenial mix of descendants of the early Yankee settlers, along with Azorean Portuguese-Americans and a few egghead summer types like ourselves—the director of the Metropolitan Museum, Francis Henry Taylor, lived across the street, and John Mason Brown, the drama critic, was a close friend.[13] Now many of the Portuguese have left, selling their houses in the booming real estate market; there are antique stores and restaurants where none existed— but an unquenchable charm remains.

Stephen Vincent Benét's father, James Walker Benét, West Point, class of 1880.

James McNeill Whistler lived in our house as a little boy.[14] My father added to its historic value when he wrote in a little attic aerie on the top floor. At that time, he was deeply into work on behalf of the developing war effort. We would listen to his "Letters to Adolf" programs on the radio; his poetic representation of an Independence Day drama appeared on the Fourth of July in *Life* magazine. We had come up to Stonington mostly through friendship with Griffith Bailey Coale, a Navy combat artist who lived next door and was out on assignment much of the time.[15] The actuality of the war suffused the period.

Stephen Benét's first love was his poetic work, and he longed to get back to completion of what was to be another epic of the American story, *Western Star*. But contributing to the American—and Allied—cause had to come first.

Who could have told in this edgy period that my father would have so little time to play his part?

Rosemary Carr: The so far unsung, and barely mentioned, person in this reminiscence is my mother. Actually, though, her presence and spirit infuse the whole thing. My father's success would have been much less, and hardly personally satisfying, without her. This only child of Scots-Irish

Tom Benét, 1998, at Stephen Vincent Benét centenary in Bethlehem, Pa.

antecedents gave him a grounding of family and love and practicality that was critical. From a bright, but disorganized and frivolous, Yale grad with a considerable talent in verse and storytelling he became a mature, balanced voice for the American muse. Rosemary competed in a rugged arena before she met him—as a reporter in the *Chicago Tribune*'s Paris office—so there was toughness and stability beneath an outwardly delicate manner. They were an affectionate couple who thoroughly enjoyed the work they did and the world they lived in. She was the rock on which his life depended. [Editor's Note: See McAndrew in this volume.]

Now what does this all add up to? I have tried to evoke the likeness of a man who died 55 years ago and the dim sides of memory's tunnel are elusive. What might he have accomplished had he lived just 25 more years—until the age of 68, say? Such speculation is idle, of course. We're lucky to have his work to read, and to sense his love of America in the words he wove so deftly. I'm lucky to remember the kindly, twinkling father, the supportive man concerned about a timid little boy. Perhaps best to wind up with his own words:

> All these you are, and each is partly you.
> And none is false, and none is wholly true.[16]

NOTES

1. Henry Seidel Canby (1878–19), literary critic, was a former Yale professor who taught creative writing, chairman of the editorial board of the Book-of-the-Month Club, a founding editor of the *Saturday Review of Literature*—along with my Uncle Bill—and an old friend of my father's.

2. Norman Thomas ran for president many times on the Socialist Party ticket.

3. *The Devil and Daniel Webster and Other Writings*, New York and London: Penguin, 1999, 373.

4. Gerald and Sara Murphy, wealthy expatriate patrons of the arts, opened their villa on the French Riviera to artists and writers, such as Ernest Hemingway, John Dos Passos, and F. Scott Fitzgerald who modeled Dick and Nicole Diver in *Tender is the Night* partly on the Murphys. Gerald (1888–1964), Yale Class of 1912, was himself a painter.

5. William Rose Benét (1886–1950) is perhaps best remembered for his *Reader's Encyclopedia* (1948) of world literature and the arts; however, he published several volumes of verse including *Merchants from Cathay* (1913), *Man Possessed* (1927), *Golden Fleece* (1935), *Day of Deliverance* (1944), and *The Spirit of the Scene* (1951). He was awarded the 1942 Pulitzer Prize in poetry for his verse autobiography, *The Dust Which Is God* (1941).

6. William Rose Benét was married four times. His first wife with whom he had three children, Teresa Frances Thompson, died in 1919. His second wife was Elinor Wylie [Hoyt] (1885–1928), a poet and novelist of some renown in the first half of the twentieth century. Her poetry publications include *Incidental Numbers* (1912), *Nets to Catch the Wind* (1921), and *Collected Poems of Elinor Wylie* (1932). Some of her prose publications are anthologized in *The Collected Prose of Elinor Wylie* (1933). After being widowed a second time, William Rose married Lora Baxter; they divorced in 1937. His fourth wife, Marjorie Flack, was born in 1897 and died in 1958.

7. Kathleen Norris (1880–1966) became known as "the grandmother of the American Sentimental novel." After marrying the novelist Charles Gilman Norris, brother of novelist Frank Norris, and moving to New York, she began publishing stories in magazines. All told, she published 88 books, 81 of which were novels. Most of her novels were first published serially in women's magazines and subsequently became bestsellers. Some of these include *Mother* (1911), *Certain People of Importance* (1922), and *My San Francisco* (1932). *The Best of Kathleen Norris* (1955) was an omnibus volume.

8. Laura Benét (1884–1979) wrote a series of biographies for young readers, such as *Young Edgar Allan Poe* (1941), *Thackeray* (1947), *Coleridge, Poet of Wild Enchantment* (1952). She also edited *Famous Poets for Young People* (1964) and *Famous Storytellers for Young People* (1968). Books of her own verse include *Fairy Bread* (1921), *Basket for a Fair* (1934), and *Is Morning Sure?* (1947). Her memoir *When William Rose, Stephen Vincent and I were Young* was published in 1976.

9. Westbrook Pegler (1894–1969), journalist, worked for the United Press, and wrote a column "Fair Enough" for the Scripps-Howard newspapers. In 1942 he moved his column, retitled "As Pegler Sees It," to the Hearst chain of newspapers. He won a Pulitzer Prize in 1941.

10. John Chipman Farrar (1896–1974), though known mostly as a publisher, also wrote poetry and drama. He published his verse in a number of volumes, such as *Songs for Parents* (1921), as well as his drama *Indoor and Outdoor Plays for Children* (1933). With Stephen Vincent Benét he wrote the plays *Nerve* and *That Awful Mrs. Eaton* (both produced 1924). Farrar was fictionalized as "Johnny Chipman" in Benét's first two novels, *The Beginning of Wisdom* (1921) and *Young People's Pride* (1922).

11. Christopher LaFarge (1897–1956) was a Renaissance man, having worked as an architect and a war correspondent, as well as painting water colors and publishing poetry and prose: *Hoxsie Sells his Acres* (1934, narrative poem), *Each to the Other* (1939, novel in verse), *Poems and Portraits* (1940), *The Wilsons* (1941, short stories), *East by Southwest* (1944, prose novel), *Mesa Verde* (1945, play in verse), *The Sudden Guest* (1946, prose novel), *All Sorts and Kinds* (1949, collection of short stories).

12. Leonard Bacon (1887–1954) began his career as an academic at the University of California but resigned after a decade to devote more time to writing. He won the Pulitzer Prize for poetry in 1941 for *Sunderland Capture* (1940). Other books of poetry include *Ulug Beg* (1923), *Animula Vagula* (1926), *The Legend of Quincibald* (1928), *The Furioso* (1932), *The Goose on the Capital* (1936), *Rhyme and Punishment* (1936), and *Day of Fire* (1943). His autobiography, *Semi-Centennial*, was published in 1939.

13. John Mason Brown (1900–1969), drama critic, war correspondent, essayist, lecturer, was most famous as the drama critic for *Theatre Arts Monthly,* the *New York Post*, the *New York World-Telegraph*, and the *Saturday Review*. His criticism is collected in such volumes as *The Modern Theatre in Revolt* (1929), *Two on the Aisle* (1938), *Broadway in Review* (1940), *Seeing Things* (1946), *Seeing More Things* (1948), and *As They Appear* (1952). He also wrote biographical sketches, such as *Through These Men* (1956).

14. James Abbott McNeill Whistler (1834–1903) is the famous American expatriate painter and etcher. He spent part of his boyhood in the Stonington house at 24 Main Street. His parents are buried in Stonington's Evergreen Cemetery, as are Stephen Vincent and Rosemary Carr Benét.

15. Griffith Bailey Coale (1890–1950) was an American painter who studied on the continent.

16. From the "Invocation" to *John Brown's Body*, Chicago: Elephant Paperbacks, Ivan H. Dee, publisher, 1990, 5.

2. Stephen and Rosemary: A Love Story

Patricia McAndrew

> The two things which were rooted in the core of his nature were the one, his love of his wife, so deeply satisfying to him that the wonder is that there was room in his affections for the rest of us, and the other his intense love of his country.
>
> *— Douglas Moore, speaking of Stephen Vincent Benét*

> It is impossible to speak of Rosemary without speaking of Stephen. They worked together as dedicated poets of the American dream.
>
> *— Mrs. John Mason Brown*

Stephen Vincent Benét was, at the time of his death in 1943, one of America's most famous and best-loved writers. His wife, Rosemary Carr Benét, was by then familiar in her own right as a poet, translator, and literary critic. Events surrounding the Benéts' meeting, courtship and mutually fulfilling marriage were well known in their lifetimes. Today they are all but forgotten, while the more flamboyant but less happy lives of their contemporaries, such as Ernest Hemingway, F. Scott Fitzgerald, and Sara and Gerald Murphy, remain endlessly fascinating to readers and writers alike. Since only one biography of Benét has been written, this article intends to shed some light on certain periods of his life by seeing him through Rosemary's eyes. It will, at the same time, serve as an introduction to the character and personality of this vivacious woman whom Benét "loved completely."[1]

One of the best ways to get to know Rosemary Benét is through her previously unpublished correspondence with her family, particularly with her mother. "I tell you things lots more frankly than I would others," Rosemary once told her, "but I have the utmost confidence in your discretion."[2] Most of the fragile sheets of onion skin, newspaper letterhead, and yellowing vellum are written in the kind of distinctive hand Stephen Vincent Benét ascribes to the heroine of his novel *Young People's Pride*: "firm and straight as any promise she ever gave, but graceful as the curl of a vine-stem."[3] Carr's hundreds of letters chronicle her days as a graduate student, her career as a newspaperwoman and aspiring writer, and most importantly, her relationship with Stephen Vincent Benét.[4]

I. Rosemary

Rosemary Carr was born in Chicago in 1898, the only child of Thomas Carr and Dr. Rachel Hickey Carr. A strong woman of Scots-Irish ancestry, Dr. Carr was one of Chicago's first woman physicians. Her daughter later wrote of her "still, Scotch look," while the Benéts' son, Thomas Carr Benét, remembers his grandmother as "a distinguished, white-haired lady who joined us for Christmases in Richmond, Virginia."[5]

Rosemary Carr's academic brilliance earned her a Phi Beta Kappa key in her junior year at the University of Chicago, where she was majoring in French. Rosemary was popular. She loved politics and action, not introspection; liked the shore better than the mountains; loved music; loved to dance; loved warmth "like a pussy cat"; hated cold and seasickness.[6] She had many friends, and her seriousness did not preclude involvement in college social societies such as the Esoterics.

In spite of her American directness and "spunk," as she called it, Rosemary had a French sensibility, an affinity for French language and literature. ("I am rarely taken for an American," she wrote during her early days in France. When someone complimented her on her command of French, however, she replied, "I have an Irish sense of imitation of sound and absolutely no appreciation of grammar and rules and exceptions.") After graduation she taught for a time at a school in Janesville, Wisconsin. By then World War I was nearing an end, and though she liked her pupils and colleagues, Rosemary—like so many other young women—was anxious to test her independence. "You know how I love variety," she told Dr. Carr, "that I believe with all my heart that variety is not only the spice but the salt and savor of this life."[7]

Rosemary Carr Benét, circa 1915.

A perfect opportunity came in the form of a French government fellowship, awarded by the Committee of Collegiate Alumnae to a select number of Americans for advanced study in France. Under the watchful though indulgent eye of a chaperone, Rosemary Carr sailed for Europe on September 19, 1919. Her destination was the École Normale at Sèvres.[8]

Photographs from the time show her with a full, oval face; clear, penetrating eyes; and an aureole of dark, wavy hair. Friends would later remark that she possessed a "fey quality"[9] and a gentleness, fragility and softness of manner which "at first suggested the Lillian Gish of the literary world,"[10] and belied the fact that she was anything but a frail reed. Writer Vincent Sheean met Rosemary Carr in 1920, when he was a freshman at the University of Chicago. He was enchanted by her beauty. "I don't mind saying," he told Benét biographer Charles Fenton, "that she remained in my mind a long time after she had gone to Paris."[11] She still wore ankle-length skirts and high-laced shoes, but Rosemary's thoughts were definitely modern.

Carr made a number of acquaintances during the crossing, and she would see some of them again in France. For the first time in her life she was overwhelmed with masculine attention. This she ascribed, in her self-deprecating manner, to the small number of young women on board the ship. A nice, clever, twenty-five-year-old Italian gentleman "was quite devoted though we didn't agree on many questions. He … told me that I was too serious and that I was always observing people and weighing them and looking for something I didn't find. One evening we had quite a heated discussion about whether women should stay home or work and have interests outside. He is fearfully conservative of course, but I knocked out all his arguments though he remained unconvinced."[12]

Rosemary adored France and later said that she would always regard the countryside around Sèvres as one of the loveliest places on earth because of its gardens. That November she wrote to Rachel Carr: "I never saw such a rainy country—it just pours continuously—but of course I love rain so I'm happy but the rest get *cafards* (black beetles) a particularly apt and lovely word to express 'the blues'…. I am dying to buy a pair of the wooden shoes the children wear on rainy days. They slip on like boats and make a most delightful noise on the stony Sèvres walks."[13] She tried to be a dutiful student, but the routine of the conservative French school system could be wearing. "We rise by chimes and go to bed by chimes and in between live a well ordered convent existence. The quiet and simplicity and lack of hurry will spoil me I know—I'll be entirely too placid for the more vigorous buoyant life that I love at home."[14] Even baths were a ritual. Students signed up for them as they did when going to the "Op–ra." For the major weekly bath, they "descended an impressive stairway to the basement, carrying our towels and soap. The baths were large, tinny, spotlessly clean, and full to the brim of boiling hot water, and reminiscent in shape of the one in which Marat had bathed so fatally."[15]

Besides differences in hygiene, there were also different aesthetic and political views. Rosemary seems to have gotten along quite well with most of the students, but on November 18 she told her mother about one "tactless" pupil who had received some cards and magazines from a friend in America. The girl came to Rosemary's room to find out the meaning of words she did not know, then proceeded to criticize the pictures. All the buildings constructed in a mixture of architectural styles "displeased her aesthetic nature." When she finally lashed out at the public buildings in New York and Washington, Rosemary could stand it no longer.

> With much self control I told her that we usually considered utility first and convenience and even cleanliness—that most of our buildings were for service.... At which she looked superior and said of course those buildings would never be allowed in Paris where everything is for beauty.... However, I have seen many things in Paris, lovely as it is and much as I love it, that I would not care to find in my home town.... Besides I'm always dying to tell them that being a democracy, we have never had a noble and cultural and royal few who could snatch the funds from the rest to decorate the landscape with lovely carved palaces; or that could send out an edict that all the houses in a certain district be torn down to make a favorable site for a public building. But I don't say anything.... Of course they have a lot we lack—tradition and history and cultuah (as Miss Scott [the English teacher] says it) but we have wealth and *comfort* and many things they need.... I seem to be getting more patriotic by the month.[16]

Even holiday activities were carefully planned for the *boursières*. Before that, though, there were lectures to be gotten through. Their literature teacher told them that in Shakespeare the characters eat and sleep and work, and it rains and snows and storms. Nothing of the kind happens in the plays of Corneille or Racine. These characters

> speak to one another in lengthy, classic speeches about love and duty and passions. I think that is why they sometimes bore me. The every day natural human happenings of life interest me a lot more than the classic—however pure and lofty—But don't tell anybody—I wouldn't dare confess it here.... We are having an unutterably boring lecture on ideas of space and time in Kant. Sometimes I wonder what good philosophy is anyway, and how a perfectly strong healthy man could devote his life to anything

so vague and impractical. Our history teacher says it is "playing tennis with ideas"—and I agree with him!! You never seem to get anywhere with it, and you get on quite as comfortably without it…. Philosophers never live up to their ideas anyway. They are like the poets who write love songs in that respect. The girls … laugh at me because I say "Believe me if all those endearing young charms" is a lovely lyric, but I don't believe in the fidelity therein averred. They sing it to me constantly and say I am a pessimist. Who wrote it? Burns wasn't it? At least he wrote several as lovely and untrue—and look at him—as fickle as the wind…. Art may be long—but philosophy is *interminable*!![17]

The school authorities were adopting a more liberal policy regarding students' visits to Paris to see the sights. Rosemary loved the Musée de Cluny best of all. When attending church she discovered that she was drawn to arches and stained-glass windows more than to the sermon; nor were the gilt and embroideries of the "fussy French style" to her taste. She much preferred carved wood to curlicues.[18]

As she experienced her first postwar Paris winter, parts of the social landscape disturbed her deeply. On December 13, Rosemary told her family, "Nowhere have I seen such dreadful old age as in France. It horrifies me. I have always, as you know, had only two fears—to grow old and to be alone…. One sees such wrecks of old men—weak, doddering, paralyzed—all stages…. They seem to be more in evidence than in America. In many cases they try to eke out some pitiful sort of livelihood by begging, or selling the thousand things that are sold here on the streets—or carrying signs on their backs and one sees them tottering about in the careless, pushing crowds. One sees them and looks away…. The Anglo Saxon has mastered much more completely 'the art of growing old,' as mother calls it."[19]

In spite of the grim reality she encountered in the Paris streets, Rosemary fell in love with the city. During the holidays she and the other scholars were entertained royally by host families. But now the new year, 1920—which would at last see women in America given the vote—brought with it serious decisions for her. The school was pleased with her work and she was invited to apply for a second year of study at Sèvres. "In some ways it is a great temptation," she told her mother, "—I love Paris and the life here [at Sèvres] is absolutely a carefree contented one—like a convent—For that very reason I think it is bad for me. It is far too sheltered and I am young and strong and ought to be battling with life as it were…. I have no ambitions to write a thesis or work for a master's or doctor's on my own initiative—for while I like and admire and aim at intelligence above all, I do not particularly aspire to be a scholar, in the true sense of the word."[20] She realized that the secluded life was making her less independent, not more.

By February she had pretty much made up her mind that at the end of the term she would either return to Chicago or try to find a job in the city and stay a few months longer. "I love to see people, *lots* of people, all kinds, and scoot around from things actively and buoyantly instead of drifting along placidly and indolently—no convent for *me*. That much is proved,"[21] she wrote home.

Salvation arrived in the person of Alice Lee Herrick Myers, an old friend from Chicago and a fellow member of the Esoterics. "Saturday Alice Lee Herrick Myers asked me to spend the afternoon with her. She was leaving next day for London so it was my only chance. She showed me her husband, who is a dear and very congenial, if impractical, [and] all her lovely wedding gifts, and told me all the gossip at home including a description of her unexpected wedding. Afterwards I went with them to poke about quaint little shops and pick out etchings. And then they took me to tea to a heavenly studio presided over by a pair of artists, delightful, cultivated ones not the long-haired variety—whom [*sic*] I am praying will invite me again…. They spent the afternoon feeding me cakes each better than the last…. Dick, Slee's husband, gave me the best kind of cake to carry home with me, and a bunch of violets." These were the kind of people Rosemary was longing to meet. The Myers would be living in London but planned to move to Paris eventually.[22]

Springtime brought treks through the French countryside with teachers, classmates and friends. Rosemary even spent a day showing a visiting young Englishman the glories of St. Cloud; this elicited a note of thanks and the enthusiastic comment, "It is ages since I have met a girl with really sound healthy ideas, who doesn't care whether her nose is powdered or not, who doesn't mind using her legs to walk not merely to show off shoes."[23] But all of this did little to quell Rosemary's restlessness.

Her youthful cynicism surfaced during a visit to La Malmaison, the country estate of Napoleon and his first wife: "I'm sure the chief reason Josephine so loved la Malmaison was the garden. It contains her very own roses—not yet in bloom of course, but the lawn was purple with violets and yellow with cowslips…. As usual also, there was an idyllic French couple wandering about in Love's Young Dream," she reported. "I never saw such an affectionate, sentimental race nor one so completely unconcerned and oblivious to others. Being Anglo-Saxon and hard-hearted, it pains me, but it can't be escaped even in the metro or tram, which is my idea of the most unromantic spot in the world. And the remarkable part of these spoony couples is that they usually turn out to be forty and ugly in which case they ought to know better. There might be some excuse if they were young and charming!"[24]

Weekend visits to the capital continued to broaden Carr's circle of acquaintances. The Myers had introduced her to Mr. and Mrs. William Francis. Francis was a newspaper man and his wife did the Paris sketches for *Vogue*. Rosemary had also met an expatriate American artist named Catharine Hopkins. The two young women got along well from the start and, little by little, as the school year waned, the center of Rosemary's world shifted from Sèvres to Paris. When in town she stayed either at the American Women's Club (located in the mysterious-sounding Hotel Petrograd) or at Catharine's pension, across from the Luxembourg Gardens. America seemed very far away.

On June 11, after more than a month of silence, Carr wrote to her family:

> Alice Lee and Dick are coming to Paris to live *permanently* July 15th and are simply singing hymns of joy and praise over the prospect. They hate London.—you should hear Dick's stories— he is without doubt the most amusing person I've ever met and I giggle absurdly as I used to in my young days, at his stream of nonsense. All anyone would have to do to write a musical comedy or a sixth best seller would be to follow him around with a note book and take down the pearls that fall from his lips. He's steadily gay and cheerful. It seems a shame that anyone so charming will probably be a wretched husband as to turning into a solid provider—has no money sense and loves a good time which can't be paid for by song-writing which is his talent. Isn't it a pity you can't find both qualities in one man—which is why I'm single still, as it were! When I think of how Alice Lee waited around engaged for centuries it makes me indignant and yet it is a case of 'with all his faults' he was worth waiting for.... The Francises and Dick took me on a very gay party Sunday. I dragged Catharine Hopkins along, too and they loved her. It was such a comfort to see how congenial they all were that I just sat back and beamed with pride at my handiwork. Catharine has been longing to meet Mrs. Francis who it seems is famous in the world of art.... You might not have approved so much of the party though I thought it most diverting. Alice and I met Dick for tea … at St. Cloud. They insisted I go to dinner with them and as Sunday night we can stay in Paris if we want to, I did.... Then we had dinner at Prunier's which is the superlative of French food—

lobster and the best ice cream I've had since the states and champagne—[25]

The big news was that Rosemary now had a one-day-a-week job. Catharine Hopkins had found her a position as a *collaboratrice* for a new magazine:

> It is called *Welcome* and is destined for all Americans abroad—quite well edited. ... [I]t amuses me and I get to type and translate, neither of which I'd refuse ever. The editor is the most English looking Frenchman I've ever seen—tall, blond, wears spats, was with British troops so he has their accent. He is young and polite and it embarrasses me—treats me like a duchess—rises when I come in and draws up my chair and hands me my pen with a bow. When I think of how some of my former employers differed in attitude it makes me laugh—Mr. Rovensky who used to say "Here sister take this letter" and Miss Hewes who treated me like part of the typewriter. Mr. Francis, who is a newspaperman, says he can get me some stuff to do if I'm here next winter probably. I'd probably starve but oh how I'd love to try![26]

By July 4, Rosemary was able to tell her family that her friend Bill Francis, of the Cross-Atlantic Newspaper Service, had offered her a job, slated to start on September 15, 1920. Some of the wealthy French friends Carr had met at school simply could not understand her desire to try a job and earn a living. She later explained, "The reason I cast aside this life of ease and luxury is because it was *too* easy. The other was harder and it seems to me the courageous thing to do.... I love their houses and gardens and manners and music. They all look expensive and cultivated, but I'm beginning to understand what it is to be weighed down by things and conventions."[27]

Almost as an afterthought in her letter of July 4, she asked her parents, "Who is this F. Scott Fitzgerald who seems to be making such a literary hit at home? He is certainly clever. These youthful geniuses who tumble into fame by one blot from their pens make me green-eyed with jealousy. I wish I could read his book."[28]

As autumn came on with its whirl of social activities, Rosemary realized increasingly how important appearance was. She was traveling in more sophisticated circles now, but still had only the things she had brought with her to Sèvres. "Catharine buys all her clothes at great designers—most at Lanvin...." She herself was not aspiring to designer fashions, but knew she must try to be less dowdy. "Americans are so bloomingly well groomed over here, too, that I'm a disgrace to the country." Nice note paper and silk stockings always went together in her mind as being essentials to gentility.

With Rosemary now based in Paris, she and Catharine, in the time-honored fashion of career girls, decided to share an apartment. They were able to sublet a lovely studio at 8 Rue de la Grande Chaumière. The large, soft-yellow and black studio had huge windows, big easy chairs, lots of books and a cream Persian rug. Catharine had known the owner, "one of those artistic birds, without being an artist, and wealthy which helps so much with taste. We don't like to think what he had this studio for, but there's no use worrying about that because in Paris one can't be too particular and after all, we do mail him cheques for the rent."[29]

Their street was "a dirty, tenementy place" and the entrance was "a horror." Yet most of the people around were nice, including "a musician graduate of Yale, preparing for concert work, a friend of Alice Lee's and Dick's…." This neighbor, who was attending the Schola Cantorum and also happened to be in Paris on his honeymoon, would play a major role in Rosemary's future. His name was Douglas Moore.[30]

Between holding down a job and trying to work out arrangements for cooking in a bed-sitter, Rosemary finally managed to read Fitzgerald's *This Side of Paradise*. She was not impressed. "It is surprising by its goodness and badness," she wrote her mother, "… but not worthy of all the commotion it has caused. And my word times have changed, according to that sophisticated youth."[31]

For Catharine and Rosemary (who often found long Sundays conducive to homesickness), weekends seem to have settled into a pattern of visiting the Myers, the Moores and some of their Yale friends. Over the next decade and beyond, Alice Lee and Richard Myers would play host to many major literary and artistic figures on the European scene. In late 1920 the group of "young geniuses" they entertained happened to include a man named Stephen Vincent Benét.

II. Stephen and Rosemary

Fresh out of Yale in June 1919, Stephen Vincent Benét had decided "I had to support myself and couldn't do it by writing poetry, so got a job in advertising and stuck with it 3 months writing about tender bleeding gums, steel-split pulleys, and sweetheart soap. Then John and Henry

Opposite: Stephen Vincent Benét and Rosemary Carr Benét, Paris, 1922.

Carter came back from Europe—and we had dinner together one night and decided we'd all go to the Yale Graduate School that winter and Paris the next summer. As we didn't have any money, this seemed rather a chimerical plan—but we followed it out to the letter."[32]

Benét sailed for France in late August 1920—part of the vanguard of what would become an invasion of American writers and artists. He and his friends Henry Carter and Stanley Hawks soon rented a small apartment in the Montparnasse district. Though a well-disciplined writer, Benét spent a good deal of his first few months in Paris hanging around Sylvia Beach's bookshop,[33] prowling the pavements of Montmartre, or pondering the meaning of life from a café table at the Dôme or the Rotonde.

"It was in the Montparnasse section of Paris that we became close friends," Douglas Moore later recalled. "This was a time in the first of the twenties, before the Hemingway era, when the Café du Dôme and the Rotonde were still neighborhood bistros where you could get breakfast chocolate and croissants and have a beer in the evening without feeling that you were part of a literary movement."[34] Benét was completing his first novel, *The Beginning of Wisdom*, and liked to work at the Moores' apartment in the Rue de la Grande Chaumière.

Sometime that fall Rosemary Carr met the young writer. "Mother, have you ever read any poetry by Stephen Vincent Benét ?" she asked in December. "We know him and he is really a dear tho' queer looking—His father is a brigadier general—funny combination." By holiday time his name was appearing regularly in her letters to her family. Just before the close of 1920 she wrote that Benét had written a poem about her name. "It is really lovely," Rosemary said, "or I should be annoyed. He is a real poet so you see I may attain immortal fame therefrom...."[35] The introduction to Benét was doubly interesting to her. She was about to join the staff of the Paris edition of the *Chicago Tribune* as a fashion and society writer, and Benét's aunt and uncle were two of the leaders of the American colony in Paris. The connection to this valuable source of society news was not to be sneezed at.[36]

Early in the new year Benét presented Catharine and Rosemary with an autographed copy of his book of poems, *Heavens and Earth*. "Steve reads it very well and would come and chant yards to us if we had the time. He is unattractive looking in some ways, but possesses the most enchanting imagination and sense of humor I have ever encountered, and a sort of childlike simplicity. This sounds as though I were much more interested in him than I am. I just mention him because he is the first poet I ever knew, and they are so apt to be diverting personages."[37] As part of this new circle in which a ready wit and spirited repartee were essential, Rosemary began to broaden her intellectual horizons. "I have two autographed volumes of poetry now," she boasted, "with little dedications and poems by the authors—the second a book of sort of Metaphysical poetry by Danford Newton Barney, called *Chords from Albireo*. I do not understand one word of it, and much prefer Steve Benét's variety, but I am very proud of them both, and am thinking of starting a collection. I have been reading a lot of things I should have, to keep up with these highbrows—most of it being modern poetry, which I have enjoyed hugely."[38]

Some holiday photographs she sent home prompted her to comment, "... this is a party given by Steve Benét and Henry Carter—time holidays. We (C & I) came forgetting to wear costumes and had to borrow them from Mr. and Mrs. Moore at whose apartment this grande fête was held. I had on a slinky dress so I borrowed Emily's veil and beads and was oriental. Catharine took Douglas's golf clothes and made a darling little boy.... Enough—except that Dick said I look like someone in the Bible with my traily veil—and someone else responded 'Jezebel'—because Emily had added two spots of rouge on my cheeks. Now S.V.B. says I have a dual personality: 'Jane and Jezebel.' I am usually Jane however. Forgive the glimpses of Jezey. *A word about my work....* I am much encouraged and enthusiastic.... Floyd Gibbons [the head European editor] said he wanted me to specialize on good society news.... Steve's aunt gives me my best society news but in great secret so don't tell—...."[39]

February brought with it the unwelcome news that the girls had had to move from their lovely studio to a less attractive but larger room. About this time, Benét's own letters reveal, his interest in Rosemary began to intensify. He sold his first poem about her, and overwhelmed her with verses and messages. Rosemary asked her mother for a critical assessment of his work. "*Don't*, I beg, *read them to people* who might misunderstand—Steve simply writes poetry about what is nearest to him ... and we have seen a lot of each other this winter and are the best of friends."[40]

By March 13 Rosemary reported that her job was going well. It was interesting and she had almost ten signed articles to her name. It bothered her to think of leaving this position to return to America just when things were starting to develop. Then there was another complication: Stephen Benét. His friends had been able to see for a long time how deeply he cared for Rosemary. Douglas Moore spent a long walk back from Montmartre with Benét trying to convince him that he was, indeed, worthy of her.[41]

The intensity of his ardor finally forced Rosemary to confront the reality of the situation. She poured out her feelings to her parents: "I realize now what a thoughtless perhaps heartless person I have been. We had lots in common so I drifted along letting him write me charming poetry until I woke up to the fact that poor Steve really means it and now I don't know what to do. Beyond the poems, he has never hardly said one silly word. We've just been good friends. But he wanders around now sort of pathetically & adoringly like a little dog. I can't be too mean and cruel; and he hasn't even enough money to ask me to marry him so I'm sure I don't know what *will* happen. It will just peter out I suppose; and he will decide after while [*sic*] that he doesn't love me. Forgive all this, but I've been quite unhappy about it lately...."[42]

Three days later Benét told Rosemary, over lunch, he had just heard that serial rights to his novel had been sold for $1,000. He beamed with delight, imagining all the things he could do with the money. Rosemary only half paid attention to him, fretting instead over a lost pass to a prizefight she was supposed to report on for the paper:

> Gradually, I thawed with Steve's pure, contagious enthusiasm and we went walking over to the Champs-Elysées nearly kicking our heels as though we were six. He'll make lots more money out of other things but he'll never be so nice and little boyish and thrilled as he was over this one—or so funnily conceited.... We are just good friends again, which I like—Steve having forgotten that he thought he was in love with me in the excitement of making money. Just like all men—success is a so much bigger game. We were talking once yesterday about F. Scott Fitzgerald who has written another novel—Steve said he supposed it was about his marriage and I said I didn't suppose he'd let that much good saleable emotion go to waste—which it seems was a Janish thing to say, and even bitter.[43]

In the final paragraph her thoughts returned to Benét: "I am making desperate resolutions to write short stories and may live up to them—If Steve can sell his, I can do others nearly as good, for I do not fall down and worship his prose as I do his poetry—which is a gift of the gods, I think and quite inexplicable."

Rosemary Carr must have written and mailed that letter on the morning of March 17. Whatever happened afterwards, by the end of the day Stephen Vincent Benét had somehow convinced her that she meant more to him than anyone or anything in the world. They decided to consider themselves engaged, and sealed their decision with a kiss. The next day, Steve Benét was still seeing the world through rose-colored glasses.

Paris, France March 18, 1921

Darling: (since I can say it now.)

I want to poke myself to make sure that I'm real. It is too incredible & wonderful.

What I want to do really is to run hotfoot to the [*Chicago*] *Tribune* office & take you away from your typewriter & make you come and have tea at 11 o'clock A.M. some place where I could kiss you. But c'est pas permis. Have a nice time on the Hilltop on the Marne. And think of me once in a while.

Would you prefer to have been first kissed in the little old back street in Paris outside of a bar, an Italian restaurant or a printing plant? I stood there in the rain this morning like a fool trying to decide which it was. All might be symbolical except the Italian restaurant. I don't know what that would stand for.

Henry is a sound sleeper. He merely swore mildly when I came in, started to sing & asked him to tell me a fairy story. Three cheers for his somnolence....

If you say any more about artistic careers, I will shake you. Remember, I fully intend to spoil yours.

There are too many things to say to write most of them. I love you. And I am so proud & happy that you love me—though I don't see how you can—that I feel as if I were mad or translated or something. I love you. You are so sweet & kind & humorous & true. I am not worthy of you, Jane, but I will try to be. I miss you & want you now and always. We will be jocular lovers & play tunes on irony's ancient ribs for fun—and ride comedy whenever we want to—you and I. I love you.

Steve[44]

For the next few weeks they lived in a lovers' paradise. But by early April the letters to their families had to be written. Well aware of what a "thunderbolt" she was hurling into their midst, Rosemary enclosed Benét's "introduction" to Mr. and Mrs. Carr in a letter of her own.

April 5 [1921]

Dearest Family

This is Steve's letter as you might have deduced without my explanatory note—It was too bulky to go with mine so I sent it separately. I hope, though, that they arrive together.

I hope you like his letter as much as I do. He put a good deal of thought into it but was dissatisfied with the result which he considered too heavy. I saw the letter to his family which was like it in subject but more amusing consisting mostly of a list of flattering remarks about me which will probably irritate them hugely.

Steve seems to think you will cable—though I said you'd have so much to say it couldn't be reduced to cable form. It would be nice if you could reassure us in a few words that you do not disapprove or want me to take the next boat home, though.

I am of course anxious and curious to see your letters and reaction. Can hardly wait.

Now I have some things to ask.

Please don't quote my letter to him. It was in strictest family council. Don't tell any of them how old I am. I am perennially 20 from now on. (That sounds silly; Steve knows but the six extra months irritate him.) Please do this to please me. It is no one's business anyway. I know I can trust you to respect my wish—at least until I see you and you expostulate about how silly my whim is. You can tell anything else about me you wish to his family or to him.

... I know you'll do just the right thing and write excellent delightful letters.... He expects you will be hard on him but I wouldn't mind if he were disappointed.

... Alice Lee is going to write mother to reassure her since she knows us & you.

Devotedly,
Rosemary

[April, 1921]

My dear Mr. & Mrs. Carr!—

As you have never seen me & know nothing at all about me except what Rosemary has said in her letters, I approach even writing you with a good deal of trepidation. But I do want to explain some things. In the first place, I am very much indeed in love with her and—though I still don't see how she can—she says that she loves me. Of course on my part it's the most natural and inevitable thing in the world. To see and have the companionship of anybody as sweet, fine, humorous, kind and wholly delightful as she is—I couldn't help loving her any more than I could help being born. In fact it seems to me at present the chief reason why I ever was born. What she sees or can see, I certainly don't know— I can only hope she keeps on seeing it. I couldn't bear losing her now.

Second—something about myself and my family. I am 23 years old (very young!) and graduated from Yale in 1919, taking an

M. A. in English in 1920. I came to France on a travelling fellowship to study at the Sorbonne and get a chance to do my own
work, which is writing. My grandfather and father were both
officers in the regular Army—the latter, Colonel James Walker
Benét, is at present in command of Watervliet Arsenal, New York
and retires this year. By blood we are Spanish and Scotch-Irish—
the first accounts for the curious name.

Third, what prospects I have—financial and otherwise. As I
said, I write for a living. I have published three books of verse
which have had fair reviews but which, of course, brought me no
money at all. The serial rights of my first novel, however, have just
been sold to "Harper's Bazaar" for $1000—serialization starting
July and ending October when it will be published in book form
by Henry Holt. As regards its success in book form, I have only
opinion to go on, but the editors & critics who have seen it seem
to think that it will be a considerable financial success. In fact, as
far as I can see and if luck doesn't run too consistently against me,
I have many reasons to believe that I will be making a good income
from my work in a reasonably short time.

Fourth—and of course the only really only important thing—
what chance there is of Rosemary's being happy with me. That's
just something that can't be known. All I can say is that I will try
to make her so with everything I've got—for she means more to
me than anything else in the world.

This has been a hard letter to write—and looking it over, it
seems simply measled with "I"s. But I thought, since I can't very
well talk to you all the way across the Atlantic Ocean, it would be
better to write as freely as possible. I hope, immensely, you'll find
me the kind of person you can trust. But that can't be decided on
letters. And, believe me, I really know the largeness of the gift I'm
asking.

All this sounds very stiff and formal on paper. But I want you
to like me—lord knows how much!—and I'm so completely in
love with your daughter that it's hard doing anything in any letter but saying what a perfect person she is. When I meet you I will
try, though rather scared, to be rather more natural & even sensible also. And I hope, infinitely, that you will be able to find things
to trust in me, as I say.

> Sincerely,
> Stephen Vincent Benét[45]

April neared an end, but there had been no reply yet from the Carr
family. Rosemary, spending a week with Alice Lee Myers while her husband was away, finally ventured a note to her mother. She loved Benét

but was still plagued with doubts: "Steve and I are still happy—I increasingly so—he about the same.... One thing worries me: I don't believe I can ever really fall in love with anyone. I am terribly fond of Steve and admire him and am congenial with him; and that ought to be enough. It has been hard on him because I always say we will be unhappy when we are married—that I hate to think of getting married at all, because I have known so few happy marriages that I am entirely a cynic and a skeptic. I try so hard not to be, for Steve is sweet and sort of trusting and I am horrid to load all these doubts on him. But I can't help it. I see nothing but disillusionment ahead in marriage—and particularly with him because he has so many illusions about me and is really in love—at the beginning."[46] Rosemary derived consolation from the fact that he was sure to make her write eventually; his whole family did it—father, mother, brother, sister. Not that she was marrying him for that.

Benét's "society Aunt" took the news in stride. "She asks Mrs. McCormick (wife of the owner of the *Trib*) if 'their little girl reporter was going to marry her nephew?'" Carr wrote. "And she has been darling to me—giving me many news items and I was always so scared both of her and that I should look self-conscious that I fled from her leaving a startled fawn impression...."[47]

Being accepted into the Benét family did not prove at all difficult for Rosemary, as is evident in a letter to her from Benét's mother:

> Dear Rosemary:
>   You are already loved by me, since my Stephen loves you so much.... It is all very, very strange & romantic—this courtship. I am thinking of you two today—a beautiful spring day here, as warm as June—& how much more lovely in Paris!—with all the love & tenderness imaginable—I send you the warmest welcome into the "Family." We are an odd group, all as different as can be, and all as devoted as can be! We hope you'll like us. We know we'll love you.... I am debarred from saying anything of your future husband, since he happens to be my son—But I'll tell you this—he is "steel true & blade straight"—and the rest you know—or rather you'll find out as you go on, for there's no limit to him—... All that is in our power to make you happy we will do. But we're not jealous, and we won't interfere. Love us a little!
>   Faithfully & affectionately
>   Frances Rose Benét.[48]

Rosemary finally received answers from America. Her parents insisted she return to the States that summer to think and talk things over. She replied that Benét himself had urged her to do so. Almost overnight her letters lose the tone of schoolgirlish chitchat and become more mature. On April 26 Rosemary wrote to her father, Thomas Carr, in a determined, but increasingly erratic, hand: "Last week I received a letter from mother, two from you, a package of newspapers ... a Life—grand! and a book.... I was delighted to get them all with the possible exception of a few parts of the letters which seem sort of dissatisfied with me. I shall try to explain—" She ascribed her failure to pay an endless round of courtesy calls on friends and acquaintances she had met in connection with her scholarship at Sèvres to the irregular hours newspaper work entailed.

> I have really worked very hard this winter. 1200 francs is not a munificent sum but it requires a lot of effort on my part to earn it. It is not bad for a girl.
> I have only one day off a week, and often not that if something interesting happens that must be reported. Often on Sundays I go somewhere that while interesting is a reportorial duty. My evenings are almost all gone, for after all on a newspaper you have to work when the news happens and cannot have regular hours....
> You say that I am absorbed in the life over here. I'm sorry but I can't help caring most for the delightful interesting American friends I have made, who have done much for me and who make allowances when I am tired and excuse me when I am working, as French people never do. After all they will mean more to me later, for I shall see them constantly.
> But it is chiefly that I have been busy—busy. I have to make an effort to fit things in my scraps of time and let those go that won't get in. I love it—a full, busy life and want it—but it means that I can't be a lady of leisure etc. I thought that you would understand that was why I let so many things slip. I'm not complaining or apologizing exactly—just explaining my seeming thoughtlessness. It is summed up in 1200 francs & a newspaper job.
> Of course I did find time to fall in love with Steve but that was inevitable and not to be slighted. Besides poor Steve has many & many a time been neglected for job as he complains at intervals.
> He received a delightful cable from his family a week ago Sunday—blessings love and good luck to us both. I am anxiously waiting word from you all now—I think I should hear in a day or two now—but my!!! the time has seemed long.
> His society aunt gave a very lovely dinner for us all last Friday, at her home—quite grand, Steve at the head of the table and me at his uncle's right—six courses, old wine, butlers and all our group of friends in the picture at their best.

Now please don't be cross at me any more and I'll try to write
more useful letters and do the errands. I can't bear to have you
dissatisfied and I'm doing the best I can

—much love
Rosemary.[49]

Declaring her independence would not be an easy job.

Shortly afterwards, Stephen Benét received the letter he had been
waiting for from Dr. Rachel Carr. From his aunt's and uncle's Right Bank
home, he replied:

[Late April or early May, 1921]
c/o L. V. Benét
1 Ave Camoens

Dear Mrs. Carr:—

Thank you very, very much indeed for your letter which I
appreciate more deeply than I can express both in its justness and
in its kindness. I think I can appreciate at least a little of what
Rosemary has been and is to you by what she is to me now and I
certainly hope will be to me in the future, though I have only
known her such a short time—and Heaven only knows, there is
nothing farther from my wish or intention than to separate her
from you and her father who love her and whom she loves so
devotedly in any way. And it is a fortunate condition of my work—
to call it such—that if I am successful in it, it will allow me to live
practically anywhere I please. On the other hand if it is to be what
I should like to make it, it will require a good deal of travel, especially in Europe, and the most favorable working conditions possible, as there are some under which I cannot work at all. This, of
course, is merely explanation—the same holds true of any one of
the arts—Germany, for instance, used to be almost a necessity to
the proper development of a musician—France & the French
schools to that of a painter. But such things, in my particular case
and Rosemary's, seem rather too far in the future at present to go
into fully now.

I realize that it is possible we may as you say, be mistaken in
thinking we love each other. I don't think it probable—certainly
not in my case—but it is only fair to Rosemary to let her consider
how a change from this environment and a return to the home in
which she was brought up may alter her feelings. I should be the
last person in the world to hold her to any past word or promise
in case they do alter—though I should be unutterably sorry. Certainly we can't consider marriage till I have some sort of a stable
income—and I won't know about that till next October at least if

then. I have wanted her to go back ever since we first became engaged. The present situation is of course very delightful & romantic—Paris and the spring & new moons & the smell of the Luxembourg Gardens—but I would much rather be sure of marrying her than of being romantic, though I am afraid I have a fatal tendency in the latter direction in most affairs of existence.

We are young—that's something that can't be contradicted and that only time will cure, if there is a cure. But I have been lucky enough to see, I think, somewhat more of various kinds of people & experience than most men of my age. And Rosemary has had a great many more opportunities to develop than fall to the lot of the average American girl. Not that, as you know, I compare her with anything but seven million miles outside of the average in every way.

As for qualities, I hope I am kind, I think I am reasonably honest, while essentially indolent by disposition I can be hardworking, especially with her to work for, and I can truly say that my life in the respects you would wish it has been absolutely clean. The last is due, no doubt partly to luck, but chiefly to the influence of a family whom it would take the lack of morals & ideals of an African gorilla to dishonor on purpose. This isn't an overstatement.

As for Rosemary she is every beauty & wish and urge in poetry and life that I have ever wanted dearly. She is also a lovely friend, a perfect companion—and a very human and humorous person. But you know that. As for kindness to her—it seems to me I have given very little and received infinitely. Her friendship has been and is so much to me—her love so much more & so beyond any words or deserving. I have tried as best I could to express what I feel in poetry—as a man will turn to his own small aptitude for help to make at least some semblance of what he loves most deeply enduring[.] (I suppose if I were an engineer I would build her an immense bridge or if I were an Ancient Briton paint myself an even more brilliant ultramarine—all in her name of course) but it is useless & always will be useless because after all she is all the best poetry in the English language already, and the men who wrote it were considerably my superiors, and at that, I will defiantly inform the universe in general and their ghosts in particular, they didn't say half enough & fell completely down on the job. Pardon this brief & rather frantic outburst. I love her so much.

She is going back in June then—and I will probably return around the same time, as what work I have at the schools here is practically finished and I must get back to New York and see various editors & publishers if I want to arrange serialization for my second novel—now well under way & to be finished in America. Also I'll have to see her occasionally if I'm to work—I couldn't otherwise any more than I could without eating or sleeping.

You can really trust me to do nothing you wouldn't approve of. I won't elope with her to Borneo & become a head-hunter— I don't think she'd like that anyway. I won't even come back on the same boat with her or buy her an engagement ring—for one thing I'd have some slight difficulty in raising the price for a proper one of the latter. This sounds very frivolous but I mean it. You can trust me. Please believe. I have a conscience—and even some common sense in streaks—if I am a minor poet.

On coming to the end of this letter I seem to have rambled all over the place & expressed myself very badly. Please forgive. I could have put it better in three or four sentences. I love Rosemary with my whole heart and I want to marry her as I've wanted nothing else in my life. If she finds out after returning to America that she has mistaken her feelings and doesn't really love me, I shan't play spoiled child and fight her decision because I know she wouldn't make it except on absolutely just grounds. I want to see both you and Mr. Carr personally immensely and I realize wholly that you can't decide whether Rosemary will be even safe with me, much less happy, until you do. I thank both you and him again & most sincerely and affectionately for your letters. As I said before I hope you'll discover something at least to trust in me when you do see me—and I can promise you on my word of honor to answer with complete frankness any questions about my self, conduct or prospects you may wish to ask.

Sincerely
Stephen Vincent Benét

Rosemary saw Stephen off to New York at the end of June. "I have never seen anyone so depressed and unhappy—partly because he is so afraid something may happen to separate us at home. Everyone has talked so much about the influence of environment etc. and the thought that we might grow apart without our lovely Paris background, terrifies him."[50] She herself sailed early in July, carrying a letter from Mr. Gibbons of the Paris *Tribune*, stating that if she applied for work at the paper's Chicago office, the *Tribune* "would be fortunate to recover the services lost to us through matrimony."[51]

While Rosemary went on to Chicago, Stephen Benét went up to Scarsdale, New York, to stay with his family while he sought opportunities for publishing his work. The lack of a dependable income now stood between him and the fulfillment of his desire to marry Rosemary. At the Myers' apartment back in Paris, Benét had had the good luck to hear about New York literary agent Carl Brandt from screenwriter Sidney Howard. Benét's friend John Farrar now arranged for him to meet Brandt. Over the next two decades, Carl Brandt would become the most important figure in Stephen Benét's professional life. Brandt looked over Benét's work and gave him sound advice about the needs and demands of the American literary market—especially the mass-circulation magazines. Benét told him quite frankly that he intended to get married that autumn and simply had to make enough money to make this possible.[52]

Benét set to work with a will. For the next four months he labored "in a tin hell of a garage," writing a novel and experimenting with the kind of short stories that would become the backbone of his income for the next twenty years. On paper, he worked through his feelings for Rosemary, and the pain caused by their separation. "No more air castles till I've earned the right to believe in 'em," he wrote her.[53]

Now that she was back home, Rosemary longed for France. She considered taking a teaching job or going back to Europe with a friend. "I know I've certainly felt ever since you went back to Chicago that it was all my fault you were there in a hot dirty city at a job you didn't like," Benét confessed. "And these last not-quite-two-months have been the hardest time I've ever had in my life, in some ways—loving you body and mind and soul and never being able to see you and tell you anything more definite than that I was working at something that might go or might not."[54]

Suddenly, in early fall, things began to happen. He shared a $500 prize from the Poetry Society with Carl Sandburg[55]; his novel *The Beginning of Wisdom* would probably do well; his new novel, *Young People's Pride*—the one he had written in the garage—would be serialized; and his short stories were starting to sell. By October he had estimated his income for the following year. "Do you think we could try it on that?" he asked. Benét knew he was asking Rosemary to take a big chance, but assured her that at least life would not be dull. Although they both wanted to live in Europe, Carl Brandt advised Benét to spend a three-month honeymoon there, then hasten back to New York to work until he had established his reputation firmly with the American reading public.

Benét wired Rosemary to get her passport in order and to make plans for their wedding. He headed for Chicago, where he was joined by his ushers and his best man—his brother, William Rose Benét, who was to represent the family. "William is always an impressive figure," Stephen's father confided to Rosemary.[56] On November 26, 1921, Stephen Vincent Benét and Rosemary Carr were married in a traditional ceremony. The "adding machine courtship" had come to an end. Shortly thereafter, the Brandt & Kirkpatrick literary agency released this simple statement:

> Mr. Stephen Vincent Benét and his bride
> are sailing for Europe on the *Adriatic* for
> their honeymoon. Mr. Benét's book is
> *The Beginning of Wisdom*.[57]

While the Benéts honeymooned abroad, the Brandt agency did its best to keep his name before the American public. Newspapers and periodicals, like the *Erie Railroad Magazine*, apprised readers of the latest standings in the collegiate literary scrimmage.

> By the appearance of *The Beautiful and Damned* Mr. *Scott Fitzgerald* has shot one lap ahead of Mr. *Stephen Vincent Benét*. It took a year of married life, however, before Mr. Scott Fitzgerald completed this book. At the moment Mr. Benét is still on his honeymoon but it's even money that Yale will catch up with Princeton just as soon as he turns from the fields of asphodel and comes back to hunt for an apartment in the big city.... He writes from Paris where he is spending a part of his honeymoon: "We have a three room studio, stone floors, candlelight, except in the cuisinette, a cellar reached through a trap in the floor that reminds one of oubliettes and the torture-chamber in *Swords*. Adrienne Lecouvreur ... lived in the apartment opposite and Racine used to visit her there ... also many other celebrated and immoral characters, so the place has associations. In fact as a French friend of my wife remarked on observing the dirty little street hardly wide enough for one taxi—this is just the place where American[s] in Paris *would* live" [March 1922].[58]

By late spring the Benéts were back in America. On August 25th Benét's novel *Young People's Pride*—the book he had written "to get married on"—was published. It bore the simple dedication "*To Rosemary*," accompanied by five stanzas of verse, ending with the poet's "gift" to her:

> Nothing can I give you—nothing but the rhymes—
> Nothing but the empty speech, the idle words and few,
> The mind made sick with irony you helped so many times,
> The strengthless water of the soul your truthfulness kept true.
>
> Take the little withered things and neither laugh nor cry
> —Gifts to make a sick man glad he's going out like sand—
> They and I are yours, you know, as long as there's an I.
> Take them for the ages. Then they may not shame your hand.

"I do hope that it sells well," Rosemary told her parents. "He will send you a copy I think. It is very beautifully and conspicuously dedicated to me and of course I burst with pride every time I look at it."[59] True to his word, Stephen Benét continued to celebrate Rosemary and his love for her in verse. He wrote her poems whenever and wherever he felt the inclination. (Many of them were published, and in 1939 composer Randall Thompson set some of the "Rosemary" lyrics to music.)

Upon their return to New York in 1922, Benét was faced once again with the task of making a living for two. For the moment he concentrated on mastering the craft of writing short stories for the lucrative magazine market. Learning the formula was one thing but, as biographer Charles Fenton emphasizes, it was a highly frustrating occupation for a man of Benét's creative abilities. The stories sold, but during the mid twenties—a boom time for many writers—Benét became less and less pleased with the kind of prose he was turning out. Seeking inspiration in American history and folklore, with its rich store of source material, Benét broadened the range of his story writing and at the same time gave the public poems like "King David" and "The Ballad of William Sycamore"—works which would help to make his fame, but not his fortune.[60]

The year 1924 was brightened by the birth of the Benéts' first child, Stephanie Jane, on April 6; it was marred by the failure of a Broadway play on which Benét had expended a great deal of energy and a little money. [See Izzo and Konkle's "Benét as Dramatist" in this volume.] He went back to the grind of magazine fiction and also began an historical novel, *Spanish Bayonet*, the story of his Minorcan ancestors. During these years Rosemary took a job at *Vogue*, and for a time hers was the only family income. To her credit, she seems never to have asked Stephen Benét to earn a living as anything other than a writer. Her brother-in-law William Rose Benét—another artist always in need of money—commended her for this in his essay *My Brother Steve*. "There is Rosemary," he wrote, "... who was born to understand just why he has wished to write exactly as he has written."[61] Benét himself was acutely sensitive to this quality in her. Through poetry, his instinctive mode of expression, he later thanked her for sustaining him even though it sometimes meant sacrifice and disappointment for her. How should he not know there was more to her than charm and grace?

> The delicate, secret courage of that face,
> So slight, so stubborn in its fortitude,
> The Irish laughter in the Irish eyes?
> I know enough that you are flesh and blood.
> I know you are a woman and distressed,
> Subject to mortal comedies and fears,

I know the heart is mortal in the breast,
I know the angry and the fruitful years.
I know all these unnecessary things
And could not love you more if you had wings,
Having once lived with these mortalities.[62]

By late 1925, Benét—and Rosemary—realized that he had reached a turning point: "When he applied for the Guggenheim Fellowship in December, 1925, he was twenty-seven years old. He had a wife, and a child under two. Another child was to be born in early fall. He lived entirely by his writing and he wanted very much to take time to write a long poem…. The backward look is easy. Too easy perhaps," she recalled in 1949. "People are apt to say to me now, 'It was inevitable for him to write a long poem.' So it was. But I remember how it was *then*, when we were trying to look forward, and there was no backward look."[63]

Benét was overjoyed to learn he had been awarded the grant and that summer, after paying farewell visits to both of their families, Stephen, Rosemary and Stephanie Jane left New York (sweltering in 97-degree heat) to return to France, where the atmosphere was congenial and the rate of exchange made the living good.

Alice Lee Myers met them at the boat and drove them on the three-hour 'short run' up to Paris. She also got them settled into a sunny, clean, modern apartment she and her husband had located in the Rue Jadin. Stephen Benét had "a little room to work in upstairs." Rosemary, having great faith in modern medicine, did not mind having her baby so far from home. She and Benét visited the American Hospital, "new, shiny, well-equipped."[64]

The Benéts enjoyed being back in Paris. Stephen worked; Rosemary rested. At the end of August she told her mother that he was "starting to work on a long poem."[65] Friends from the States came to visit while passing through. On September 28, 1926, Rosemary gave birth to a son, Thomas Carr. "Poor Steve worried greatly as usual," she told Rachel Carr, "and is jubilant that it is over."[66] With a toddler, the new baby, a cook and two adults, the apartment had become quite crowded, so Benét rented a place across the street to work in.

By January 1927 the family had moved to a new apartment at Neuilly, just outside the gates of Paris. The atmosphere was quieter and Rosemary could report that "Steve is working hard. I think his long poem is going well"; by March she was able to add that "his new poem is about the Civil War. I think it is very interesting, but then, I am a partial audience."[67] Benét's request for a six-month extension of his fellowship was granted, and he settled down to completing and revising the manuscript. Rosemary, too, was working. Her friend Emily Kimbrough had asked her to write for the Marshall Field magazine, and she contributed a monthly letter to *Town & Country*. On May 12 they dined with James Joyce at Archibald MacLeish's, and on the 27th witnessed the excitement of the Lindbergh flight. The end of the month brought a move to southern Normandy and the completion of Benét's poem, now called *John Brown's Body*. "It is nearly done and I am to help him type it," she wrote. "It costs so much to have it retyped in Paris."[68]

As the manuscript neared completion, Rosemary offered her opinion: "I think it is a great poem in spots, but being poetry will not make money. But if it is a satisfaction and pride to Steve and a few people it will be worth it."[69] It was a great satisfaction to publisher John Farrar: "Congratulations. Poem magnificent," he cabled on November 19. The book was not to be published until the following year, but Farrar hinted that it might become a selection of the recently formed Book-of-the-Month Club. He told them not to get their hopes up,[70] but the following August Rosemary told her mother, "We have good reports from the book which is out by now. A large number have been ordered tentatively—something like 45,000."[71] A week later the ads were saying 70,000 copies had been sold. "I *do* hope so. He worked so hard over it without ever thinking he would make money out of it. It is comforting and encouraging to have it so well received."[72]

The publication of *John Brown's Body* changed the Benéts' lives. Stephen Benét became a national celebrity, almost overnight. "He really is a grand person if he is my own husband, kind, loyal, full of courage and modesty," Rosemary declared to her mother. "I admire him more all the time! This sounds silly put into words—and any way you know it already."[73] Stephen and Rosemary would draw on every one of those reserves in the years ahead.

About a year later, they returned to America. Sometime after that, Rosemary's poem "Bon Voyage" appeared in the *New Yorker*. Lighthearted in tone, it painted a series of word-pictures of "their" Paris:

> Caped police,
> Saint-Sulpice,
> Musée Cluny,
> Café au lait,
> Lovers moony
> Along the quais,
> Sainte Chapelle,
> Streets old and catty
> Cecile Sorel

In a new Bugatti,
Punch and Judy,
Chestnut trees,
Soldiers dudy
In the Tuileries.
Stone Gambett
The people's choice,
Mistinguett
In an old Rolls Royce,
Crowds at the races,
Chantilly laces,
Paris sun!
Paris rain!
God's will be done!
I'll see them again.[74]

They were ready to come home. The children were growing and it was time to think of finding a permanent place to live. "We all have a little of it, I think, the born Americans—even the city born—the nostalgia, the sickness of the frontier," says a character in Benét's novel *James Shore's Daughter*. "It's a different curse from Europe's and a different fate."[75]

The Benéts' fate willed that they should return to the United States in late summer 1929. A few months of comfortable living, at the home of their friend Leonard Bacon in Rhode Island, were followed by weeks of separation when Benét went to Hollywood as a screenwriter for D. W. Griffith, because the money was good, even with the Depression going on, and the Benéts were again in need of money since virtually all of his earnings for *John Brown's Body* were lost in the stock market crash. However, Benét's health was undermined by the California dampness, and for almost two years the family divided its time between Manhattan and the sun and sea of Rhode Island.

In spite of financial constraints—shared by most of their fellow citizens—and an increasing awareness of the plight of the country as a whole, the Benéts' family life appears to have been a happy one. On October 22, 1931, a second daughter, Rachel Felicity, was born. Photos show Stephen, Rosemary and the children enjoying afternoons in the park, relaxing in their back yard, or chatting with friends. Editor Basil Davenport recalled being with them: "His talk ranges over everything he has read (and he has read everything) ...; while from time to time his wife Rosemary puts in a wise and charming word as she sits serenely sewing—looking like an unusually humorous version of the housewifely Athena, as Steve behind his spectacles looks like an unusually humorous version of Athena's owl."[76]

As she had predicted, Rosemary became one of "the writing Benéts." She admitted that she was not a born poet; she had ideas, but Stephen helped her with the rhymes. Several of her poems and short stories were eventually published in the *New Yorker* and the *Saturday Review of Literature*, and during the early 1930s, as the nation slowly recovered from the Depression, Rosemary put her knowledge of French language and literature to good use. She seems to have been drawn particularly to the writings of Colette, whose whole life had been spent in the study of love and lovers; and from Rosemary's pen came translations of her *Lesson in Love* and *The Gentle Libertine*. (Later, when Andre Maurois was in the United States as an exile from occupied France during the early days of World War II, Rosemary Benét translated his book *Fatapoufs and Thinifers*.)

Stephen and Rosemary were very much a part of the New York literary scene. Together they wrote portraits of other writers for *Herald Tribune* editor Irita Van Doren's review section, "Books." But it was a chance occurrence that finally gave them the opportunity to collaborate on an amusing little work that was destined to become a children's literary classic. Benét enjoyed reading aloud to his two older children, and a New York Public Library exhibition on children's literature in May 1933 led to discussions with their friend from Paris days, artist Charles Child about the possibility of doing an illustrated book of verses about famous Americans. Child, John Farrar and the two Benéts were enthusiastic, and in just a few months *A Book of Americans* was published. Stephen wrote about the men, Rosemary about the women. "Nancy Hanks," one of the book's most popular poems, is Rosemary's work.

The mid 1930s, biographer Charles Fenton points out, became years of personal and professional crisis for Benét—and, by extension, for Rosemary. He was torn between writing serious novels like *James Shore's Daughter*, and committing himself to the commercial stories most of his readers had come to expect. The serious writing took time but did not make money to support the lifestyle he had come to prefer. Benét, while altruistic—as his son Tom explains—was also fascinated with the American dream. Fenton writes, "There were private schools, and a maid, and a good New York address; there were Rhode Island summers and Brooks Brothers clothes, and one had to return the dinners and entertainment received from friends who lived on their unearned incomes or were as prosperous as the Barrys."[77]

Both Benéts had been longing for a real home ever since their return from Europe. In 1940, with another war on the horizon, they found what they were looking for at Stonington, Connecticut. The old house had a long history and had been the childhood home of American painter James

McNeill Whistler. Here, Rosemary was finally able to indulge her love of gardening and decorating, as a lavish "Day-in-the-Life-of" magazine feature shows,[78] while Benét could write in his third-floor study.

Even before World War II began, Benét's devotion to the Allied cause was tireless. His arthritis had gotten progressively worse, but he refused to complain or allow it to affect his work. He attended meetings, spoke at rallies, and wrote and wrote and wrote. In February 1943 he was hospitalized with a heart attack. Stephen Benét had begun to resume his writing when, during the night of March 13, he suffered a heart seizure. Within minutes he lay dead in Rosemary's arms.

III. Rosemary

The shock of Benét's death was enormous for his family and close friends. Philip Barry summed up their grief and anger in a short tribute in the *Saturday Review*: "It is too soon to write about him. The sense of indignation, of actual anger, at this deprivation is still present."[79] For Rosemary, one of her great fears had been realized. They had been so close, and he had been relatively young. "This is the end of Everything for me— More than for him—for he will live in his writing. Oh my darling. I cannot face it," she wrote in Benét's diary.[80]

Rosemary Benét was far from alone, however. She had her children to console and to counsel, and she could take comfort in the tremendous outpouring of sympathy from public and private individuals. An especially meaningful telegram came from the White House. On April 27, Rosemary thanked Franklin Delano Roosevelt for his thoughtfulness.

> Dear Mr. President,
>   Your telegram of sympathy meant a great deal to me and to my children—I cannot begin to express to you in words how proud I was, and how deeply touched that, with all the cares of the moment, you thought of us at this sad time and sent us words of comfort…. Like you, he loved his country with loyalty and selfless devotion. Aside from my personal grief and aching loss, it makes me sad to think of the words that will not now be written about America which he loved so much…. Your telegram will be kept among my treasures. It is a source of great pride and comfort to me. It would have meant so much to Steve that you remembered. I can only say thank you from my heart.
>   Gratefully,
>   *Rosemary Benét*[81]

The Benéts' friends—the Myerses, the Barrys, the MacLeishes, the John Mason Browns, and others—surrounded Rosemary with support and affection. Thanks to Amy Loveman, one of her old friends and an editor at the Book-of-the-Month Club, she reentered the literary world.[82] She served on the club's editorial board, specializing in poetry, short stories, and French literature and, from time to time, wrote about authors for their monthly newsletter. Her judgment was highly regarded by writers and critics alike.[83] During these years the Benéts' son, Tom, would often go down to her Madison Avenue office and join her for lunch at a nearby French restaurant.

The old Rosemary whom Benét had loved and celebrated—she who was neither meek nor mild and could "shake the pride of angels"[84] with her scorn—still existed, though she was tempered now with a touch of sadness. Thomas Benét does not remember that his mother ever indicated feeling sorry for herself. "She was a realist, and it took great strength of spirit to live out her life as she did," he says. "Among the many gifts she gave me, aside from her unquestioning love, was the prod to be independent. She was not at all clinging, and always urged me on—to the Field Service, the Army, to California."

Besides her concern for her children's futures, Rosemary Benét's interest lay in keeping her husband's legacy alive. "She kept his memory green," said Mrs. John Mason Brown, "quoting him, remembering him, admiring and honoring him."[85] She was delighted in the 1950s when Charles Laughton adapted *John Brown's Body* into a popular stage presentation starring Benét's old friend Raymond Massey, and when the short story "The Sobbin' Women" was made into the classic film *Seven Brides for Seven Brothers*.

There was still the historic house in Stonington. In later years, Rosemary Benét spent more and more time there, enjoying the town and its people, and even helping a local theater group adapt Benét's Civil War epic for the stage. With thirteen grandchildren, she remained quite active until she was stricken with cancer in the early 1960s. Even then she continued to serve the Benét name. Only a few weeks before her death, an obviously frail Rosemary traveled to Watervliet Arsenal in upstate New York, at the U. S. Army's request, to help dedicate the Benét Laboratories.

On August 18, 1962, she died at New York City's Columbia-Presbyterian Hospital. She is buried next to Stephen Vincent Benét in Stonington's old Evergreen Cemetery. After her death it was discovered that Rosemary Benét had written her own "Little Epitaph":

Say only this of me
When I have died,
She's where she loved to be
There at his side.

That November, her friend Cassie Brown spoke about Rosemary to
members of the "Junior Fortnightly," to which she had belonged. She
began her remarks by saying that some years before, Philip Barry had
asked her when she had come to love Rosemary. Startled, she countered
with, "Well when did you?" Playwright Barry, noted for his quick wit and
sparkling dialogue, replied, "The moment I realized she was far from being
just sweet."[86]

NOTES

1. See Benét's poem "Little Testament," *The Last Circle* (New York: Farrar, Straus and Company, 1946), 309.
2. RCB to RHC, June 17, 1920.
3. Benét, Stephen Vincent, *Young People's Pride* (New York: Henry Holt
and Company, 1922), 29.
4. Unless otherwise indicated, Rosemary Benét's manuscript letters to her
mother are from the Benét Family Papers at Yale University's Beinecke Library.
In these notes, Rosemary Carr Benét is referred to as RCB; her mother, Rachel
Hickey Carr, as RHC; and Stephen Vincent Benét, as SVB.
5. In her poem "Advice to my Daughter" (*Saturday Review of Literature*,
n. d.), RCB writes about disciplining her child and then being taken aback when
the little girl looks at her with a reproachful gaze that reminds her of her own
mother: "That still, Scotch look that ranked / My youthful sins...." Thomas Benét's
recollection was a personal communication to the author.
6. RCB to RHC, Jan. 27, 1920.
7. RCB to RHC, Feb. 8, 1920.
8. Rosemary Carr received her appointment through the American University in Paris as part of an exchange program for French and American teachers.
9. Nancy Redpath, personal communication to the author.
10. Eulogy of Rosemary Benét given to the "Junior Fortnightly," Nov. 12,
1962, by Cassie Brown, wife of critic and biographer John Mason Brown.
11. Fenton, Charles A., *Stephen Vincent Benét: The Life and Times of an American Man of Letters, 1898–1943* (New Haven: Yale University Press, 1958), 104.
12. RCB to Family, Oct. 6, 1919.
13. RCB to RHC, Nov. 18, 1919.
14. RCB to Family, Jan. 29, 1920.
15. Bennett, Rosemary Carr, "Order of the Bath," *New Yorker*, n. d.
16. RCB to RHC, Nov. 18, 1919.
17. RCB to RHC, Dec. 13, 1919.
18. RCB to RHC, Jan. 27, 1920.

19. RCB to RHC, Dec. 13, 1919.

20. RCB to Family: Jan. 3, 1920.

21. RCB to RHC, Feb. 8, 1920.

22. RCB to Family, Mar. 1, 1920. For accounts of the Myers' friendships with Sara and Gerald Murphy and writer Frederick Faust (Max Brand), see Amanda Vaill, *Everybody Was So Young: Gerald and Sara –Murphy, A Lost Generation Love Story* (New York and Boston: Houghton Mifflin Company, 1998) and Robert Easton, *Max Brand: The Big "Westerner"* (Norman: University of Oklahoma Press, 1970).

23. RCB to RHC, Apr. 27, 1920.

24. RCB to Family, Mar. 22, 1920.

25. RCB to Family, June 11, 1920.

26. RCB to Family, June 11, 1920.

27. RCB to RHC, July 4, 1920. Rosemary's 'declaration of independence,' however, was less than complete. At the end of a letter on Aug. 31, she asked her mother to promise she would always keep enough money in the bank for her trip home. "I want to feel I can cable any time and leave instantly or I should be lost."

28. RCB to Family, July 4, 1920.

29. RCB to Family, Nov. 7, 1920.

30. Douglas Moore, American composer. His musical works were influenced by his acquaintance with writers such as Benét, Archibald MacLeish and Vachel Lindsay. During 1937-38 he and Benét fashioned a highly successful folk opera from the latter's classic short story "The Devil and Daniel Webster." Moore's best-known operas are *Giants in the Earth* and *The Ballad of Baby Doe*. Moore's second symphony, written in 1945, is dedicated to the memory of Stephen Vincent Benét.

31. RCB to Family, Nov. 7, 1920.

32. Autobiographical sketch done for Brandt & Kirkpatrick Literary Agents in 1921. Original in Files of Brandt & Hochman Literary Agents, Inc.

33. See Fenton, Charles A., *Stephen Vincent Benét*, Sylvia Beach's autobiography, *Shakespeare & Company* (New York: Harcourt, Brace, c1959), and Noel Riley Fitch, *Sylvia Beach and the Lost Generation* (New York: W. W. Norton & Company, 1983) for accounts of SVB's early days in Paris.

34. Moore, Douglas, "Reminiscences of Stephen Vincent Benét," originally broadcast on CBS radio in June 1953; printed in the *Dictionary of Literary Biography Yearbook 1997*, 309–11.

35. RCB to Family, Dec. 28, 1920.

36. Laurence Vincent and Margaret Cox Benét. "Uncle Larry" was the European representative for the armaments firm of Hotchkiss & Company.

37. RCB to Family, Jan. 8, 1921.

38. RCB to Family, Jan. 1921.

39. RCB to Family, Jan. 1921. Letter from the collection of Thomas Carr Benét. In many of Benét's letters and love poems, Rosemary is addressed as 'Jane,' his pet name for her.

40. RCB to RHC, Feb. 27, 1921.

41. Moore, "Reminiscences," *Dictionary of Literary Biography Yearbook 1997*, 309.

42. RCB to Family, Mar. 17, 1921.

43. RCB to Family, Mar. 17, 1921.

44. *Selected Letters of Stephen Vincent Benét*, Charles A. Fenton ed. (New Haven: Yale University Press, 1960), 47–8.

45. RCB to Family / SVB to Mr. and Mrs. Carr, Apr. 5, 1921.

46. RCB to RHC, Apr. 21, 1921.

47. RCB to RHC, Apr. 21, 1921.

48. Frances Benét, April 16, 1921, at Watervliet Arsenal.

49. RCB to her father, Thomas Carr, Apr. 26, 1921.

50. RCB to Family, June 30, 1921.

51. Floyd Gibbons to RCB, June 29, 1921. Collection of Thomas Carr Benét.

52. Fenton, *Stephen Vincent Benét*, 109–112. Charles A. Fenton's biography must be the starting point for anyone wishing to write about SVB. It is, to date, the only full-length life of Benét. Fenton, writing in the 1950s, was able to get many of the poet's friends to speak "for the record." See also, Parry Stroud's literary biography, *Stephen Vincent Benét*, Twayne's United States Authors Series 27 (New York, Twayne Publishers, Inc., 1962).

53. SVB to RCB, Aug. 4, 1921.

54. SVB to RCB, Aug. 1921.

55. For Benét's book *Heavens and Earth*; for Sandburg's book *Smoke and Steel*.

56. James Walker Benét to RCB, Nov. 17, 1921.

57. Brandt & Kirkpatrick File on SVB.

58. Undated clipping in Brandt & Kirkpatrick Benét file. Sometime the previous autumn, F. Scott Fitzgerald had sent Maxwell Perkins his "prognostications" for books that fall. Though he had not read it, the fourth book on his list was "*The Beginning of Wisdom* by Stephen Vincent Benét. Beautifully written but too disjointed and patternless. Critics will accuse him of my influence but unjustly as his book was written almost simultaneously with mine." *The Letters of F. Scott Fitzgerald*, Andrew Turnbull, ed. (New York: Charles Scribner's Sons, 1965), 149.

59. RCB to Family, Aug. 28, 1922.

60. See Fenton, *Stephen Vincent Benét*, Chapter 6, "Ballads in Grub Street," for a detailed account of SVB's life and work during this period.

61. Benét, William Rose, "My Brother Steve," *Saturday Review of Literature*, Dec. 15, 1941.

62. Benét, Stephen Vincent, "Today I Saw You Smiling," *The Last Circle*, 305.

63. Benét, Rosemary Carr, Introductory remarks to "Epic on an American Theme: Stephen Vincent Benét and the Guggenheim Foundation," *The New Colophon* (New York, 1949), 1.

64. RCB to Family, Aug. 11, 1926.

65. RCB to family, Aug. 30, 1926.

66. RCB to RHC, Oct. 6, 1926.

67. RCB to RHC, Feb. 1927; RCB to RHC, Mar. 10, 1927.

68. RCB to RHC, July 6, 1927.

69. RCB to RHC, Aug. 29, 1927.

70. RCB to RHC, June 18, 1928.

71. RCB to RHC, Aug. 2, 1928.

72. RCB to RHC, Aug. 18, 1928.

73. RCB to RHC, Oct. 5, 1928.

74. Undated clipping from the *New Yorker*. Collection of Thomas Carr Benét.

75. Benét, Stephen Vincent, *James Shore's Daughter* (Garden City, New York: Doubleday, Doran & Company, Inc., 1935), 28.

76. Davenport, Basil, "Stephen Vincent Benét," Introduction to *Selected Works of Stephen Vincent Benét*, Two Vols. (New York: Farrar & Rinehart, Inc., 1942).

77. Fenton, *Stephen Vincent Benét*, 267.

78. *House & Garden* magazine, November 1942, 36–37. Copy in the Philip Barry Papers, Georgetown University.

79. Barry, Philip, "As We Remember Him," *Saturday Review of Literature*, March 27, 1943.

80. Benét, Stephen Vincent, *The Devil and Daniel Webster and Other Writings*, Edited with an Introduction by Townsend Ludington (New York: Penguin Books, 1999), x.

81. Roosevelt, Franklin D.: President's Personal File, 8348, Stephen Vincent Benét, Franklin D. Roosevelt Library and Museum.

82. Amy Loveman (1881–1955) was one of the founding editors of the *Saturday Review of Literature*, along with Henry Seidel Canby, William Rose Benét and Christopher Morley. She was an associate editor of Book-of-the-Month Club, and was with it from its inception.

83. In 1948, for instance, John O'Hara wrote to his Random House editor, "The title of my novel is A RAGE TO LIVE. I have tried it out on everybody from Rosemary Benét to Eric Hatch's mother, an enormous range, believe me. Several persons who didn't like it at first changed their minds days later. The best thing about it, or one of the best, as Rosemary pointed out, is the unusual juxtaposition of simple words." *Selected Letters of John O'Hara*, Matthew J. Bruccoli, ed. (New York: Random House, 1978), 207–208.

84. "Difference," *The Devil and Daniel Webster and Other Writings*, 349–350.

85. From Cassie Brown's eulogy of Rosemary Benét, Nov. 12, 1962.

86. Cassie Brown eulogy, Nov. 12, 1962.

3. The Yale Club of Stephen Vincent Benét, Archibald MacLeish, and Thornton Wilder: The Writer as Liberal Humanist and Public Activist

David Garrett Izzo

> I love the heroic. I hate the game of puncturing heroics which people think so clever nowadays.
> —*Vachel Lindsay (qtd. in Graham 162)*

A well-known, successful actor—and a middle-class child of school-teachers—appears on PBS to defend government spending for the National Endowment of the Arts: The artist as public spokesman is a rarity today. A legendary singer forsakes a lucrative rock 'n' roll tour to sing folk songs about the put-upon and disenfranchised. The artist as populist is rarer still. Today, expedient neutrality overrules urges to get involved, which might alienate or possibly offend someone.

There was a time, however, when being an artist or man of letters did not preclude one from speaking or writing on public issues. There were moments when writers had opinions about more than just their art and felt a duty to give them. There was an era, one which now is relegated to poignant memory, when a writer could be a liberal humanist *and* patriot without these seeming to be mutually exclusive qualities subject to jaded derision as they would likely be today. This era saw writers—journalists, critics, artists—who could love their country right or wrong and actively work within the system to defend the right, but also confront the wrong and ask their country to fix it.

Between the great wars, the children of the last generation of the nineteenth century grew up amidst such tumultuous change as the world has not seen before or since. In New England, this first generation of the twentieth century was imbued with an inherited sense of duty and public service derived from a subliminal aura of pragmatic Protestant ethic melded with the more metaphysical motives of transcendentalism's unified consciousness. This combination of Emerson's self-reliant oversoul and Thoreau's civil disobedience could only result in writers who assumed their art was just one aspect of a required public-spiritedness. Many of these writers went to Yale and Harvard. The Yale Club of 1915–1919 yielded three in particular who exemplified the writer as a multifaceted, gregarious public entity who was artist, man of letters, and an activist just as inclined to give a speech as write one: They were Stephen Vincent Benét, Archibald MacLeish, and Thornton Wilder.

Each was an artist who entered into and thrived in the public arena, unabashedly working within the system to use their artistic achievement as a staging area for civic-minded purposes. This was a stance not always appreciated by many in the literary milieu who cynically looked askance at those who associated with the established infrastructure; they somehow believed this cast them as "impure": i.e., business/government should stay out of the arts and artists should stay out of business/government.

In the 1930s and beyond, Benét, MacLeish and Wilder, as New Deal Democrats, demonstrated blatant—but not blind—patriotism, choosing to love their country by challenging it to do better. All three were very public men who did not draw a line in the sand separating their artistic personas from their personas of activists in the greater world. Often, this attempt to balance the creative spirit with public responsibility became the subject of their art as, collectively, many of their poems, plays, stories, novels and essays considered this prevalent theme: the conflict of the public activist in an indifferent or even hostile world. Indeed, it seems there was a price to pay for Benét, MacLeish, and Wilder in choosing to be public men. All three are not given their just due as artists, with Benét and MacLeish neglected and Wilder, though recognized, not fully respected here as he is in Europe.

The more public they became, the less their work was considered as "serious" by many of the "purists" who had earlier praised them; taken together, they form a case in point as to why there are so few like them today willing to speak out. It's safer to be quiet.

Each was imbued in youth with an ethic of dutiful service, both public and private. (Private benevolence is herein included because it is important to see that much of what they did was unpublicized so as to understand that their public activism was sincere and not strictly motivated by any self-serving need for grandstanding which, of course, they were accused of anyway.) Their writing was an extension of their public selves rather than their public selves being an extension of their work. Moreover, their art reflects their personalities—Benét: American Visceral; MacLeish: American Stoic; Wilder: American Metaphysical.

Stephen Vincent Benét: American Visceral

> I suppose the only way to describe Steve would be to say that if I had a chance to be some other person whom I had known in my lifetime, I would have preferred to have been Stephen Benét, not anyone else.
>
> —Benét's friend William Sloane
> (qtd. in Fenton 302)

Stephen Vincent Benét (1898–1943) in his time was as popular as any writer in America, principally through his short stories in mass circulation periodicals such as the *Saturday Evening Post*. He was first and foremost an entertainer who wore his heart on his pen. He wrote for the popular audience and gave them what they wanted—poignant, heart-tugging, exhortatory fables with direct narratives, archetypal caricatures, and punchy finales. Countless teenagers have read his most famous and widely anthologized short story, "The Devil and Daniel Webster" (1936). Little else is remembered. Even his Pulitzer Prize–winning Civil War epic in verse, *John Brown's Body* (1928), is known mainly by name only and considered quaint when considered at all. This is ironic because when he graduated from Yale in 1919, he was known as a "wunderkind" all over the northeast. Wilder recalled that at Yale, Benét was "the whole power" of the *Yale Literary Review* (qtd. in Harrison 52). He was the youngest of the three, but the first to achieve literary recognition with a well-praised first book of poetry, *Five Men and Pompey*, when he was just seventeen years old. More poetry followed and a first novel, *The Beginning of Wisdom*, 1920, solidified his emerging reputation.

Critic John Peale Bishop included the novel in a review that also considered F. Scott Fitzgerald's *The Beautiful and the Damned* and John Dos Passos's *The Three Soldiers*. Of *Wisdom*, he said, it "is a picaresque novel of a young man who successively encounters God, country and Yale." Bishop, while having some reservations (Benét was only twenty-two) said that throughout, Benét had "the courage and skill to write beautifully. He has so rare a skill with color, so unlimited an invention of metaphor, such humorous delight in the externals of things, so brave a fantasy ..." (230). Praise was customary for Benét, at least until he became a public activist.

Stephen Vincent Benét (of Spanish, not French ancestry) was the son of a military man, Colonel James Walker Benét, about whom he said, "I cannot agree with those who say that the military mind is narrow and insensitive" (Fenton 1). His father was "articulate, civilized, and widely read." His mother, Frances, was "talented and lovely; the fluency of their children [as writers] was foreshadowed in her immense correspondence and occasional verse" (Fenton 3). Indeed, Stephen's older siblings, William and Laura, also became writers.

As a son of the army, Benét moved about: Bethlehem, Pennsylvania, Watervliet, New York, Rock Island, Illinois, Benecia, California, Augusta, Georgia and more. This diverse view of the United States would later inform his writing. He graduated from Yale in 1919. (In 1918 he had enlisted in the army, but was honorably discharged due to very poor vision and a fragile health derived from a childhood attack of scarlet fever, which would follow him through life and result in his early death.) Benét earned an M.A. from Yale in 1920 and received a traveling fellowship, which enabled him to go Paris in 1920-21. He married Rosemary Carr at the end of 1921 and began his career as a writer of poems, short stories, novels, and book reviews. He received a Guggenheim Fellowship in 1926-27, which enabled him to write *John Brown's Body*, winner of the Pulitzer for poetry in 1929. Southern poet-critic Allen Tate said of it, "If professional historians, particularly those of the Northern tradition, will follow Mr. Benét's Davis, a distorted perspective will soon be straightened out. Nowhere else has Lee been so ably presented..." (Fenton 214). The best-selling epic earned him substantial income for the first time and Benét invested it in stocks. By the end of 1929, he lost all of it in the stock market crash.

For Benét, as well as MacLeish, Wilder and the rest of the Western world, the 1930s demanded attention be paid to, first, the Depression, then, the rise of fascism and Stalinism in Europe. Here begins the public activism for the Yale trio that they pursued to the end of their lives. Still, the true measure of service is not just what a person does in the general forum, but the personal, private gestures that signify true, egoless magnanimity. All three were prodigiously generous with or without fanfare.

Benét is recalled as a benefactor to emerging writers, particularly in the early 1930s when he was the editor of the Yale Series of Younger Poets. Among them were: Edward Weismuller, Norman Rosten, Muriel Rukeyser, James Agee, Margaret Walker, Joy Davidman, and Paul Engle. Weismuller said in 1956, "It seemed to me that I owed the real beginning of my career to him. He was a very wise person, utterly kind; only seeing him and having him glad to see me, willing to talk to me, meant a great deal. A great man, talking to me as though we were both quite ordinary people! Obviously it was possible to be a poet and a human being too; I had hoped it was, but how, at that time, is one to know?" (Fenton 263).

Benét, far from affluent after the crash, understood the young writer's struggle. "I have been thinking about the Yale series," he wrote to the Yale Press, "to this effect. It seems rather disproportionate to pay me $250 for reading the mss. when the lucky boy or girl who wins the competition can only make, at the most, $100 if he completely sells out the 500 copies of his book. I therefore suggest that you pay me $150 and pay the winner of the competition the other $100 ... after all, I'm old and tough" (Fenton 264). And so it was.

In fact, due to Benét's own need for income, he was forced to sacrifice a quest for "pure art" for commercialism and wrote, to the best of his ability, short stories that were good, but would also sell. He fully understood the struggle to make a living, especially in the Depression, which aroused the first stirrings of his public consciousness:

> He could not insulate himself against the grim depression winters in New York. He was stricken by the sight of white-collar workers wielding relief shovels in their shabby overcoats. "They were not used to digging," Benét wrote. "You could tell by their shoulders." [Archibald] MacLeish, far better informed about the national scene than most American writers [as editor of *Fortune* magazine] was living in New York now. The two couples were congenial and saw a good deal of each other socially. MacLeish's own poetry was shifting from the personal concerns of his earlier verse; now he was formulating his concept of public speech as the role of the poet in time of national emergency. In the fall of 1933 Benét spent [an] evening with MacLeish. "Talk[ed] about really doing something about what we believe in," Benét noted in his diary, "both as regards literature and democracy" [Fenton 277].

This meant *liberal* democracy. With his support given to the New Deal, he said, "At the moment every element I dislike most in the country [Marxists, fascists, and the rich] is allied against Roosevelt [who] has made his purpose plain and united all the pigs and Bourbons against him, which is fine" (Fenton 278). This meant Benét was *for* him. Liberalism was something very concrete and very American to believe in and share: "If you're a liberal, that means you're always out on a limb. It isn't very comfortable, on the limb, but then God never intended liberals to be comfortable. If he had, he'd have made them conservatives. Or radicals" (Fenton 279).

As time went on, however, Benét's frustration began to sound, if not radical, angry: "It is horrible to see the nervous violence of the comfortable ones once they get the idea that one cent of their precious money is being touched. It makes you feel degraded. The patriots and lovers of America who put their money in Newfoundland holding companies—the descendants of signers who talk about people on relief as if they were an inferior breed of dog. What a sorry class of rich we have here—their only redeeming feature is their stupidity" (Fenton 282). The energy of Benét's anger was put to good use. For the first time, his stories and verse began to use the American past as parables to the present.

His story about the young Washington, "Man from Fort Necessity," appeared in the *Saturday Evening Post,* and in it the unwarranted vitriol aimed at Washington is meant to be compared to the attacks on FDR. In "Silver Jemmy" Jefferson and Aaron Burr are meant to parallel Roosevelt and Huey Long. So began a steady output of stories using the spirit of a liberal America to proselytize for the New Deal as the model of democracy in action. In 1936, Benét's *Burning City* was a verse outburst of patriotic indignation. Here—in addition to reminding Americans of their populist heritage in an "Ode to Walt Whitman" and "Do You Remember, Springfield?" about the evangelistic poet Vachel Lindsay—Benét considers the threat to the U.S. of totalitarianism. In "Ode to the Austrian Socialists," "Litany for Dictatorships," "Metropolitan Nightmare," and more, he tells not only of the actual European situation, but also warns of the potential for a homegrown fascism that could evolve out of a public indifference resulting from the alienating effects of the mechanized city. In "Nightmare with Angels," an angel in a gas-mask warns:

> You will not be saved by General Motors or the pre-fabricated house.
> You will not be saved by dialectic materialism or the Lambeth Conference.
> You will not be saved by Vitamin D or the expanding universe.
> In fact, you will not be saved [*Burning City* 75].

Increasingly, Benét's work took on the responsibility of the writer as citizen:

> If the artist believes, I think he should state his belief. It will never be earlier. He ought to think and think hard. For neither his freedom of speech nor his liberty of action will automatically preserve themselves. They are part of civilization and they will fall if it falls. And he has a responsibility to his own art, and that is to make it great. I doubt if he can do so by blacking himself out [from social awareness] [Fenton 357].

In 1936, Benét's role of parabolic storyteller took on more importance with the publication of "The Devil and Daniel Webster" in the *Saturday Evening Post.* The demand for it soon saw the story come out in book form, then an operetta, and later a film. Its enormous popularity "consolidated the national role which had slowly been materializing for Benét" (Fenton 293). With the increasing fascist threat in Europe, this was a role Benét readily responded to in his stories and verse. When, in 1939, the conflict there began, he said, "I hope we stay out of it. On the other hand, I'd sell the allies all the munitions possible—I don't want us to have to build a two-ocean fleet against time" (Fenton *Letters* 330). Prophetically speaking, Benét had hit the mark; the U.S. was put exactly in this position after Pearl Harbor.

Benét, without apology, now became a writer for democracy at the service of his country. "If what I am writing today ... will hurt my eventual reputation as a writer—very well, then let it. [And it did.] I can't just sit on my integrity as a writer, like a hen on a china egg, for the duration" (Fenton 357). He far from sat, writing pro–American, antifascist fiction and verse. He also wrote radio scripts for national broadcast: "We Stand United," "Listen to the People," "Letter from a Worker," *Dear Adolf* (a continuing series), "They Burned the Books," and much more. He requested that any fees he received be given to the USO. While Benét wrote for the public about a national democratic government being a service to its people—as compared to those who wanted less government—he also contemplated this privately in a letter to a friend:

> If national government is merely a "necessary evil" why the hell should anybody bother trying to set up any sort of *international* government? I think one of our great troubles has been this idea that "government" is something high-sounding and far-off and scary that gets after you with a club—that it's outside of and removed from the normal life of the citizen—that it's something you yell [to] for help in a very bad jam and curse out the rest of

the time. It isn't. Government is the people and the people are government. It isn't something some man from Mars called a "politician" does to you—it's what we do to and for ourselves to get the way of life we want and believe in. If we don't like the men who run it, we can get them changed—if we don't like the laws they make we can get laws changed—but we can't do either by sitting back on our rears and remarking, "The best government is the government that governs least." That was never true of any civilization more complex than that of the free hunter—and while I might like to be a free hunter, I know I can't be.... I don't know how you get an ideal government—but I'm perfectly sure you don't get it by regarding it as a dose of salts or an inevitable doom overtaking the innocent taxpayer. To the men who founded this union, the republic they envisaged and the government they devised meant something—a great and daring experiment and a roof for the people and a flag out on the wind. I want to get back to that idea and to the pride that was in that idea. I am tired of apologizing for the American experiment. In addition, that American government is precisely and exactly a howling success by any standard now existing on the planet. It is full of defects, it is still what we make it. But it works [*Letters* 392].

On March 13, 1943, this man of fragile health, who tirelessly worked for his country, died of a heart attack at the age of 44: "Orators and editorial writers [said] he had been killed in uniform as surely as if he had burned up in a B-17 or fallen at Guadalcanal" (*Letters* 362). Two days earlier, the last entry that this patriot for the common man wrote in his diary stated: "FDR sends social-security plan to Congress which immediately raises a storm of hate from the inept and reactionary" (Fenton 373).

MacLeish: American Stoic

Archibald MacLeish (1892–1982) was "a playwright, a lawyer, a teacher, a journalist, a Librarian of Congress, an assistant secretary of state, and, above all, a poet. The author of more than forty books of poems, plays, essays, and speeches, he won the Pulitzer Prize three times and received numerous other awards. Amy Lowell was for a time his mentor; Ernest Hemingway and Dean Acheson were among his closest friends. Adlai Stevenson once worked for *him*. He was called a fascist by communists and a communist by Senator Joseph McCarthy. Though Ezra Pound disdained his poetry, MacLeish was responsible, as much as anyone else, for Pound's release from long confinement in St. Elizabeth's [mental] Hospital" (Winnick xi).

The most public of these three public men, MacLeish was a lawyer who became a poet; an editor of *Fortune* magazine while writing articles for it that exhorted corporate America to respond more compassionately to the Depression; an assistant secretary of state and librarian of Congress under FDR; and a Harvard lecturer who wrote essays debunking McCarthyism. (Of the three writers, MacLeish was the most prolific essayist on specific social issues.) His experience with the law, business, and government made him a pragmatist, and his art, compared to Benét's visceral patriotism or Wilder's metaphysical parables, reflects this pragmatism with a starker, more stoic recognition of reality.

His art was well-praised, but the more he engaged in public activism, moving facilely from boardroom, to stateroom, to Harvard classroom, the more he was sniped at by those who implied that "true" art could not emerge from such "compromised" activities. The vitriol seemed excessive at times, and even envious of a man who could move in these circles so fluidly. Of course, MacLeish was not introverted and his outspoken opinions invited vociferous responses.

MacLeish was born to a progressive, upper-middle-class family in Illinois. His New England heritage came from his mother, who was from Connecticut. After attending Yale—where he was a poet *and* football player—then Harvard Law, MacLeish would make Conway, New Hampshire, his home base thereafter. In 1923, he gave up the law and with his wife, Ada, went to Paris—as did so many of his artistic contemporaries. There, he read and wrote poetry while Ada studied voice, being a very talented soprano. His first volume of poems, *The Happy Marriage*, came out in 1924. In 1929, Henry Luce, cofounder of *Time*, hired MacLeish to be the first editor of *Fortune*. In 1933, he won his first Pulitzer Prize for *Conquistador*, an epic poem, in vogue after the success of Benét's epic, *John Brown's Body*. His writing, both as journalist and artist, became increasingly activist *and* liberal. His poems and verse plays dealt with the Depression, fascism, and the poet's role as spokesperson. This is exemplified in the verse from the volume *Public Speech*, 1936, in which social issues are front and center.

Disturbed by *Time*'s conservative coverage of world events and the antipathy towards his pro–FDR/New Deal articles, MacLeish resigned from *Fortune* in 1938 and was asked to be Librarian of Congress in 1939. There, he modernized the library, sought greater recognition and salaries for all librarians, and "helped to redefine the profession by urging librarians to see that their proper place in the modern world was as champions to a cause: freedom of speech, freedom of thought, and, ultimately, human liberty" (Winnick xv).

In 1940, MacLeish's controversial essay *The Irresponsibles* asserted,

> History—if honest history continues to be written [compared to the rewritten history of totalitarianism]—will have one question to ask of our generation, people like ourselves. It will be asked of the books we have written, the carbon copies of our correspondence, the photographs of our faces, the minutes of our meetings in the famous rooms before the portraits of our spiritual begetters. The question will be this: Why did the scholars and the writers of our generation in this country, witnesses as they were to the destruction of writing and of scholarship in great areas of Europe and to the exile and the imprisonment and murder of men whose crime was scholarship and writing—witnesses also to the rise in their own country of the same destructive forces with the same impulses, the same motives, the same means—why did the scholars and writers of our generation in America fail to oppose those forces while they could—while there was still time and still place to oppose the enemies of scholarship and writing? [3]

Literary critic Van Wyck Brooks aligned himself with MacLeish, adding that too many writers emphasized gloom and doom without trying to do anything about it. The ensuing furor of the MacLeish-Brooks controversy was enormous:

> To many observers it seemed that MacLeish was wrapping himself in the flag. Dwight MacDonald accused him of "patrioteering." Bernard DeVoto spoke of him as a "crisis patriot." [Ignoring the fact that MacLeish had been writing on these issues for years.] In the fall of 1941, the *Partisan Review* solicited reaction to the "Brooks-MacLeish thesis." [They] were nothing more than "ideological policemen" and "frightened philistines," James T. Farrell asserted. MacLeish had dwindled into an apologist for official public policy, others commented. The dispute had barely quieted down by April 1942, when Stephen Vincent Benét wrote Farrell what may have been the most evenhanded assessment of the literary quarrel. On the one hand, Benét wrote, he "did not believe in throwing overboard a lot of the best writing of the past thirty years because it was 'gloomy' or 'depressing' in tendency" [nor did MacLeish]. On the other hand, he could not agree with Farrell that Brooks and MacLeish "wish to 'politicize' writing, set up a certain kind of State writing, put artists in uniform or do the

various things of which they have been accused." Farrell had also objected that lyric poetry [meaning MacLeish's] was hardly an appropriate form "in which to predict historic events." Why not? Benét wondered. "I don't think poetry should put its head in a bag—I don't think it should be the exclusive possession of an intellectual few." Of course, he would burn no books and suppress no writers—and neither would MacLeish [Donaldson 337–38].

Moreover, by 1942 MacLeish had been proven correct; there had been reason for concern and many of his critics would never forgive him for having been right.

After the war, never again did MacLeish receive the critical praise he had before it. In fact, his work was largely ignored. The notable exception was his first and only Broadway play, *J.B.,* 1958, an allegory about Job and man's place in the universe. It won the Pulitzer Prize for drama, and was a commercial success.

In 1949, MacLeish went to Harvard as Boyleston Professor of Rhetoric and Oratory. For thirteen years he taught, befriended and encouraged students who became his friends. In his advanced writing course were future writers William Alfred, Ilona Karmel, Edward Hoagland, Donald Hall, George Plimpton and Robert Bly. Bly recalled that he, young and rebellious, antagonized MacLeish constantly. Years later, Bly realized that "Archie could have exacted revenge; he could have dressed me down or turned me in to the dean for insubordination or embarrassed me in front of others, but he did none of those things." His teacher even nominated him for a poetry prize. "He," Bly said, "taught me something about nobility" (qtd in Donaldson 406).

As was Benét and, to come, Wilder, MacLeish was a kind and generous benefactor who privately lent his support to individuals and causes. He brought St. John Perse to the U.S. by securing him a consultancy at the Library of Congress; he played the major role in rescuing Pound and let others get the credit; he quietly paid the medical bills for a student who had a crippled leg; he intervened for a teacher who had been arrested for a charge relating to homosexuality that today would not even be illegal; he gave parties for friends and students where, the poet May Sarton said, "he had a genius for drawing people out, for making everybody feel they were brilliant." Most of all she found him selflessly generous (qtd. in Donaldson 423–24).

Even as a teacher, MacLeish still could be aroused to public action, especially to confront injustice. In the late 1940s, early 1950s this meant Joseph McCarthy. He did so in published letters to editors ("the greatest menace the American liberal tradition has faced in our lifetime"), essays and satiric doggerel verse befitting McCarthy's ranting. McCarthy retaliated by accusing MacLeish of having "been affiliated with as vast a number of communist fronts as any other individual whom I have ever named" (qtd. in Donaldson 430). Archie was honored.

In the 1960s he publicly argued against the Vietnam War, as did his lifelong friend Thornton Wilder.

Finally, through all of his varied life, he was first and last, a poet of just causes:

> Art exists in the context of life; that art is an action on the scene of life; that art is a means of perceiving life; of ordering life; of making life intelligible; and thus also of changing it. Only in poetry does *man* appear, man as he really is in his sordidness and his nobility. Elsewhere in the University man is a clinical specimen, or an intellectual abstraction, or a member of a mathematical equation, or a fixed point in a final dogma. Only with [poets] is he himself ... himself in all his unimaginable—unimaginable if literature had not perceived them—possibilities [qtd. in Donaldson 416].

Thornton Wilder: American Metaphysical

> I am happiest in loving and being loved by human people, and next to that in writing words and being commended for them, and next to that in mysteries of the spirit, into which I penetrate more every year.... I am continually surprised at people's lukewarmness: I am perpetually enthusiastic over some composition or book, some person or friend.
> — *Thornton Wilder, at age 20,*
> *in a letter to his brother Amos*
> *(qtd. in Harrison 8)*

Thornton Wilder's (1897–1975) self-confident fervor shows that his lifelong enthusiasm was not merely an aftereffect of public success, but began much earlier as an integral aspect of his nature.

Archibald MacLeish, fellow Yale graduate and lifelong friend, recalled that Wilder "was the most felicitous talker in America on almost any subject, particularly American culture" ("Isolation..." 177).

Wilder's enthusiasm for life was a key to his personality as a public persona. Yet, the integral Wilder was the man who devoted his life to studying the "mysteries of the spirit." He was a metaphysician on a consistent quest in a particular study: Thornton Wilder's lifelong pursuit was to inquire into the nature of goodness and consider how he could teach parables that conveyed what he learned. Unlike Benét and MacLeish, who are rarely read or performed, Wilder's legacy—even if he is not necessarily as esteemed by U.S. critics as he is revered in Europe and Russia—is secure. Why? Because as this is being read, *Our Town* is being performed somewhere in the world. He said, "Of all the forms of goodness, genius has the longest awkward age" (*Woman* 55). America is still awkwardly trying to catch up with Wilder's genius, which is revered elsewhere.

Wilder's art was a conscious methodology of parabolic wisdom: In his earliest work, the playlets of *The Angel That Troubled the Waters*, Wilder established metaphysical themes that he would develop and extrapolate thereafter for the rest of his artistic life. He wrote novels and plays of ideas that never strayed far from his first love, which was teaching: His art was a sequence of lessons, but lessons disguised as entertainment as he believed that formal didacticism repelled readers rather than encouraged them. "One knows that in these matters beyond logic, beauty is the only persuasion" ("Preface..." xv). Wilder was a public activist, just as much as Benét and MacLeish, but he chose not to use his art to engage specific contemporary issues; instead, he dealt with universal themes of love and brotherhood, which might inspire readers or playgoers to practice these virtues that he had helped them to see.

Wilder, like Benét, grew up moving around. His father was alternately a journalist, diplomat, prohibitionist, and devout Congregationalist; his mother was the daughter of a minister. Hence, the "mysteries of the spirit"—a liberal spirit—imbued his youth. Wilder was born in Wisconsin. From 1905 to 1909, his family lived in China (Shanghai and Hong Kong); from 1910 to 1915 they resided near Berkeley, California; Wilder did his first two years of college at Oberlin of Ohio, the last two at Yale, his father's alma mater; there he worked on the *Yale Literary Magazine* with Benét with whom he later founded, with others, a literary review, *S4N* ("space for name"). After graduation, he went to Rome to study archaeology; this experience greatly informed Wilder's existential bent. From 1921 to 1926, he taught at a preparatory school in Lawrenceville, New Jersey. In 1926, his first novel was published, *The Cabala*, which drew on his Roman expedition. In 1927, *The Bridge of San Luis Rey* won the Pulitzer Prize for fiction and was an enormous bestseller and turned Wilder into an international celebrity. This was both a blessing and a curse.

Critics then, no differently than today, were skeptical of commercial success (i.e., if it plays to the mass, can it be "real" literature?). The novel had received good reviews, which predominantly categorized it as a "romance" albeit a superior one. The critical apparatus was not yet ready to see the full import of the book's metaphysics, which "between the lines" considered issues hued with both Eastern and existential philosophy. Hereafter, Wilder, despite his future accomplishments—*Our Town, The Skin of our Teeth, The Matchmaker* (later, the musical *Hello Dolly*), the screenplay for Alfred Hitchcock's *Shadow of a Doubt,* and many more novels, plays and essays—was never given the careful scrutiny he deserved. There have been more appraisals of him in Germany alone than in the United States. An aspect of this lack of appreciation is that Wilder was a very public man; he was gregarious and loquacious, and enjoyed the benefits of his celebrity—not in the financial sense, although he did enjoy making money so that he could give it away to family, friends, and causes—but for the freedom to travel and the chance to meet people he admired. He was frequently mentioned in the newspapers in the company of other famous people and thus didn't fit into the critics' idea of a "serious" artist who cloistered himself in solitude to await his muse. Frankly, Wilder was enjoying himself; he was also, privately, and without publicity, dispensing habitual benevolence:

> As his income increased so did his charities. A check went to Janet [his youngest sister] with a note, "sew this into your corset-cover. Travelers—especially girls—should always have lots of extra dough concealed on their person. Things happen. Sudden downpours. No taxis. Airplanes are boarded by pirates and directed to Cuba. Purses are snatched. If no 'call' is made on this money, do *anything* with it except mention it to me." He called this "mad-money," spending-it-on-anything money. He brought food and drink to [school] gatherings [the University of Chicago, 1931–36], sent flowers to hostesses, … $500 … to a young actor, money to a negro baritone from Hamden [Connecticut] High School, to Yale. Leftover travelers checks were handed to impecunious students. A thousand dollars went to the American Civil Liberties Union, $250 to a struggling painter … $100 to someone in Texas who had written him a despairing letter…. There would be gifts to hospitalized veterans, to the Thacher school [of his youth], a Brooklyn church, German refugees, a godson for travel ($2,000), a preservation society, the Red Cross, Recordings for the Blind, Berea College, and of course to the Wilders. He never wanted to think about or be reminded of what he earned. [In 1930 this was $78,000 (before taxes), mainly royalties from *The Bridge,* of which he gave away at least $24,000 which can be accounted for, and probably much more out of pocket.] It gave him pleasure to give pleasure and he devised ingenious ways of doing it [Harrison 134].

At the end of 1930, however, Wilder found out about the downside of celebrity, learning that he was fair game for critics.

The huge success of *The Bridge* afflicted Wilder with the "curse of the bestseller." This inevitably meant that whatever followed it would be subject to the severe scrutiny that comes with high expectations. *The Woman of Andros*, 1930, set just before Christ on a Greek isle, is very short—really a novella—and its style is fairy tale. There are thematic metaphysics consistent with Wilderian cosmology, but it is still *The Cabala* and *Bridge* "light." With more of an epic follow-up expected, combined with the temper of this now-depression era, which wanted more in the way of current events, this fable, for many critics, smacked of "escapism" and a denial of reality. Writers were now supposed to be engaged and Wilder's new novel seemed—to them—rather *dis*engaged. Romanticism was out—particularly for Communist literary critic Michael Gold.

Gold knew that an attack on Wilder would give him the most publicity. Gold, in his *New Republic* article "Prophet of the Genteel Christ," called *The Woman of Andros* "a daydream of homosexual figures in graceful gowns moving archaically among the lilies." (There are no homosexual characters; this was 1930. Rather, it appeared to be a cheap stab at Wilder's orientation—one that was very private.) Further, Gold said that the book's spiritual motives were grounded in a religiosity of

> Anglo-Catholicism, that last refuge of the American snob ... that newly fashionable literary religion that centers around Jesus Christ as the first British Gentleman. Is this the speech of a pioneer continent? Will this discreet French drawing-room hold all the blood, horror, and hope of the world's new empire? ... Where are the cotton mills...? Where are the child slaves of the beet fields? Where are the stockbrokers' suicides, the labor racketeers, or passion and death of the coal miners? ... Is Mr. Wilder a Swede or a Greek, or is he an American? No stranger would know from these books he has written [qtd. in Kuner 90-91].

"Mr." Wilder, definitely a proud American, did not respond directly, but as he was normally a loquacious person, the vociferousness of his answer was in the silence. As for the so-called lack of reality of this "French drawing room," *The Woman of Andros* has three deaths (two young women and an infant); oppressed minorities, workers, and slaves; conniving capitalists and politicians; bigotry; a victim of mental illness; and a heroine, Chrysis, who is a former slave, becomes a working girl (prostitute), starts an intellectual "salon" to disseminate egalitarian ideals, takes in the homeless and the crippled, and dies young. Gold apparently couldn't see these allegorical correlations to the present unless Chrysis was renamed Bess and relocated to the present of Anytown, U.S.A.

Gold's politicized attack was self-serving; he had chosen himself to be spokesman for the oppressed and argue for more social—preferably Communist—activism from the literary front. Choosing Wilder as his negative exemplum was easy and, as expected, the most likely choice to arouse the controversy—and publicity—he was looking for. In effect, he was accusing Wilder of a naivete so egregious as to be insensitive by omission. Wilder could live with being accused of naivete, but insensitive was too much for a man who *needed* to be thought otherwise and acted on this need with profligate gestures of kindness and generosity. Wilder did not respond in kind, but did so in the way he knew best—through his art as parable. Moreover, despite the unfairness of the attack, it could only have made an already sensitive Wilder even more so to the needs of the world around him.

In 1931, Wilder wrote his first works with American settings, a sequence of one-act plays collected under the title *The Long Christmas Dinner*. Some critics thought that these and his next novel, *Heaven's My Destination*, published in 1935, were responses to Gold. In part, they may have been influenced by Gold's attack, but all had been in progress before it. The novel, his fourth, is set in contemporary America and concerns the blundering adventures of a twenty-three-year-old traveling salesman named George Brush, an evangelistic Christian who is also a follower of Ghandi and Tolstoi. His escapades are the result of an enormous naivete like that which Gold had accused Wilder of. Brush is, in part, autobiographical, plus a little of Wilder's father and a lot of the poet-performance artist Vachel Lindsay, 1879–1931, whom Wilder had met at Yale in 1918. Lindsay, like Brush, was also a naive evangelist who admired Eastern philosophy and Tolstoi. He killed himself when the public, hardened by the Depression, no longer appreciated his patriotic, Whitmanesque poems about love, freedom and brotherhood.

Wilder never did respond to Gold directly, but through Brush—and Lindsay—he used his conscious method of parable art to teach this lesson: How well-meaning idealists, even if perceived as naive, should receive patience and kindness rather than callous rebukes that could destroy them.

Wilder survived. Moreover, in 1938, *Our Town* was first performed. This American metaphysical classic is as homespun as the corner candy store, but one where we soon realize the sage man behind the counter, like *Our Town's* Stage Manager, dispenses the wisdom of the ages. Throughout the 1930s, Wilder continued his private kindnesses, but was as yet not the public activist he would become. One event changed him.

In 1940, his good friend MacLeish had been asked to attend an international writer's conference in London to represent the U.S. and, in effect, show support for England's war effort. MacLeish could not attend and asked Wilder to go in his place. Wilder (and John Dos Passos) arrived in London at night during the blackout and then experienced the blitz of German air attacks. He returned to America determined to report what he saw and get involved with the war effort; this included enlisting in the Air Force, serving in its Intelligence division. Hereafter, Wilder was a civic participator:

> Increasingly, beginning in 1941, Thornton would be drawn into nonliterary public activities. He would aid refugees fleeing Nazi Germany and Austria, providing affidavits of support enabling them to obtain American visas, welcoming them at the dock in New York, handing them five hundred dollars, arranging hotel accommodations, taking them to dinner and sending them theater tickets; he would accept the presidency of a committee raising funds for Albert Schweitzer's hospital in Africa; serve on the American delegation to a UNESCO Conference in Venice; join a national committee supporting the election of Senator John F. Kennedy for president; sign a petition to Congress demanding that American troops be brought home from Vietnam; protest the practice of racial discrimination in theaters and auditoriums in Washington, D.C.; write a get-out-the-vote appeal for the American Veterans' Committee; prepare a script for the National Conference of Christians and Jews honoring America's religious diversity [Harrison 210].

Wilder was also an early *feminist*, telling his unmarried sister, Isabel, in 1937, "Don't overdo the notion that a woman has nothing to say or be or give unless she's wife-mother-and-home-decorator. *We're all people before we're anything else*, even before we're artists. The role of being a person is sufficient to have lived and died for. Don't insult 10 million women by saying a woman is null and void as a spinster" (Harrison 176).

After the war, Wilder received more attention than MacLeish did, but mainly in Germany and Russia rather than at home. There, his apocalyptic play *The Skin of Our Teeth* (1942), which is about man rising from his ruins, poignantly moved postwar audiences. Wilder, like MacLeish, also had a hit play, *The Matchmaker*, 1954, and published three more novels: *The Ides of March*, 1948, *The Eighth Day*, 1967, and *Theophilus North*, 1973. The novels did moderately well, and *The Eighth Day* even had a good critical response, winning the National Book Award, for its existential murder mystery. Still, the critics who appreciated the metaphysics in it seemed to think Wilder had caught up with modernity when, in fact, modernity had caught up with him. The themes in *The Eighth Day* were the same as those he had initiated over fifty years before in *The Angel That Troubled the Waters*. Europeans already knew this. There, the Wilderian cosmology, with its *New Age* elements, is fully appreciated; here, it still awaits the elucidation that it has deservedly received overseas. In fact, all three members of the Yale Club deserve better than they have gotten; and this neglect is not due to their art, which holds up just fine, if anyone would read it. There is another reason.

Wilder, MacLeish, and Benét were too public, too patriotic, and hence, too "uncool" for the purists. This writer believes that the Yale Club was largely ignored after the war because of their public roles before and during it when they were among the most popular writers in the country. In the U.S., large-scale acceptance is greeted with great skepticism by "serious" critics. In fairness, the correlation is often correct, but one that has become an assumption of always being correct. Early in their careers, before the national emergencies of the Depression, followed by World War II, all three had received praise from such esteemed critics as Conrad Aiken, Arnold Bennett, John Peale Bishop, Van Wyck Brooks, Malcolm Cowley, Allen Tate, Edmund Wilson, and many more. After the war, all three suddenly were no longer nearly as credible as serious artists for a combination of reasons: from 1945 to 1950, people wanted to forget the war and this required forgetting the previously popular patriots; in the 1950s, the cold war and the bland Eisenhower era didn't pay too much attention to anything—especially issues; the 1960s created a new set of issues, but also a new set of heroes and this baby-boom, youth-oriented decade didn't trust anyone over thirty.

What are the lessons to be learned from Benét, MacLeish, and Wilder? Apparently, that too much popularity and public activism are bad for one's long-term artistic reputation.

MacLeish, Wilder, and Benét were artists who believed they had a civic responsibility as American citizens to assert their democratic option to speak out for themselves, but even more so, for others. If a doctor, salesman, fireman, teacher, mechanic, seamstress, bus driver, bank teller does this, no one complains. Public figures are different; they're celebrities, living in a fantasy that fascinates us. The public shrouds them in mystery and does not want reality to intrude into that vicariousness of "otherness" that takes them temporarily out of their own lives. When public figures speak out, the illusion is broken; they remind people of the real world they are trying to forget. Sometimes, the public reacts to these reminders by hostile rejection. Today, with the media practically reporting from celebrity bedrooms almost immediately after anything happens, writers, actors, musicians, even the nearly extinct men of letters, are afraid to say something that might come back to haunt them. So they don't say anything at all—even when they should.

Stephen Vincent Benét, Archibald MacLeish, and Thornton Wilder did the sixties thing in the thirties and far past that tumultuous decade, and it seems they too had to pay a price for doing so. They should be admired as role models. We, like they, should believe it's okay to care about our fellow citizens—the common men and women, to speak out for them, to defend them, to respond to their detractors. We, like the activists of the 1930s and 1960s, should think it's "cool" to be a liberal humanist who is a public activist. What writers of or about literature today are civic participators? Where are the men or women of letters today with a social consciousness? This writer lives near three major universities, the English faculties of which seem to be invisible—even the tenured members. Don't rock the boat! The pattern seems to be that it is better to cast silently about than risk making waves. The more silent and cloistered men or women of letters are, the poorer we all are. It is easier to respect a person who takes a public position even if disagreed with, than to respect someone who whines in private but disappears otherwise. It seems also that when someone does go public, many of the private whiners, even if agreeing with this person's views, snipe anyway, perhaps resenting the other's courage that they themselves cannot find.

WORKS CITED

Benét, Stephen Vincent. *Letters of Stephen Vincent Benét*. Ed. Charles Fenton. New Haven: Yale UP, 1960.

_____. "Nightmare with Angels." *Burning City*. New York: Farrar & Rinehart, 1936.

Bishop, John Peale. *The Collected Essays of John Peale Bishop*. New York: Scribner's, 1948.

Donaldson, Scott. *Archibald MacLeish: An American Life*. Boston: Houghton-Mifflin, 1990.

Fenton, Charles. *Stephen Vincent Benét*. New Haven: Yale UP, 1958.

_____, ed. *The Letters of Stephen Vincent Benét*. New Haven: Yale UP, 1960.

Graham, Stephen. *Tramping with a Poet in the Rockies*. New York: Appleton, 1922.

Harrison, Gilbert. *The Enthusiast, A Life of Thornton Wilder*. New Haven: Yale UP, 1983.

Kuner, M.C. *The Bright and the Dark*. New York: Crowell, 1972.

MacLeish, Archibald. *The Irresponsibles*. New York: Duell, Sloan, Pearace, 1940.

_____. *"The Isolation of the American Artist."* A Continuing Journey. Boston: Houghton-Mifflin, 1968.

_____. *Public Speech.* New York: Farrar & Rinehart, 1936

Wilder, Thornton. "Preface." *The Angel That Troubled the Waters.* New York: Coward-McCann, 1928.

_____. *The Woman of Andros.* New York: Albert & Charles Boni, 1930.

Winnick, R. H. "Introduction." *The Letters of Archibald Macleish.* Boston: Houghton-Mifflin, 1983.

4. The Charmed Circle of Stephen Vincent Benét: Philip Barry, Jed Harris, Thornton Wilder

Laura Shea

When Stephen Vincent Benét arrived at Yale in September 1915, he made friends who would last a lifetime. Among his contemporaries were the playwrights Philip Barry and Thornton Wilder, who became part of his circle, as did the director and producer Jed Harris. The circle turned out to be charmed. In the years between the wars, American drama, once a provincial enterprise, achieved world-class status. This was due in no small part to the talents of Barry, Wilder, and Harris, who represented and revolutionized the theatre of the 1920s, 1930s, and 1940s.

During their college years, when the stratification of Yale society was set in stone, most of Benét's associates organized themselves around the *Yale Literary Magazine* with the Elizabethan Club as the base of operations. While theirs was a noble undertaking, they did not aspire to, nor could they expect entry into the Skull and Bones or Scroll and Key, the upper reaches of the collegial social scene. This was the domain of the sons of privilege who enjoyed unquestioned social superiority: those related to a president or an Auchincloss or a du Pont; followed by the sons of the captains of industry. Prosperous merchants, ministers, lawyers, and physicians sent their sons to Yale, as did the genteel Protestant middle class. Finally, there were those who would not be considered for membership in any society—the sons of immigrants, usually Irish or Jewish, for whom a quota, rather than a social, system was firmly in place. Usually, their goal was to study hard for a degree in law or medicine (Goldstone 27). Among the socially unsolicited, one of twenty-five Jewish freshmen in a class of 375, was Jacob Horowitz, from Newark, New Jersey. During his short time at Yale, he began the transformation of Jacob, quickly renamed Jake, Horowitz into Jed Harris, the theatrical *wunderkind* of the 1920s.

From the genteel Protestant middle class came Thornton Wilder. Wilder's father, Amos, had matriculated at Yale. After several childhood years spent in China, where his father for a time held the post of consul general for Hong Kong, Wilder hoped to enter Yale as a freshman. Although his father had ended his diplomatic career and moved his family to New Haven, where he served as the executive secretary for the Yale-in-China program, Amos Wilder thought the school too worldly for his son. Thornton and his older brother, Amos, were sent to the more egalitarian Oberlin College, which based its educational pursuits upon a strong moral foundation. Wilder's disappointment was assuaged by the fact that at Oberlin he found like-minded individuals interested in literature and theatre, and he stood out among them. After his sons spent two years at Oberlin, Amos Wilder changed his mind. Always uncertain of Thornton's potential for success and eager to end the family's separation and save a little money, Thornton's father enrolled him at Yale, where his brother Amos also became a student. As at Oberlin, Wilder found his way into the literary and dramatic circles. According to his classmate John Farrar,

> The artistic life of the college centered around the Elizabethan Club, where undergraduates, graduates and professors gathered ... of an afternoon or evening to smoke and talk. Here one would find most of the English faculty.... It was a volatile and eager gathering and in this crowd Wilder was a somewhat retiring but decidedly definite figure.... His wit was sudden and devastating, and while it made him close friends, it frightened away the dullards [qtd. in Simon 30].

Benét was not among the intimidated; the first meeting between Benét and Wilder suggests that the reverse was true. Wilder's early acquaintance with Benét is transcribed in a letter from "Thorneybush" to Wilder's mentor at Oberlin, Dr. Charles H. Wager, chairman of the English department. Wilder writes of his early impressions of Yale:

> This evening, the young [Stephen Vincent] Benét asked me over so that he could read some of my stuff as potential for the *Yale Lit* of which he is the whole power, although not printed as even on

the staff. He is a perfectly unromantic looking person, although not commonplace. His hair is short and light and curly. His face is round and quizzical and snubbed and his eyes are mole's eyes. He rocks his shoulder from side to side while talking. He was somewhat late for our appointment, so I went into his room and made myself at home. Everything was in an awful disorder. Clothes and books covered the floor. I found out later that four boys used this room as their library. There were hundreds of titles: an awful lot of Zola, Samain and Maupassant. *Sinister Street* and Lord Dunsany galore, Synge and Fiona, Lionel Johnson, Francis Thompson, *Alice in Wonderland*—the eternal affectation of the sophisticated—and so on…. Soon Steve came in and devoted himself to my paper [and] while my smudgy typewritten sheets were passed silently between them, I again was left to my thoughts. They were wealthy boys; all the books I have named were bought at our little deluxe Brick-Row Bookshop where you ask for Yeats and he takes it for granted that you want the autographed copy on Japanese paper…. They had been reading [my] *Angel on the Ship* and *Solvs inter Deos Potens* and when Benét finished he got up and said some very nice things and showed me all the way out down the hall…. I myself was obsequious and Uriah Heepish the while, but you doubt not that I shall assert myself in time. But what a glimpse I got of what I thought I would have to go to Oxford for. And I don't suppose they ever let it occur to them that they are so perfect. It takes one from the jaded middle class, one too used to pinching and window shopping and chatting with grocers' sons, to really appreciate the amenities and timbres of such a group [qtd. in Harrison 52–54].

Following this introduction, Wilder began to write for the *Yale Lit* and to socialize with Benét and his friends at their gatherings on Sundays, when Wilder recited his poetry. In an interview with the *Boston Traveler*, December 14, 1955, Wilder identified Stephen Vincent Benét, Harry [Henry R.] Luce and himself as the outstanding poets at Yale (qtd. in Simon 30), though it was Wilder who composed the college's Ivy Ode.

Like many of his era, Wilder's education was interrupted by military service. His friend Benét had joined the Army, passing the eye exam only by memorizing the chart. Benét was sworn in, but the oversight was noticed the next day by a sharp-eyed sergeant who watched him peel potatoes and thought him in danger of cutting off his nose. A second eye exam was ordered, using a different chart, and he was recommended for immediate discharge, his military career ending after three days. Benét was subsequently appointed to the State Department as a clerk, followed by a year as cryptographer for Military Intelligence (Fenton 73). Poor eyesight did not keep Wilder out of military service, though it did limit his participation. Instead of experiencing the war overseas, Wilder was assigned to a division of the Coast Artillery at Fort Adams, in Newport, Rhode Island. Among the boarded-up "cottages" of the very rich, Wilder served for a year (1918-19) as a clerk typist and successfully defended Narragansett Bay.

Following his military service, Wilder returned to Yale to complete his degree. Wilder's four-act play *The Trumpet Shall Sound*, the winner of the Bradford Brinton Award, was published one act at a time over four months in the *Yale Literary Magazine* (1919-20). Borrowing from Ben Jonson's *The Alchemist*, the play follows two servants as they attempt a takeover of their master's house. It was the first of Wilder's plays to receive a professional production, off–Broadway in 1926. Wilder graduated from Yale in 1920, but never fully left the place, living for many years in close proximity to the college.

While teaching at Lawrenceville Academy, Wilder gained fame in 1927 when he wrote the novel *The Bridge of San Luis Rey*. But he is best known for his dramatic works, particularly *Our Town* and *The Skin of Our Teeth*. The former is kept alive by innumerable high-school productions, and the latter is frequently revived by amateur and professional groups. At the time of their composition, both plays offered an experimental approach to drama, defined by John Gassner as "theatricalism" as opposed to the realism often associated with American drama. Gassner wrote in *Form and Idea in Modern Theatre*:

> The fundamental premise of realism is the Aristotelian one that drama is an imitation of an action; realists held, therefore, that the most desirable theatre is that in which imitation is closest. The fundamental premise of theatricalism is that theatre is not imitation in the narrow sense, which Aristotle never could have held, since the Greek drama upon which he based conclusions in his *Poetics* was not realistically imitative. For the theatricalist, the object of action and all other "imitative" elements is not imitation but *creativeness*, and a special kind of creativeness at that. The realists would agree, of course, as to the value of creativeness. But the theatricalist goes one step further, and that step is the truly decisive one for the theory and practice of pure theatricalism. He maintains that there is never any sense in pretending that one is not in the theatre; that no amount of make-believe is reality itself; that in short, theatre is the medium of dramatic art, and the effectiveness in art consists in *using* the medium rather than concealing it [141-42].

Frustrated by what he saw as the theatre's failed attempts to be real, Wilder employed dramatic techniques in *Our Town* and *The Skin of Our Teeth* that shatter the invisible fourth wall of realism. The Stage Manager in *Our Town*, a role Wilder played on several occasions, and Lily Sabina, a stage manager of sorts in *The Skin of Our Teeth*, speak directly to the audience, frankly admitting that what the audience sees is only a play. Staged with a minimum of sets and props, as opposed to the often cluttered stage picture of realism, Wilder's plays attempt to imbue the smallest details of everyday life with a metaphysical significance. According to Wilder, "Molière said that for the theatre all he needed was a platform and a passion or two. The climax of this play needs only five square feet of boarding and the passion to know what life means to us" (48).

Our Town, written in 1938, shows how the people of Grover's Corners, New Hampshire, particularly the Webb and Gibbs families, grew up, married, lived, and died. Human beings in Grover's Corners never "realize life while they live it," and only the deceased Emily Webb, and perhaps the theater audience, who watch the scenes of everyday life from different perspectives of time and space and from a position outside the action, come to this understanding. (As the Stage Manager adds, "The saints and poets, maybe—they do some" [72].) A connection between the quotidian and the cosmic is suggested in a letter addressed to Jane Crofut, as described by Rebecca Gibbs to her brother, George:

> REBECCA: It said: Jane Crofut; the Crofut Farm; Grover's Corners; Sutton County; New Hampshire; United States of America.
>
> GEORGE: What's so funny about that?
>
> REBECCA: But listen, it's not finished: the United States of America; Continent of North America; Western Hemisphere; the Earth; the Solar System; the Universe; the Mind of God—[31].

The Stage Manager describes the Dead, who sit onstage in Act III, at different stages of indifference to life on earth, as "waitin' for something that they feel is comin'. Something important and great. Aren't they waitin' for the eternal part in them to come out clear?"(59). This occurs after death when the earthly part of them, their human identity, dissolves, and they merge with that final piece of Jane Crofut's address: the Mind of God. This action, according to Wilder, is both commonplace and remarkable.

In *The Skin of Our Teeth*, written in 1942, Wilder enlarges the scope of the everyday by presenting the 20,000-year-old man and his wife and family. The Antrobuses of Excelsior, New Jersey, encounter every disaster in human history, both natural and man-made. Average Americans and universal types, Mr. and Mrs. Antrobus, Adam and Eve, and their two children, Gladys and Henry, a son who bears the mark of Cain, must survive fire, flood, the Ice Age, and each other. Not the least of the challenges to the Antrobus marriage is their own snake in the garden, the maid Lily Sabina, who often steps out of character to express her dissatisfaction with her role. Rather than approximating life as lived, *The Skin of Our Teeth* is littered with falling scenery and the onstage presence of a dinosaur and a mammoth, pets to the Antrobus family, with another Stage Manager who makes frequent appearances to move the action forward and to remove the detritus left in the wake of catastrophe. Through it all, the Antrobuses, like humankind, survive, as the title suggests, by the skin of their teeth.

The comic theatricalism of *The Skin of Our Teeth* masks the more serious issue debated by Mr. Antrobus: whether the human race, with all its flaws and failures, is worth saving. Luckily, he decides that it is, although Antrobus' forbearance, and the man himself, is sorely tested. With the successful production of *The Skin of Our Teeth*, Wilder found himself embroiled in a controversy which challenged his own forbearance, regarding the use by the former schoolmaster of literary sources. At this point in his career, Wilder was an enthusiastic reader of the revolutionary works of James Joyce. *Finnegans Wake*, perhaps the most difficult of Joyce's novels, was read and understood by a very small audience when it first appeared in 1939. In that number of mostly professional readers were two scholars, Joseph Campbell, then a professor at Sarah Lawrence, and Henry Morton Robinson, a former academic and playwright. Working together on a book entitled *A Skeleton Key to Finnegans Wake*, the two accused Wilder in the *Saturday Review of Literature* of extensive borrowing from Joyce's work. While not a direct accusation of plagiarism, "The Skin of Whose Teeth? or The Strange Case of Mr. Wilder's New Play and *Finnegans Wake*" describes the play as "an Americanized re-creation [of the Joyce novel], thinly disguised" (3). There are similarities between the two works in the circular pattern of the action and the repetition of the opening lines at the end of the play and the novel. The Antrobuses, like the Earwickers of *Finnegans Wake*, compress the history of humankind into the present day, and each work includes an "other" woman, Lily Kinsella in *Wake* and Lily Sabina in *Skin*.

Biographer Richard H. Goldstone insists that Wilder was well aware of the similarities, identifying two specific references to the novel. Wilder interpolates a line from *Finnegans Wake* into the text of *The Skin of Our Teeth*, when Sabina quotes almost verbatim from the novel: "What I think is that there are certain charges that ought not to be made, and I think I may add, ought not to be allowed to be made" (qtd. in Goldstone 174). The second reference is when Mrs. Antrobus displays a bottle she plans to throw into the ocean. The bottle contains a letter that describes all the secrets a woman knows and has never told any man. Both of these instances play a larger role in the novel than in the play. Goldstone sees these similarities as an acknowledgment of the Joycean influence: "No reader of *Finnegans Wake*, seeing or reading *The Skin of Our Teeth*, could fail to receive Wilder's signals, just in case the connection had not already been established" (174). And as Wilder himself writes in the Preface to *Three Plays*,

> The play is deeply indebted to James Joyce's *Finnegans Wake*. I should be very happy if, in the future, some author should feel similarly indebted to any work of mine. Literature has always more resembled a torch race than a furious dispute among heirs [xii].

The theatre community, most of whom did not read Joyce's novel, was mixed in its reaction to the controversy. Although *The Skin of Our Teeth* did not receive the New York Drama Critics Circle Award, it was honored with the more prestigious Pulitzer Prize.

A more notable influence on Wilder's work in the theater was the director and producer Jed Harris, whom Wilder met at Yale. In his largely self-serving memoir, *A Dance on the High Wire*, Harris offers one assessment that has the undeniable ring of truth:

> I don't need anybody poking around in my past for the origin of my prejudices against the rich. I got them legitimately in New Haven, Connecticut, and it's probably the most important thing I learned at Yale [13].

There was a point in his life when Harris loved Yale, but for reasons that had little to do with the reality of the place. Between the ages of ten and twelve, he was a voracious reader of the stories by Burton L. Standish, Jr., depicting the exploits of Frank Merriwell. Though he created part of its culture, Standish never actually visited Yale, and until his matriculation, neither did Harris. He was accepted after arriving in person, well past the application deadline, with transcript in hand and an alternative plan for satisfying the foreign language requirement, after failing third-year French in high school. He suggested and received a test in Hebrew. A two-hour exam followed, on which Harris received a perfect score. He was immediately accepted for admission (Gottfried 19).

This was the last form of acceptance Harris enjoyed at Yale. Sequestered with other Jewish students, Harris was an outsider even within this group, coming from a family of modest means, while his friends enjoyed more comfortable circumstances. Harris made extensive use of the library, but it was an article in one of the college magazines, *The Record*, that really got his attention. It began, "When Jews and other scum beyond human ken make Yale fraternities ..." (Harris 15; see also Gottfried 20–22). The anti–Semitism on campus was not unknown to Harris or to his friends, who advised Harris not to dignify the statement with a response, representing as it did not only the opinion of its author, but also that of the faculty advisors who allowed the article to be published.

Harris' break with Yale came as a result of his infrequent attendance at classes and less frequent attendance at the required college chapel. Though suspended, Harris took his final exams and passed, just barely in geology and economics, and with honors in philosophy, the only area of real interest to him and the only class he regularly attended. In response to Harris' essay on the origins and development of Christian philosophy, Professor Charles Allen Bennett wrote on the exam booklet, which received a grade of an A++, "For maturity of thought and terseness of style, the best paper I have ever had from an undergraduate" (Gottfried 24). When summoned to the dean, who informed the student that the suspension had escalated to an expulsion, Harris denied any knowledge of the matter, insisting that he had never been informed in writing. The boldness that would serve him well during his life in the theatre assisted him here, for he was never officially expelled, and the choice to leave Yale was his own.

Harris had always liked and respected Thornton Wilder, whom he knew slightly as an undergraduate. After Harris' departure from academe, they would not meet until ten years later when Harris, a successful theatrical director, and Wilder, the author of the best-selling novel *The Bridge of San Luis Rey*, met on a train going from Florida to New York. Their careers would intertwine on several important occasions, most notably in 1937, when Harris produced and directed Wilder's translation of *A Doll's House*, adapted for Ruth Gordon, followed by Harris' directing *Our Town*. Typical of his working style, Harris alternately charmed and bullied Wilder during the rehearsal period. Enthused about the prospect of directing a play that was experimental in technique, Harris was also determined that the play would succeed in its commercial run, and suggested many cuts to the text in order to make it more "entertaining." Though Wilder enjoyed the collaborative nature of theatre, he was not convinced that Harris understood his play, certain that the director was creating a New England daguerreotype that appealed to audience nostalgia at the expense of theatrical innovation. A brief tryout in Princeton went well, but in Boston the critics were not impressed. According to the actor William Roerick, one of the Boston reviews consisted of a single paragraph:

> Last night, Thornton Wilder's new play, *Our Town*, opened at the Colonial Theatre. When we arrived, the curtain was up and there was no scenery on the stage. We wondered if there was going to be a play. After watching it for two hours, we still wondered [qtd. in Gottfried 173].

Despite the grim tidings, Harris chose to open the play a week ahead of schedule in New York. The play was an immediate success, winning accolades for Harris and a Pulitzer for Wilder. Despite this success, their working relationship was damaged, and in 1942, when Wilder sent Harris *The Skin of Our Teeth,* the director was unable to clear his calendar for a play that failed to capture his imagination, even with the promise of rewrites by Wilder. The play was offered to director Elia Kazan, who used all of his considerable skill supervising a complex production and a cast that included Tallulah Bankhead, Florence Eldridge, and Fredric March.

Their differences over *Our Town* did not end the working relationship between Wilder and Harris, whose opinion Wilder continued to respect on matters theatrical. Harris was blunt, outspoken, and certainly one to hold a grudge, but he held no permanent ill will toward Wilder. Not all of his Yale classmates were as fortunate. Philip Barry, the author of the "society" plays *Holiday* and *The Philadelphia Story,* represented to Harris, inaccurately, as it turned out, the moneyed gentility that snubbed him at Yale. Harris, in 1936, did produce Barry's adaptation of *Spring Dance,* a comedy of college life by Eleanor Golden and Eloise Barrangon. The play ran for only twenty-four performances, and was a failure for all concerned.

Barry's lineage was, in fact, working-class Irish Catholic. Born in Rochester, New York, he came to New Haven from East High School, not one of the elite prep schools where many of his classmates matriculated. Like Wilder and Benét, who became a lifelong friend, Barry joined the Elizabethan Club and wrote for the literary magazine, though little that Barry published in the *Yale Lit* foreshadowed his success as a writer. Like his friends, Barry attempted to enlist in the armed services, but poor eyesight kept him from serving his country in this capacity. Barry did manage an appointment to the State Department, where he was briefly attached to the American embassy in London. Returning to Yale, he wrote plays for the Dramatic Club. His first produced effort was a one-act entitled "Autonomy," a satire of President Wilson's theory of the autonomy of nations, which shared the stage with "Nerves," by John Farrar, and "Poor Old Medusa," by Stephen Vincent Benét. The positive audience reaction encouraged Barry to pursue playwrighting. After graduation in 1919, he enrolled in the prestigious Writing Workshop directed by George Pierce Baker at Harvard, where Barry learned to write for the commercial stage. Professor Baker encouraged Barry to make use of his glib facility with words to investigate character and situation in his plays.

Philip Barry's witty style is prominently displayed in the social comedy *Holiday*, originally titled *The Dollar*, set in upper-class America, where a line is drawn between materialists and idealists. The self-made Johnny Case wants to hold tight to both his money and his ideals, but he must choose between his desire for the extended holiday he has earned and the beautiful Julia Seton, with whom he has fallen in love. The daughter of a millionaire, Julia plans to live life according to her father's wishes, which include Johnny's immediate installment as a banker. Luckily, Julia has a sister, Linda, who shares Johnny's point of view and encourages him to follow his dreams. Subsequently, Linda joins Johnny on his holiday.

Without completely rejecting material success, *Holiday* holds tight to its own dream that each individual can and must define life for him- or even herself. The play does not celebrate money as an end in itself, but punctures the pretensions of those who do. A social comedy concerned with the foibles of the upper class, *Holiday* made it just under the wire. Produced in 1928, the play predates the stock market crash of 1929, when the holiday was over and the decade-long party of the twenties came to an abrupt end, as did any short-term investment in the problems of the very rich. With the Great Depression following the crash, America had problems of its own.

In the decade that followed *Holiday*, Barry wrote more serious plays like *Hotel Universe* and *Tomorrow and Tomorrow*, which allude to Shakespeare's *King Lear* and *Macbeth* respectively. They did not enjoy the success of *Holiday*. In the late 1930s, Barry began work on another comedy of manners. A scribbled idea in a pocket notebook led to his best-known work, *The Philadelphia Story*: "The family in the process of being studied for a piece in 'Fortune.' Most unfortunate" (qtd. in Roppolo 90).

As in Shakespeare's *A Midsummer Night's Dream*, *The Philadelphia Story* takes place in a "green" world where interchangeable lovers seek suitable partners, the happy ending helped along by a transforming power which temporarily blurs, but finally clarifies, all that the lovers hold dear. Shakespeare's woods outside Athens may be protected by the power of magic, but money rules in the outskirts of Philadelphia. Due to her father's philandering, Tracy Lord has chosen to exclude him from the preparations for her second marriage to the suitable, if dull, George Kittredge. Seth Lord does have a say in the matter, however. He does not question his daughter's choice of a husband, but whether she should marry at all, telling her, "… you have everything it takes to make a lovely woman, except the one essential—an understanding heart. Without it, you might as well be made of bronze" (Barry 98). Her father's weakness for women and her first husband's weakness for alcohol are inexcusable in Tracy's estimation, until an evening of too much champagne reveals to the heiress her own potential weakness, and more importantly, her capacity for forgiveness. Reunited with her father and her first husband, Tracy also gains an awareness of her own humanity. Barry fashioned the part of Tracy Lord around the talents of Katharine Hepburn, who was in need of a success at this stage of her career. Labeled "box-office poison" after a string of failures, and still smarting from the critical drubbing she received in a play called *The Lake* several years before, Hepburn received enthusiastic reviews, as did her castmates Joseph Cotton, Van Heflin, and Shirley Booth. Reviewers did not fail to note the author's moral commentary just beneath the high comedy, but this did not keep audiences away, and Barry enjoyed another success, both critically and financially. Having purchased the movie rights to *The Philadelphia Story*, Hepburn played Tracy Lord in the critically acclaimed film version with a cast that included Cary Grant and Jimmy Stewart.

His social comedies made Barry a wealthy man and enabled him to enjoy the lifestyle about which he wrote. Splitting his time between homes in New York and Cannes, Barry often played host to Benét and his family. The friendship that took root at Yale extended to the end of Benét's life. Biographer Charles A. Fenton recreates a conversation between the two old friends that took place at Barry's place in the Hamptons about a year before Benét's death:

> They sat on the porch and somehow their talk drifted toward epitaphs. "I know what yours should be," said Barry. "Even Stephen." Benét said he liked that. Barry developed it further. "Even Stephen? *He* must go? Even Stephen. Even so." Benét grinned. "I like that too," he told Barry, "but it's sort of scary" [367–68].

Benét's death in 1943 closed the circle, but its charms remain. Drawing upon talents as diverse as the group itself, Philip Barry, Thornton Wilder and Jed Harris each made a unique contribution to American theatre. To know the members of his circle is to know Stephen Vincent Benét; like him, they left an indelible imprint on the world in which they lived.

Works Cited

Barry, Philip. *The Philadelphia Story.* New York: Coward-McCann, 1939.

Fenton, Charles A. *Stephen Vincent Benét.* New Haven: Yale UP, 1958.

Gassner, John. *Form and Idea in Modern Theatre.* New York: Holt, Rinehart, Winston, 1956.

Goldstone, Richard H. *Thornton Wilder.* New York: Dutton, 1975.

Harris, Jed. *A Dance on the High Wire.* New York: Crown, 1979.

Gottfried, Martin. *Jed Harris: The Curse of Genius.* Boston: Little, Brown, 1984.

Harrison, Gilbert A. *The Enthusiast: A Life of Thornton Wilder.* New York: Tichnor & Fields, 1983.

Robinson, Henry Morton, and Joseph Campbell. "The Skin of Whose Teeth? or The Strange Case of Mr. Wilder's New Play and *Finnegans Wake.*" *Saturday Review of Literature* 25 (Dec. 19, 1942): 3–4.

Roppolo, Joseph. *Philip Barry.* New York: Twayne, 1965.

Simon, Linda. *Thornton Wilder: His World.* Garden City, NY: Doubleday, 1979.

Wilder, Thornton. "A Platform and a Passion or Two." *Harper's Magazine,* Oct. 1957: 48–51.

_____. *Three Plays.* New York: Harper & Row, 1957.

POETRY, FICTION, DRAMA

5. 123 College Street: Stephen Vincent Benét and the Development of an Historical Poetry for America

Jared Lobdell

In those days, the address of the Elizabethan Club was 123 College Street, in a house built in 1804 on a block off the New Haven Green. The house is still there, still in the same place on College Street, but the number is now 459.

Back in 1894-95, Yale Professor William Lyon Phelps taught his first undergraduate course on Elizabethan drama. Among his students in that class was an apparently unremarkable junior named Alexander Smith Cochran, of the Yale Class of 1896, whose family owned a woolen mill in Yonkers. In 1906, Cochran wrote Billy Phelps from England, "saying that the course in Elizabethan Drama had awakened in him an acute interest in the literature of the period; that he had amused himself with collecting some rare books; and that in a few days he would send me his manuscript catalogue" (Phelps 292). Professor Phelps was "quite unprepared" for what followed, which was a catalogue of books worth (even in 1906) several hundred thousand dollars: "Shakespeare quartos, a copy of the first edition of the *Sonnets*, of Bacon's *Essays*, and so on."

The next year, Cochran wrote Phelps that he had a plan, that he was coming back to the United States, and that he wanted to discuss his plan with Phelps. Billy Phelps takes up the story:

His plan was a good one. He wished to found at Yale an Elizabethan Club, because the one thing he had most missed at Yale
was good conversation; that if there were an undergraduate club,
with a remarkable library as a nucleus, he thought students who
loved literature and the arts would be glad to meet there, and talk
informally and naturally about literature, both with their contemporaries and with congenial members of the Faculty. He would
donate the club building, the library, and the endowment [293].

He did, and not only that. By the time the Club opened in 1911, he
had added more books to the collection, and at the great Huth sale in that
year he bought all four Shakespeare folios, including (of course) the first—
along with quite a number of other items. The club took off with "club
nights" with distinguished guests, many of them English, in the years
1911–1914. Then it continued mostly bereft of its contacts with England
through the war years, until 1919, when the English visitors streamed in
once more—to meet an undergraduate population, some of whom had
fought with the AEF in France, and some of whom were experimenting
(at least in their minds) with the question of the American identity—no
longer the Anglo-American identity, as with Henry James, or indeed with
Alexander Smith Cochran.

To this club in the World War I years came a young undergraduate,
Stephen Vincent Benét, born July 22, 1898, in Bethlehem, Pennsylvania,
son of General (James) Walker Benét (b. 1857) and grandson of General
Stephen Vincent Benét, sometime chief of ordnance, U.S. Army. (He was
also brother of William Rose Benét, b. 1886, and nephew of Laurence
Benét, 1863–1948, Yale 1884, and at this time commandant, American
Ambulance and Hospital Service in France.) When Phelps wrote his autobiography, he remembered three undergraduates in particular from 1917-
1918: "Three of my undergraduate students, who were in college at the
same time, and intimate friends, have now [1939] become famous through
creative literary work. The playwright, Philip Barry, 1918; the poet, Stephen
Vincent Benét, 1919; the novelist Thornton Wilder, 1920" (661). But Barry
graduated before the war was over, and there were others in the postwar
group, Amos Niven Wilder (Thornton's older brother), Alfred Bellinger,
and John Chipman Farrar (all three of them being among the first poets
published in the Yale Series of Younger Poets)—and a nonpoet named
Robert Coates, to whom we will return later. It is worthwhile to look at
these other figures in this group, that we might call the Yale Renascence
and that met at 123 College Street, and worthwhile to acknowledge poems
written by those three of its less well-known figures, Bellinger (1893–1978),
Farrar (1896–1974), and Amos Niven Wilder (1895–1993).

Alfred Bellinger taught classics and numismatics and history at Yale. He taught me the history of the later Roman Empire in graduate school in 1961-62, the year of his retirement. Chip Farrar founded the publishing house that still bears his name. My father was once his investment advisor, and he was by way of being a family acquaintance, though not a family friend. Amos Niven Wilder (son of Amos Parker Wilder) was a distinguished churchman whom I knew as the father of my friend at both Yale and Wisconsin, Amos Tappan Wilder, Yale 1962. The reason I mention the "nonliterary" ways I came to know these men is to suggest that in these years after World War I they were amateur writers, occasional writers, or scholarly writers, so that their eventual careers were in different (though related) areas: they wrote their poetry as part of the intellectual ferment of a sunshine age.

Bellinger's poem is a song from his collection *Spires and Poplars* (1920): "Bright as a single poppy in a field," is about the youthful joy of collegial bliss. Farrar's is another joyful song in classical meter from his *Forgotten Shrines* (1919): "Come to me, Pan, with your wind-wild laughter." (Compare Benét's dochmaics and other classical meters in his "The First Vision of Helen" noted in Basil Davenport, "Stephen Vincent Benét" in *Selected Works of Stephen Vincent Benét*, Vol. I, x).

I spoke of Amos Niven Wilder as a churchman: he was indeed a graduate of the Yale Divinity School (1924), a Congregationalist minister, editor of the *Journal of Religion*, president of the Society of Biblical Literature, and secretary to Albert Schweitzer. Perhaps "churchman" is an inadequate word. He was also the author of a long poem deriving from his experience in the First World War, *Battle-Retrospect* (1923), and a memoir of that experience, *Armageddon Revisited* (published after his death in 1993)—and a number of other books, some of them on the relationship of religion and poetry. Incidentally, he played tennis in the All-England Tournament of Wimbledon in 1922. In *Battle-Retrospect*, an initial bliss and joy give way to a terrible reality of a war in trenches. "That fluctuating roar, its rise and fall." There follows an extended Classical simile of a second-rate eighteenth-century variety: I, but probably no one else, am reminded of Akenside. But the point here is Wilder's translation of the experience of wartime France into the neo–Classical mode.

"And I have seen, or thought I saw, the gods." Once again, this is neo–Classical, and it may escape us that the imagery is that of the Angels of Mons or of Chesterton's "Ballad of St. Barbara." Now that is not to say that Wilder's poem is better than Chesterton's or better than Arthur Machen's story, but it is to say that Wilder has made a poet's attempt to recollect in tranquillity and form the recollection in a Classical mode: in that sense this is more a poem, more a made thing, and Wilder more a *makar*, more a conscious poet, than Chesterton or Machen. This is similar to what Bellinger did with his poppy (already a World War I image), or Farrar did in general in his *Forgotten Shrines*.

Here is what the historian of the Yale Younger Poets series, George Bradley, says about these poets in his introduction to *The Yale Younger Poets Anthology*. He begins by quoting a comment by C. M. Lewis, the Classicist who was the editor of the Yale Series of Younger Poets from 1918 to 1923: the comment is from Lewis's introduction to *A Book of Verse of the Great War* (New Haven, 1917), and we will see its importance to our consideration of Benét and his historical poetry for America. "A critical curse lies upon the poetry of patriotism and war. The passion of patriotism is common to all right-minded men, and Criticism wants the uncommon.... The poet whose sole aim is to rekindle ... old ardors will be fortunate if he escape the ninety-nine ways of banality; and even the hundredth way, unless he is a consummate artist, will hardly lead him to the very peaks of Parnassus" (xxvi). Bradley then goes on to say that "No survey of the Yale series [of Younger Poets] can avoid the assessment that its early volumes were banal, even if Lewis's ninety-nine ways to banality rather overestimates their variety. Put simply, these authors tried to say too much and thereby said too little. The first Yale Younger Poets knew that they were witnesses to history, and they believed they had been touched with fire as surely as Oliver Wendell Homes, Jr., and his Civil War companions before them" (xxvii).

They could not communicate their wartime experiences, however, because in any art, skill at the art must precede meaning, and "unexceptional imitation" of Classical verse is not sufficient skill for the meaning they wanted their poems to bear. William Rose Benét put it well in his review of volumes 5–8 of the series, in the *Yale Review* of October 1921, when he hoped of the poets "that they'll all learn thoroughly to put what they think in the way they actually think it and not in the way they think precedent demands that it should be put" (qtd. in Bradley xxx). Admittedly, it was the older and not the younger Benét brother saying this, but their attitudes were much the same. Though it is going outside the bounds of 123 College to look at this, the choices Stephen Vincent Benét made when he was editor of the series, from 1933 to 1942, show clearly how he welcomed poets who said what they thought in the ways they thought it, including James Agee, Muriel Rukeyser, Joy Davidman, Margaret Walker, and Reuel Denney. Not that Benét never wrote imitative verse, or even imitative poetry: "The General Public" is an example to the contrary. But it was done with impish humor—so much so that, in his Yale days, much of his purest imitative (and impish) verse found its way into the *Yale Record* (the humor magazine) and not the *Yale Lit.*

In other words, the poetry of this sunshine age right after World War I was largely derivative and even the sunshine was arguably that of an Indian summer. But the ferment was unmistakable, and the principal location was 123 College Street. Cochran was right, and there's more. If I hold the first printing of *Othello* in my hands, or Ben Jonson's own copy of his *Works*, or Izaak Walton's copy of the first edition of Milton's *Lycidas*, there bubble up in my mind not only thoughts for conversation with my like-minded friends but—more slowly and from deeper levels—thoughts of greater moment, about history and the nature of language and the peoples of this Earth. If I hold *Othello* and look at the Reynolds portrait of David Garrick in the front room of the club, I can be transported back in my imagination to Johnson's eighteenth century and history becomes a palpable thing. I can fancy Dr. Johnson there, dribbling snuff. So could—and did—Benét and his friends.

That's not American history, of course. Yet I believe the experience with *Othello* and Garrick carries over into experience with other histories, other rooms. Moreover, I believe that Benét had a similar experience in those rooms at the Elizabethan Club, with those books and those pictures and the visitors from England. One piece of evidence comes from a passage in *John Brown's Body*, Book Four, the passage on Wingate Hall: "So Wingate found it, riding at ease / The cloud edge lifting over the trees / A white-sail glimmer beyond the rise ... Mounting, mounting, the shining spectre / ... / The cloud expanding, the topsails swelling" (*Selected Works* 142). Now this is a description of Wingate Hall, but one can hear Alfred Noyes in "The Highwayman," and see Steve Benét sitting there in the front room at 123 College, listening to Noyes read his poem (which he did there during his visit to this country in 1919): "The moon was a ghostly galleon, tossed upon cloudy seas...." Phelps said Noyes was the best public reader of his own poems of any poet he had ever heard (304).

Even if this gives us a source for the imagery, however, it might be asked why bring it up in this context. The answer lies in the fact that Noyes himself was historian as well as poet and he wrote historical poetry—"The Highwayman" is an example—speaking to what I have elsewhere called the Edwardian interest in "the past alive in the present" (18–19, 23). This is not only an Edwardian characteristic—it informs Rupert Brooke's "If I should die ..."—and it is not only an English characteristic. The Americans who went to France during the "Great War" were immensely conscious of French history—recall the cry "LaFayette, we are here!"—as indeed Amos Niven Wilder, in particular, makes clear.

When they came back, they brought that consciousness with them. It had been in the poetry they grew up on—Noyes or Newbolt. It was in the poetry they read or heard at Yale. It was in the approach Phelps took to Shakespeare (and to the Age of Johnson). It had been borne in on the returning servicemen by their service in the war, fighting in and across the immemorial countryside of France. Now it was brought home and nurtured in a United States of America suddenly excited and conscious of a new literary destiny of its own.

One can remember Benét's lines in the Invocation to *John Brown's Body*, describing both his characters and the genesis of the poem: "This flesh was seeded from no foreign soil / But Pennsylvania and Kentucky wheat" (*Selected Works*, I, 7). That is true, but the method of the seeding was formed by conversation and reading at 123 College. Yes, Benét had published a volume of verse at seventeen, before he came to Yale: the volume was *Five Men and Pompey*. But it was at Yale that he fell under the sway of Yale's sense of history, and especially of the sway of a sense of the past alive in the present. *Whose* sense of the past alive in the present? Along that line of inquiry, one can look at possible poetic connections with William Morris and the Pre-Raphaelite Brotherhood. But for the moment let us imagine a scene at 123, before the United States entered the war in the Spring of 1917.

The door to the club opens into a hall, with the stairs going up on the left and the entry to the front room on the right. There is a duty table in the hall, and the hall leads to the tea room. To the right of the tea room and behind the front room is the vault room: it is in the vault that the rare books are kept (including, as of 1998, first editions of Benét's books). Steve Benét is sitting, owlish or perhaps chipmunklike behind his round glasses, round-faced and round-cheeked, legs twisted schoolboy-fashion around the legs of the chair, cigarette at the ready, in the corner just inside the door to the front room.

The chair is one of a pair flanking the table where current issues of *Punch* are kept. (The bound volumes are upstairs on the shelves in the writing room.) Under the front windows of the room is a couch, with a coffee table in front, flanked by two armchairs. A couple of straight-backed chairs are against the walls. Today Chip Farrar and Amos Niven Wilder are on the couch, Bellinger in the chair on Farrar's side, Thornton Wilder (I think he may be visiting his brother) in the chair on his brother's side, Bob Coates in the other chair flanking the *Punch* table. Benét is reading. He begins by quoting Browning's line, "And did you once see Shelley plain?" in his squeaky, oddly inflected voice, smiling at the emphasis his inflections give.

"Shelley? Oh, yes, I saw him often then," / The old man said. A dry smile creased his face / With many wrinkles, "That's a great poem, now! / That one of Browning's! Shelley? Shelley plain? / The time that I remember best is this—... Round about / Struggled a howling crowd of boys, pellmell, / Pushing and jostling like a stormy sea, / With shouting faces ... They all had clods, / Or slimy balls of mud. A few gripped stones. / And there, his back against a battered door, / His pile of books scattered about his feet, / Stood Shelley while two others held him fast, / And the clods beat upon him ... all his face / Was white, a whiteness like no human color, / But white and dreadful as consuming fire. / His hands shook now and then, like slender cords / Which bear too heavy weights. He did not speak. / So I saw Shelley plain." "And you?" I said. / "I? I threw straighter than the most of them, / And had firm clods. I hit him—well, at least / Thrice in the face. He made good sport that night" (*Selected Works*, I, 342–343).

The poem, "The General Public," was written when Benét was a freshman, but he was as prone to read old poems as new, sitting there in the front room, and "The General Public" is a good example of what differentiated Benét from his peers. It is of course derivative, but it is derivative in a way that we might now link with the idea of intertextuality: he is using Browning's style in picking up from Browning's line and twisting it rather like a Moebius strip or Escher print. Not at all the same thing as youthfully imitating Housman's classicism (or even that of Gilbert Murray, or that less-tutored classicism of Rupert Brooke), which is what Bellinger and Farrar and even Amos Niven Wilder were all doing in some degree. It doesn't very much matter if it is intertextuality or Benét's "impish humor"—or both.

Impish or not, Benét had a passion for patriotism. What distinguished him from Bellinger and Farrar and Amos Niven Wilder, and half a dozen other poets of the time (and the Yale Younger Poets series), was that he was the poet who found a new way to sing his passion, eventually with consummate artistry. How did this happen. There may be a clue in the fact that the late Ian Ballantine (1916–1995), Benét's editor for his 1943 Pocket Books collection of short stories, included in the brief biography of Benét on the cover, the simple statement that Benét was a patriot. I asked Ballantine about this some years ago (at a science-fiction convention in Tarrytown, New York), and was given to understand that it had to do not with any doubts of Benét's patriotism (in light of his sometimes leftward politics), but with finding a single word to describe Benét's literary motivation. At the time I was surprised at the answer, but I am convinced he spoke truthfully.

In short, Benét was very much of his generation, the same generation as Bellinger and Farrar and Amos Niven Wilder. But he was not an occasional poet whose career was elsewhere, and he had that impish humor. Yet in the end, what influenced him as much as anything else to take the path so much different from the paths his peers took was his status as an "army brat" who spent his summers in Carlisle, Pennsylvania, and, more important and more germane to this essay, his appreciation of history, nurtured by the Elizabethan Club and by two others among his friends there. These are Thornton Niven Wilder (1897–1975), Amos's younger brother, and Robert Coates. Coates, like Alfred Bellinger, became an historian (but what a different kind of historian!), while Wilder's first books were historical novels, one Roman, and one based in the Americas—albeit in South America. Bob Coates's *magnum opus* was *The Outlaw Years: The History of the Land Pirates of the Natchez Trace* (1930, reprinted Bison Books 1986). Alfred Bellinger's *magna opera* included *Troy: The Coins* (Princeton 1961, reprinted 1979) and *Essays on the Coinage of Alexander the Great* (likewise reprinted 1979): the same year Bob Coates published *The Outlaw Years*, Bellinger was publishing a modest item in the American Numismatic Society's *Notes* (No. 42), "Two Hordes of Attic Bronze Coins." As I say, it was a very different kind of history, but history nonetheless, and Bellinger was devoted to it over a sixty-year career.

Wilder's South American novel was the one for which he won his first Pulitzer prize, *The Bridge of San Luis Rey* (1927), which plays off the "real history" of the memoirist who died in the collapse of the bridge against our knowledge of her two hundred years later. The Roman novel was *The Cabala* (1926), which plays off contemporary Rome against Virgil and the eternal city, and which Farrar in his review (*The Bookman*, 1926) called "brilliant, bitter, imaginative"—of which the second word is the one that should give us pause. It may be worthwhile here to quote what Wilder's mother wrote to Phelps after *The Cabala* and *The Bridge* were published— noting that Wilder dedicated *The Bridge* to his mother: "As for Thornton, I always knew him for a gifted and altogether a choice spirit. But I confess to you that I feared that his very fastidiousness might separate him from the common lot. I mean make him superior and highbrow. Now I know the humanity in him is strong enough to balance the other. So I am not so much 'proud' as thankful and content" (qtd. in Harrison 106). Wilder immersed himself in history—more in *The Bridge* than in *The Cabala*—and the reward was a loss of bitterness and a gain in humanity. (Nor was Phelps's contributions to this gain in humanity negligible.) In Benét, as later (almost) in Wilder with *The Skin of Our Teeth*, the bitterness dissolved in impish laughter, in intertextual humor, and (possible, given the time) in the use of history as objective correlative.

Wilder accepted the interidentification of times and places as the keynote or cornerstone of his vision—as in *Our Town* or *The Skin of Our Teeth* or even *The Merchant of Yonkers* (*Hello Dolly!*). That is almost the exact opposite of Benét's historical consciousness, one might say the mirror image of Benét's historical consciousness (on this interidentification, see my essay "Thornton Wilder and the Science-Fiction Anti-Paradigm" in *Patterns of the Fantastic II*, Mercer Island WA 1985, 29–38). But it comes from the same root, the same concern over the relationship of past and present. One could argue that Wilder's father's move from the shores of Lake Mendota, Wisconsin, to China, in 1906 (when Thornton was eight) opened Thornton Wilder to almost a Spenglerian view of culture and history, while Benét's youthful summer visits to the area around Carlisle, including Gettysburg, and his "army brat" status, opened him to a sense of history inherent in the countryside. But in the 1920s the line of demarcation was not so clear: *The Cabala* and *The Bridge of San Luis Rey* both celebrate the past alive in the present, in almost the same way as Benét's freshman poem "The General Public."

I mentioned that Benét wrote much of his strictly imitative (and "impish") verse for the *Yale Record*. There was his "The Game and the Poets" in which Horace, Robert Burns, and John Masefield consider the Yale-Princeton game: I quote from the Masefield *pastiche* ("John Masefield Extends the Everlasting Mercy to the Tiger"): "By then I'd used up all my tricks, / 'I'm bloody in a bloody fix!' / I said—and searched the law-books through / To find some final crime to do, / The one huge, unforgiven sin / That bloody rots the heart within! / The sin that like a steel-tight jersey / Removes you from eternal mercy! / I bloody shrank a bit at first / To crown my horrors with a worst! / But soon I yielded. Vileness filled me, / I went to Princeton—and it killed me!" (*The Yale Record Book of Verse* 17). There were half a dozen others in the 1922 collection of *Yale Record* verse: he has more poems in that collection than any other poet. Finally, my favorite when I first read it in 1951, his "Wander Song (From any of the popular magazines.)": "Give me the curlews calling on the gypsy patteran, / The pine-smoke whirling, falling, and the battered, open van! / Give me the fires of spring, lass, your warm red mouth to kiss! / (But, for Gawd's sake, gimme the twenty bucks I get for writing this!)"—I quote only the first of the three stanzas (*The Yale Record Book of Verse* 24).

What happened with Benét had something to do with his coming to Yale, and to 123 College Street, without an intermediary stop. The Wilder brothers went to Oberlin before they came to Yale, and Amos Niven

Wilder was an ambulance driver in France, under Benét's uncle Laurence. For Amos, perhaps, the experience in France brought him to see that France existed as a kind of Blakean entity: I'm thinking of that passage in *The Marriage of Heaven and Hell* (Plate 11) where Blake writes that "The ancient poets animated all sensible objects with Gods or Geniuses, calling them by the names and adorning them with the properties of woods, rivers, mountains, lakes, cities, nations, and whatever their enlarged and numerous senses could perceive. And particularly they studied the genius of each city & country...." Thornton Wilder found an odd Spanish colonial *genius* in his creation of the Marquesa de Montemayor and Father Juniper and the collapse of a bridge on July 20, 1714. But Benét carried that realization into the creation of an historical poetry for the United States of America, seeking the American *genius*, the American spirit. (Yes, I know "Art has no nations—but the mortal sky / Lingers like gold in immortality" [*John Brown's Body, Selected Works*, I, 121–122]. So should we say *Ars longa, natio longior?*)

Not all at once did Benét begin this creation. If we read his poetry from his time at Yale we find an historical sense applied derivatively or intertextually in "Three Days' Ride" (*Selected Works*, I, 389–392), where the text is Browning's "How They Brought The Good New From Aix to Ghent"—and I believe, with Basil Davenport, that this is one of Benét's best early poems, with the increasing stress accompanying each variation within the refrain, up to "From Belton Castle to Solway side, / Though great hearts break, is three days' ride!" We find the same sense in "The Retort Discourteous (Italy—sixteenth century)" (*Selected Works*, I, 387–389). Listen to the last three quatrains: "Roll your hands in the honey of life, / Kneel to your white-necked strumpets! / You came to your crowns with a squealing fife / But I shall go out with trumpets! / / Poison the steel of the plunging dart, / Holloa your hounds to their station! / I march to my ruin with such a heart / As a king to his coronation. / / Your poets roar of your golden feats— / I have herded the stars like cattle. / And you may die in the perfumed sheets, / But I shall die in battle."

It is worthwhile pausing over this because the technique is similar to that of Benét's humorous verse, as well as of "The General Public" and, indeed, of the later short stories. We might call it the technique of pointed contrast, and it is not much different from the classic *Punch*-line in the jokes in those copies of *Punch* on the table there in the front room of the Elizabethan Club. "Advice to persons about to marry—'Don't!'" Fife and trumpets, ruin and coronation, die in bed or die in battle, seeing Shelley plain to hit him, "Though great hearts break, is three days' ride"—all these have a twist at the end, a point, almost a *Punch*-line, to draw the pointed contrast. Also, there is the progressive increase in stress in the opening beats of the second line of the "Three Days' Ride" refrain, beginning "From Belton Castle to Solway side, / Hard by the bridge, is three days' ride" and going on to "Strive as you may, is three days' ride," then "Ride how you will, is three days' ride," then the dragged beat of "Though great hearts break, is three days' ride" (*Selected Works*, I, 387). (This is the progress noted by Basil Davenport in his Introduction to *Selected Works of Stephen Vincent Benét*, I, ix–x). The point is that Benét uses what one might call the tricks of poetry (or the tricks of verse) as part of his technique of pointed contrast. Moreover, he had this technique at hand in his undergraduate days, as indeed he had the techniques of classical meter shared by the rest of the young poets at 123 College Street—and some of them (whether in the *Lit* or the *Record*) could work the tricks of verse to the same end.

Benét, however, had something else, something shared more by young Coates than by his fellow poets. He had his interest in American history, and particularly in the history of the area of the first push westward. Doubtless some of this came from his father's Army career, his status as an Army brat, his summers in Carlisle. Doubtless also, there is a friend of Phelps, a colleague of his in the English department at Yale, a colleague in the Elizabethan Club, to whom we ought to devote brief attention here. His name was Henry Augstin Beers (1847–1926), and he was a short-story writer (stories collected in *A Suburban Pastoral*, 1894), historian of American letters (*Nathaniel Parker Willis*, 1885, and *The Connecticut Wits*, 1920), an historian of Yale (*The Ways of Yale in the Consulship of Plancus*, 1895), and an historian of American thought (*Four Americans: Roosevelt, Hawthorne, Emerson, Whitman*, 1919). What is particularly important for our endeavor is that in the years Benét was an undergraduate at Yale, the retired Professor Beers, a regular at the club, was thinking, and writing, about the interrelationship of the push westward and the American character. This not only in his consideration of Teddy Roosevelt (who, after all, wrote *The Winning of the West*), but also because of his friendship with the Harvard philosopher Josiah Royce. It is Royce's book on California in the American Commonwealths Series (1889) that is, I believe, the *textus receptus* for the interrelation of American West and American character, not least for its philosophical portrait of John Charles Frémont.

We may see some of the influence of this concern if we look briefly at a few of Benét's poems from a little after the Yale days, around the same time as *John Brown's Body* (to which we will come shortly). In particular, let us look at "American Names" (*Selected Works*, I, 398–402) on Jefferson,

Audubon, and Daniel Boone. From "American Names" let us look particularly at ll. 10–15, ll. 23–25, and (simply because they are the best-known lines and put the rest in context), ll. 31–36: "... I will remember where I was born. / I will remember Carquinez Straits, / Little French Lick and Lundy's Lane, / The Yankee ships and the Yankee dates / And the bullet-towns of Calamity Jane. / And I will remember Skunktown Plain. / ... It is a magic ghost you guard / But I am sick for a newer ghost, / Harrisburg, Spartanburg, Painted Post. / ... / I shall not rest quiet in Montparnasse. / I shall not lie easy in Winchelsea. / You may bury my body in Sussex grass, / You may bury my tongue in Champmedy. / I shall not be there, I shall rise and pass. / Bury my heart at Wounded Knee."

Here are a few quatrains from *A Book of Americans* (note the title): "Thomas Jefferson, / What do you say / Under the gravestone / Hidden away? / ... / I liked queer gadgets / And secret shelves, / And helping nations / To rule themselves / Jealous of others? / Not always candid? / But huge of vision / And open-handed / ... / I got no riches. / I died a debtor. / I died free-hearted / And that was better ..." (*Selected Works*, I, 398). Or on Audubon, "Some men live for warlike deeds, / Some for women's words. / John James Audubon / Lived to look at birds / ... / Drew them all the way they lived / In their habitats. / (Lucy Bakewell Audubon / Sometimes wondered 'Cats?') ..." (*Selected Works*, I, 400). In addition, there is the single quatrain on Daniel Boone, going—with a kind of reverse twist—from the almost comic lines on Audubon and the imitation schoolboy mnemonics of the lines on Jefferson (admittedly both of these show something of Rosemary Benét's hand) to the haunting "When Daniel Boone goes by, at night, / The phantom deer arise / And all lost, wild America / Is burning in their eyes" (*Selected Works* I, 402). I think it is not accidental that these are all three men of the push westward, even (though Audubon is late) of the first great push westward. Then there are Benét's lines on "French Pioneers 1534–1759": "They came here, they toiled here, / They broke their hearts afar, / Normandy and Brittany, / Paris and Navarre / ... / Marquette and Joliet, / Cartier, LaSalle, / Priest, corsair, gentleman, / Gallants one and all. / France was in their quick words, / France was in their veins...." (*Selected Works*, I, 397–398).

Now let us look at Robert Myron Coates (1897–1973). After he graduated from Yale, Coates, like his friend Thornton Wilder, was a part of the circle that gathered in Paris around Gertrude Stein. His first published book (Paris 1926) is *The Eater of Darkness*, and in the Yale Library is a presentation copy of his *Yesterday's Burdens* (1933), inscribed to Gertrude Stein. He was a Leftist expatriate much of his life, a friend of Nathaniel West, and among his other books are *All the Year Round* (1943), *The Hour*

After Westerly and Other Stories (1957), *Beyond the Alps* (1961), *The Man Just Ahead of You* (1964), and *The Farther Shore* (1966). But his important book for our purposes, as we noted, is his single sustained work of history, *The Outlaw Years: The History of the Land Pirates of the Natchez Trace* (1930). The major piece in the book is on Murrell and his conspiracy in the 1830s, but Sam Mason and the Harpes and other earlier figures appear in the earlier part of the book. These are Pennsylvanians (or northwest Virginians) turned Kentuckians, a part of the trans–Appalachian frontier in the years 1775–1820. It happens that I have worked a good bit in the manuscript sources for this period, and I have wished there was something on the northwest part of that frontier comparable to Coates's book on the Southwest part. (The distinction is between the Territory Northwest of the River Ohio in the Northwest Ordinance of 1787 and the Territory Southwest of the River Ohio at the same time.)

The Pennsylvania Rifle of 1775 became the Kentucky Rifle of 1800. Frontiersman Sam Mason left Youghoughania for "Caintuck" (one step ahead of a law particularly hard on horse thieves), and "This flesh was seeded from no foreign soil / But Pennsylvania and Kentucky wheat." The sources for *The Outlaw Years* are all in the Yale University Library, and so far as I have been able to tell, were there in 1920. "American Names" is, in a way, Benét's answer, from Yale and from his sense of American history, not only to the Great War French experience of Bellinger and Farrar and Amos Niven Wilder (and Uncle Laurence), but to the postwar French experience of Bob Coates and Thornton Wilder.

It is in a sense also an answer to the achievement of another Elizabethan Club member of an earlier generation (closer to William Rose Benét), a frequent visitor in Steve Benét's years, Brian Hooker: the name may not be familiar now, but a few years ahead of the Great War Hooker was the brilliant translator of Rostand's heroic comedy *Cyrano de Bergerac* for the 1924 production starring Walter Hampden (a production Benét saw with his brother and also, I believe, at the Keith-Orpheum in Washington with his uncle Laurence Benét: my parents were there). See how Hooker (or Rostand in the original) uses the French names: "We are the Cadets of Gascoyne, the defenders / Of Carbon de Castel-Jaloux. / Free fighters, free lovers, free spenders, / The Cadets of Gascoyne, the defenders / Of old homes, old names, and old splendors, / A proud and pestilent crew, / The Cadets of Gascoyne, the defenders, / Of Carbon de Castel-Jaloux." And the wonderful scene where Roxane is introduced to the Gascon Cadets (195): "Baron de Peyrescous de Colignac! ... Baron de Casterac de Cahuzac—Vicomte de Malgouyre Estressac Lesbas d'Escarabiot—Chevalier d'Antignac-Juizet—Baron Hillot de Blagnac-Salechan de

Castel-Crabioules—" (which should be enough names to set a thousand scenes—but note Benét's use of names in "French Pioneers").

Then there is here, from Act IV of *Cyrano*, when the piper begins to play a Provençal melody, "Listen, you Gascons! Now it is no more / The shrill fife—It is the flute, through woodland far / Away, calling—no longer the hot battle-cry, / But the cool quiet pipe our goatherds play! / Listen— the forest glens ... the hills ... the downs ... / The green sweetness of night on the Dordogne ... / Listen, you Gascons! It is all Gascoyne!" (178). It is worth remembering that 1998 was not only Benét's centennial but the centennial of *Cyrano*, which opened in Paris with Constant Coquelin in the title role on December 23, 1897, and in New York with Richard Mansfield in the title role on October 3, 1898 (both in French). Its translation by Brian Hooker seventy-five years ago was part of the Francophile days after World War I, along with James Branch Cabell's creation of Poictesme and Dunsany's stories of Carcassonne. Now, with all this in mind, let us listen again to the last stanza of "American Names." (Cabell was a favorite of Benét.)

"I shall not rest quiet in Montparnasse. / I shall not lie easy in Winchelsea. / You may bury my body in Sussex grass, / You may bury my tongue in Champmedy. / I shall not be there, I shall rise and pass. / Bury my heart at Wounded Knee." The last line, of course, has taken on a different meaning since Dee Brown used it as the title of his book on the tragic history of native Americans: its point for Benét is the contrast between the European graves, and especially the British and the French, of the war and the war poets, and the scenes of war in the United States. He picks up from the second stanza: "Seine and Piave are silver spoons, / But the spoonbowl-metal is thin and worn, / There are English counties like hunting-tunes / Played on the keys of a postboy's horn, / But I will remember where I was born." As it happens, I have visited (or even lived in) a number of the places Benét names in the poem—"Harrisburg, Spartanburg, Painted Post" among them—and I know something of the historical significance they had for him. The references may seem general or even generic, but for him they were specific, as specific as the reference in the next-to-last stanza, "Henry and John were never so / And Henry and John were always right? / Granted, but when it was time to go / And the tea and the laurels had stood all night, / Did they never watch for Nantucket Light?"

Henry and John, so far as I know, are Henry James, the American expatriate novelist, and John Singer Sargent, the American expatriate painter. James visited Phelps in New Haven in 1911 (*Autobiography* 551), but that was before Benét's time: he died in early 1916 in his flat in Chelsea.

Sargent lived until 1925, but I have no idea whether Benét met him. In both cases, I suspect the references came through Phelps (or, to style him as he styled himself in his signature, "Wm Lyon Phelps"). Indeed Phelps plays a significant role in Benét's development of an historical poetry for America. Shortly after he first taught his course in Shakespeare at Yale, Professor Phelps (in 1897-98) taught a course in Chaucer and Browning. When he retired from teaching at Yale in 1933, Professor Chauncy Brewster Tinker, who had been an undergraduate member of that class, presented him with the autographed copy of Walter Savage Landor's 1845 sonnet on Browning, "with its fine reference to Chaucer" (*Autobiography* 909). Moreover, at his retirement dinner at the New Haven Lawn Club that year, he was presented with a collection of unpublished Browning letters. For all his connection with Shakespeare in Alexander Smith Cochran's mind (and it was a true connection), Phelps was pre-eminently—in the Yale mind—a devotee of Robert Browning.

There is a tradition in English letters that runs from Chaucer to Dryden to Browning, and another that runs from Langland to Bunyan to Robert Smith Surtees, and then to Tolkien, who was of Benét's generation. The traditions sometimes intermingle in a given author—Kipling and William Morris are examples—and one may recall Morris's approach to history as a possible influence on Benét. My attention was called to this point by Basil Davenport (in his Introduction to *Selected Works*, I, ix), where he notes that the influence of Morris was at the point "where he is least dangerous as an influence, in the mood of mediaevalism combined with the brutal realism of 'Shameful Death' or 'The Haystack in the Floods'—and, making allowance for some youthful romanticism, the mood, here, of 'Three Days' Ride.'" In other words, what Benét took from Morris is the application of imaginative detail in the re-creation of history, which is not unlike what he took from Browning. Benét himself recognized the influence, in his first novel, *The Beginning of Wisdom* (Davenport ix).

The evidence in Benét's undergraduate poetry (as, for example, "The General Public") is that Browning had a significant effect on his writing, perhaps the most significant effect, in his developing a poetry out of history. He is part of that tradition from Chaucer to Dryden to Browning. But there was another of Phelps's poets who had nearly as much effect, and who helped make Benét's an historical poetry *for America*: that was (Nicholas) Vachel Lindsay, a guest at the Elizabethan Club in 1916, and indeed on at least two subsequent visits to New Haven (Phelps 629–632). Professor Phelps called Lindsay's best poems—"General William Booth Enters Heaven," "The Congo," and "The Santa Fe Trail"—"truly great, both in their soaring imagination and in their felicity of diction" (629). It is not hard to hear them behind Benét's historical poetry, and particularly his use of meter in the Wingate sections of *John Brown's Body*. The point here is that both Browning and Vachel Lindsay came to Benét in his undergraduate days through Phelps and (certainly in Lindsay's case, arguably in Browning's) 123 College Street. There was a quirk in Benét, linked to his manner and voice and intonation, possibly emphasized by Browning's humor and Lindsay's meter, and even by the issues of *Punch* there in the front room and upstairs on the shelves, a quirk which led to a curious result in his writing. A quirk, also, that links him with Chaucer and Dryden and Browning.

When we read *John Brown's Body*, we, like Basil Davenport (in his Introduction to *Selected Works*, I, x–xi), find that the long, loose, five- or six-beat line that carries the bulk of *John Brown's Body* at times comes perilously near prose, though "it can carry casual conversations without incongruity, or at need can deepen without any sense of abrupt transition for the nobility of Lincoln or Lee" (xi). Benét, like Brian Hooker in his translation of *Cyrano*, was striving to solve what Davenport calls "one of the primary problems of verse in our day, the finding of a form which may bear the same relation to our easygoing talk that, presumably, blank verse did to the more formal speech of an earlier generation" (x). But look how Hooker handled the problem. Here is the last passage of *Cyrano*, where he brilliantly uses "my white plume" to render *mon panache*: "What's that you say? Hopeless?—Why, very well!— / But a man does not fight merely to win! / No—no—better to know one fights in vain   / You ther   who are you? A hundred against one— / I know them now, my anci   nemies— / Falsehood! ... There! There! Prejudice—Compromise— / Cowardice—What's that? No! Surrender? No! / Never!—never! ... Ah, you too, Vanity! / I knew you would overthrow me in the end— / No! I fight on! I fight on! I fight on! / Yes, all my laurels you have riven away / And all my roses; yet in spite of you, / There is one crown I bear away with me, / And tonight, when I enter before God, / My salute shall sweep all the stars away / From the blue threshold! One thing without stain, / Unspotted from the world, in spite of doom / Mine own!—And that is—that is— my white plume!" (255–256).

I was younger when I saw José Ferrer in the title role in *Cyrano* on Broadway than Benét when he saw Walter Hampden, but I know from conversations with some of Benét's friends and acquaintances that he came from the theatre quoting Hooker's text as I did (and as they did). But what is curious—what is part of this quirk I mentioned—is that Benét did not use his loose line to achieve the romantic heights that Hooker climbed. Instead, it is in his ruminative prose in the 1930s, which we will only touch on here, that he climbs those heights—as in "The Devil and Daniel Webster" or "Jacob and the Indians"—or plumbs the romantic depths. In *John Brown's Body*, which is his pre-eminent historical poetry for America, he asserts the American character in his long loose lines (or in his experiments in meter), not in the manner of Rostand's romantic look at France, or that of his own confreres, or even Browning's detached or quizzical look at times longer past. Davenport (xi, xiii) especially notes two of Benét's lines from *John Brown's Body*: first, as an example of Benét's individual meter, "It is over now, but they will not let it be over" and second, as a translation of a Roman epitaph "*Saltavit. Placuit. Mortuus est,*" "He danced with me. He could dance rather well. He is dead." It is good to pick out memorable lines, and there are many: I would add, "They came on to fish-hook Gettysburg in this way, after this fashion / / Over hot pikes heavy with pollen, past fields where the wheat was high ..." (*Selected Works*, I, 247). Fish-hook Gettysburg and fish-shaped Paumanok, and Walt Whitman is not only a character but an influence in *John Brown's Body*—yet Whitman was a lyric poet, and *John Brown's Body* is by way of being an epic (at least an epic ode), though there are lyrics in it. It is from lyrics or elegies one picks out the memorable lines.

Here's a Browning loose-lined lyric in the epic, Benét quizzical, remembering his own youth, on a visit to Gettysburg: "You took a carriage to that battlefield. / Now, I suppose, you take a motor-bus, / But then, it was a carriage—and you ate / Fried chicken out of wrappings of waxed paper, / While the slow guide buzzed on about the war / And the enormous, curdled summer clouds / Piled up like giant cream puffs in the blue / ... / And it was hot. You could stand and look / All the way down from Cemetery Ridge, / Much as it was, so clam and hot, / So tidy and great-skied. No men had fought / There but enormous, monumental men / Who bled neat streams of uncorrupting bronze ..." (*Selected Works*, I, 260). I too have stood, with cold fried chicken, wrapped in wax paper, under the great-skied enormous summer clouds, looking down on Cemetery Ridge, looking at the monuments, in the deserted heat of a summer day before the centennial changed Gettysburg. I nod and say, yes, indeed, that is the way it is: I do not weep as I weep at the end of *Cyrano*. Here is one reason why. Here is the end of the ode that ends *John Brown's Body* (and listen! You may hear Tennyson's "Ode on the Death of the Duke of Wellington" and you may hear a little of William Butler Yeats— two more Phelps favorites, though Yeats visited the club before Benét's student days).

"So when the crowd gives tongue / And prophets, old or young /

Bawl out their strange despair / Or fall in worship there, / Let them applaud the image or condemn / But keep your distance and your soul from them. / And if the heart within your breast must burst / Like a cracked crucible and pour its steel / White hot before the white heat of the wheel, / Strive to recast once more / That attar of the ore / In the strong mold of pain / Till it is whole again, / And while the prophets shudder or adore / Before the flame, hoping it will give ear, / If you at last must have a word to say, / Say neither, in their way, / 'It is a deadly magic and accursed,' / Nor 'It is blest,' but only 'It is here.'" Say not America is blest, or curst, but we are here. So ends the epic that began with the invocation, "American muse, whose strong and diverse heart / So many men have tried to understand / But only made it smaller with their art, / Because you are as various as your land...." (One may recall how, in that invocation, Benét turns away from Rupert Brooke, as he has turned away from France, "They planted England with a stubborn trust. / But the cleft dust was never English dust." The implicit reference is to "There shall be / In that rich earth a richer dust concealed, / A dust whom England bore, shaped, made aware, / Gave once her flowers to know, her fields to roam ..." from Brooke's most famous sonnet.)

I mentioned Tennyson and his "Ode on the Death of the Duke of Wellington": here is an earlier part of the ode that ends *John Brown's Body* ("this man" in the first line is John Brown). "Bury the South together with this man, / Bury the bygone South. / Bury the minstrel with the honey-mouth, / Bury the broadsword virtues of the clan, / Bury the unmachined, the planters' pride, / The courtesy and the bitter arrogance, / The pistol-hearted horsemen who could ride / Like jolly centaurs under the hot stars. / Bury the whip, bury the branding-bars, / Bury the unjust thing / That some tamed into mercy...." And then, eventually, "Bury this destiny manifest, / This system broken underneath the test, / Beside John Brown and though he knows his enemy is there / He is too full of sleep at last to care." Tying Benét to Tennyson through Phelps is a slightly dicey business, I admit: although reading Tennyson's *Maud* was the greatest poetic experience of Phelps's young life (*Autobiography* 144), he said later that "Tennyson was a great poet, but he did not have an interesting mind" (205). Still, Phelps did particularly direct attention to Tennyson's elegies—see his comparison of Tennyson with Milton in *Autobiography* 204–205—and it is important to remember that Phelps was an enthusiastic teacher and Benét an enthusiastic learner in matters of technical form and meter, odes, elegies, sonnets, anapests, dochmaics, and so on. Benét was not only a conscious but a conscientious formal experimenter in verse. The quirk was that his search for the pointed contrast or the ironic twist or the *Punch-*

line meant that even the long loose lines of *John Brown's Body* could not be used as Hooker used his similar lines in *Cyrano*.

Now let us set against the tone of *John Brown's Body* these two scenes from the short stories of the 1930s. First is the trial scene in "The Devil and Daniel Webster," and the second is a double scene, Jacob's sojourn in the wilderness and his times at the house of Raphael Sanchez in "Jacob and the Indians." In "The Devil and Daniel Webster," Dan'l looks at the hell-bound judge and jury, and sees their eyes glittering like hounds before they get the fox, and he sweats like a man who has just missed falling into a pit in the dark. He speaks of common things, and how the jury are all men, and American men at that, and about the things that make a country a country and a man a man, about the freshness of a fine morning when you're young, and about the taste of food when you're hungry, and how these things sicken without freedom. He speaks of the wrongs that have been done, and how, out of the wrong and the right, the suffering and the starvations, something new has come, and even the traitors played a part in it. And as he speaks, he feels, all down his back and through his chest, the strength of being a man, and the voice speaking through him is like the forest and its secrecy, like the sea and its storms, like the cry of the lost nation, like the scenes of childhood (*Selected Works*, II, 32–45). There, in prose—and in a semihumorous cautionary tale at that—, is Benét's closest approach to unabashed Romanticism.

Or in "Jacob and the Indians," where he calls up a vision of the paths in eighteenth-century America, dark with the shadow of the forest and green with its green and through the green ran trails and paths that were not yet roads and highways, without the dust and scent of the cities of men, but with another look. There were pleasant streams and wide glades, untenanted but by the deer, and pressing in, huge and vast, the promise of a continent, a great and open landscape, life in it and death, the landscape Raphael Sanchez has described to young Jacob Weiss (*Selected Works*, II, 9–16). "They think this is a mine to be worked, as the Spaniards worked Potosi, but it is not a mine. It is something beginning to live, and it is faceless and nameless yet. But it is our lot to be part of it—remember that in the wilderness, my young scholar of the law" (*Selected Works*, II, 9).

All of which leaves us—where? Briefly summarizing, Benét came to Yale as a freshman in fall 1915, already a published poet. He shortly fell in with a group of students gathering at the Elizabethan Club at 123 (now 459) College Street, and under the influence of William Lyon Phelps, "America's favorite professor" and the literary doyen of the club (though the painter John Ferguson Weir, brought up at West Point before the Civil

War, may have been the senior member). While his confreres looked to their experience in France in World War I for inspiration and history, and while the club itself focused (obviously) on English history, Benét and—on occasion—some of his friends (particularly Bob Coates in *The Outlaw Years*) looked toward American history for inspiration, and particularly the history of Pennsylvania and Pennsylvanians in the first push westward. Billy Phelps brought Browning and (among others) Vachel Lindsay to the table. Benét took them from the table, took them from the shelves, took them from Billy Phelps, and made them part of his great work.

I believe, as I said earlier, that books in the Yale Library (such as Augustine Walton's *A History of the Detection and Trial of John A. Murel*, 1835, or Charles Sealsfield's *Frontier Life*, 1860) played a role in the interest in the push westward. That helps explain (in part) some of the subject matter for Benét as for Coates. More to our point on form and technique, the circle in which Benét moved at Yale was a circle of conscious *makars*, creators of poems and *made* things. Because of Phelps's influence (and that of *Punch* and writing for the *Record*), and, through Billy Phelps, Browning's influence, Benét neither sought nor achieved the immediacy in his historical poetry that he achieved in his prose fiction. He remained in some ways the Classicist who translated "*Saltavit. Placuit. Mortuus est.*" This was not a weakness: it helped make possible the highly formal structure of *John Brown's Body* that I believe will help it to endure. I had the great good fortune in my teen years to hear Judith Anderson, Tyrone Power, and Raymond Massey in Charles Laughton's production of *John Brown's Body*. Its structure made that dramatic reading possible. There is more.

There is always, in America, the question of our part in the European tradition—European history or European literature. One may recall that George Washington believed a formal structure for the Continental Army necessary for us to take our place in the concert of nations. In somewhat the same way, Benét constructed a formal (if loose-lined) historical poetry for America, so we might take our place in the concert of history, and playing an equal part with England (but revealing our own *genius*) in a concert of letters.

WORKS CITED

Bellinger, Alfred R. *Spires and Poplars*. New Haven: Yale UP, 1920.
Benét, Stephen Vincent. *The Selected Works of Stephen Vincent Benét, Poetry and Prose*. 2 vols. New York: Farrar & Rinehart, 1942.

Bradley, George. "Introduction." *The Yale Younger Poets Anthology*. New Haven, 1998, xxvi–xxxii.

Bronson, Francis W., et al (eds.) *The Yale Record Book of Verse 1872–1922*. New Haven: Yale UP, 1922.

Davenport, Basil. "Stephen Vincent Benét." *The Selected Works of Stephen Vincent Benét, Poetry and Prose*. New York: Rinehart and Co., 1942, vii–xii.

Farrar, John Chipman. *Forgotten Shrines*. New Haven: Yale UP, 1919.

Harned, Joseph, and Neil Goodwin (eds.). *Art and the Craftsman: The Best of the Yale Literary Magazine 1836–1961*. New Haven: Yale UP, 1961.

Harrison, Gilbert. *The Enthusiast: A Life of Thornton Wilder*. New York: Ticknor & Fields, 1983.

Lobdell, Jared. *England and Always: Tolkien's World of the Rings*. Grand Rapids, Mich.: W. B. Eerdmans Publishing Co., 1981.

Phelps, William Lyon. *Autobiography, with Letters*. London: Oxford UP, 1939.

Rostand, Edmond. *Cyrano de Bergerac. an heroic comedy in five acts. A new version in English verse*. trans. Brian Hooker. New York: H. Holt & Co., 1924.

Wilder, Amos Niven. *Battle-Retrospect*. New Haven: Yale UP, 1923.

_____. *Armageddon Revisited: A World War I Journal*. New Haven: Yale UP, 1994.

6. *John Brown's Body* and the Meaning of the Civil War

Gary Grieve-Carlson

When Henry James asked William Butler Yeats to contribute a poem for a collection intended to raise money for the Allied cause in World War I, Yeats replied, "I think it better that in times like these / A poet's mouth be silent, for in truth / We have no gift to set a statesman right...." Yeats plays to the common assumption that poetry is not the place where politics or history may be understood. But of course Yeats never believed that, or he never could have written "Easter 1916," "Nineteen Hundred and Nineteen," or many of his most powerful poems that deal with political and historical themes of Ireland and its quest for independence from England. Poetry's capacity to tell the truth about history, however, remains controversial. Stephen Vincent Benét's *John Brown's Body* (1928) appears after Ezra Pound's "Near Perigord" (1915) and the early *Cantos*, and after T. S. Eliot's *The Waste Land* (1922), poems which radically challenged our conventional thinking about history, not only in ideological but also in epistemological terms. The iconoclastic examples of Pound and Eliot are followed by Hart Crane (*The Bridge*, 1930), William Carlos Williams (*Paterson*, 1946–58), Robert Penn Warren (*Brother to Dragons*, 1953), and Charles Olson (*The Maximus Poems*, 1953–75). Benét's poem belongs in this modernist tradition because of certain stylistic elements, such as its multiple and fragmented narrative lines, but in many ways *John Brown's Body* is closer in spirit to the great narrative poems of the past, such as Longfellow's "Evangeline" or "The Midnight Ride of Paul Revere." Benét is also closer to Longfellow than to the twentieth-century poets mentioned above in his refusal of historical iconoclasm. Epistemologically, he believes the past has a stable meaning, and that we can know it, and ideologically, he believes that the Civil War reflects the values of liberal democracy. Essentially he sees the meaning of the War as Lincoln saw it: the war results in "a new birth of freedom," a redeemed nation, a re-unified people. From our perspective in the twenty-first century, it is easy to forget how important and healing such an attitude toward the war was, even in 1928. The divisiveness spawned by the war was bitter, recriminatory, and enduring, and one of Benét's poem's great strengths is its honoring of both sides in the conflict and its affirmation of the restored union that emerged from the conflict. In order to achieve this, he emphasizes certain romantic, even sentimental, elements and evades certain troubling questions, and these aspects of the poem, along with its refusal to conform fully to the modernist aesthetic, have resulted in its precipitous fall from popularity. Although his poem has remained in print, it is rarely assigned in high school or college classes, and Benét is difficult to find in either American literature anthologies or the MLA bibliography. Nevertheless, *John Brown's Body* remains a signal achievement in American poetry.

In 1926 Benét (1898–1943), a Yale graduate who had also studied at the Sorbonne, won a Guggenheim grant—the first ever awarded for poetry—to research and write a long poem on the American Civil War. He moved to Paris, where the cost of living was more manageable, and wrote *John Brown's Body*, a poem of over three hundred pages and almost 15,000 lines, in less than two years. Benét was unsure of its quality; after 135 manuscript pages, he wrote to his brother, "… sometimes I think it will be the most colossal flop since Barlow's *Columbiad*" (Fenton 192). But the book's first readers felt otherwise. The Book of the Month Club selection for August 1928, *John Brown's Body* proved incredibly popular. It was Doubleday's biggest moneymaker between 1924 and 1934, selling over 130,000 copies in its first two years, and well over 200,000 copies to date (Fenton 219). In 1929 the book was awarded the Pulitzer Prize for Poetry, and at that time Benét was probably the most widely read poet in the United States. Sinclair Lewis mentioned *John Brown's Body* in his 1930 Nobel Prize acceptance speech as evidence of an American literary renaissance, and Allen Tate called it "the most ambitious poem ever undertaken by an American on an American theme." As late as 1962 Parry Stroud called the poem "decisively the closest approach to Homer and Vergil that an American poet had ever made" (46). To his credit, Benét was more modest than some of his critics. "A poet of greater faculties," he wrote to his publisher, John Farrar, "would have avoided my failures in it and my superficialities—and there are many of both" (Fenton 199). Later: "If the poem is to stand eventually, in any sort of way, it will do so because of a few passages in each

Book and the mass-effect of the whole. The faults are many and glaring. But I could do no better, given such brains as I had" (Fenton 209). Benét's judgment has proven more accurate than Parry Stroud's.

However, despite its waning popularity, *John Brown's Body* has genuine strengths, particularly in its cataloguing of vivid emotional images: Ulysses Grant seeing that the Confederates have lit bonfires to celebrate the birth of George Pickett's son, and ordering his Union troops to do the same, then sending the baby a silver service several days before attacking the Confederate position; the secessionist Edmund Ruffin, who fired the first gun against Fort Sumter, walking in his garden after hearing the news of Lee's surrender, cloaking a Confederate flag around his shoulders, and shooting himself in the heart; Lincoln visiting Pickett's widow in Richmond, just before the surrender at Appomattox. In early reviews both Allen Tate, who refers to *John Brown's Body*'s "motion picture flashes," and Harriet Monroe, who calls the poem "a kind of cinema epic" (91), praise Benét's powerful and effective juxtaposition of images.

Benét is also a good storyteller, especially in terms of his ability to tell the tale of a complicated war in a coherent and engaging manner—the major battles, the broad political issues involved, character sketches of the chief figures on both sides (similar to John Dos Passos's short biographies in the *U.S.A.* trilogy). Unlike, say, *The Cantos* or *Paterson*, *John Brown's Body* is absorbing reading, almost novel-like in its ability to pull the reader along. Benét read voluminously as he worked on the poem—regimental histories, diaries, memoirs, autobiographies—and complained that he wanted still more to read. Both Samuel Eliot Morison, who wrote to Benét for permission to quote from *John Brown's Body* in his *The Growth of the American Republic*, and Lee's biographer Douglas Southall Freeman praised the poem for its historical accuracy (Fenton 182). Bruce Catton has called it the single best book, in some respects, ever written on the Civil War (Griffith 14), a judgment shared by Henry Steele Commager (Jackson 73).

Benét, however, insists he is not a historian; in his note prefaced to the book, he writes, "this is a poem, not a history," explaining the absence of notes and bibliography. However, he protests too much, for he then goes on to cite his chief sources and to explain his approach to history: "In dealing with known events I have tried to cleave to historical fact where such fact was ascertainable. On the other hand, for certain thoughts and feelings attributed to historical characters, and for the interpretation of those characters in the poem, I alone must be held responsible" (vii). Thus for Benét history is essentially a matter of fact, not interpretation. He complains in a *Saturday Review* essay of 1932:

> A good many of our recent biographies—or biografictions—what-
> ever you choose to call them, have [been] rather like Mark Twain's
> reconstruction of the dinosaur, "three bones and a dozen barrels
> of plaster." The author might not always take the trouble to find
> out just what his subject did and when he did it—for that often
> requires a tiresome amount of research. But, as regards what the
> subject thought and felt, there the author was not merely all-wise
> but all-seeing... [Fenton 184–85].

The sharp distinction between "what his subject did and when he did it"
and "what his subject thought and felt," and Benét's preference for the
former, suggests that history ought to be comprised primarily of ascertainable fact, and that interpretation ought to be minimal. At another
point Benét writes, only half in jest, "I wish prominent historians wouldn't
contradict each other as much as they do. How's a poor poet to know
which is right" (Fenton 348). If they'd take the time to do the "tiresome
research" and resist the speculative interpretation, Benét implies, the contradictions would disappear.

Benét imagines history as essentially a stable, linear narrative whose
meaning is accessible. Historical meaning is a function of accuracy, massive detail—what Ezra Pound called "the method of multitudinous detail,"
in contrast to his own "method of luminous detail"—and a variety of
points of view subsumed within a coherent master narrative. Benét works
hard to tell a story that both North and South can agree is true; to be
objective, for Benét, is to be nonpartisan, and he treats both Northern
and Southern historical characters with respect, depicting heroic behavior motivated by genuine, if somewhat obscure, ideals on both sides of
the conflict. His fictional storylines are sentimental and sometimes simply unbelievable, and we might wonder why Benét, with his insistence on
the supremacy of the fact, would include them. The answer lies in his
inability to get the historical facts by themselves to generate the kind of
meaning he wants to impart to the war. The fictional storylines tell accessible, romantic tales that end happily, tales in which suffering and destruction become redemptive and purposeful. In other words, Benét can make
the war meaningful in his fictional storylines in a way that he cannot in
the historiographic parts of the poem. As Aristotle says in the *Poetics*,
poetry can tell universal truths, while history is confined to particular
truths. Benét's scrupulous adherence to the particular truths of the Civil
War prevents him from twisting history to suit his thematic goals, and so
he relies on fictional narratives. But the war itself, in all its complications
and refusal to conform to neat or simple meanings, keeps getting in his
way.

Benét's difficulty with the war's meaning becomes clear early in the book when he considers the question of the war's cause. He points to the usual factors, especially the slavery question—the poem's preface describes a Bible-quoting New England sea captain carrying a cargo of slaves from Africa to North America, and Book One describes John Brown's raid on Harper's Ferry. But rather than represent the war as the result of political, economic, and moral decisions made by particular human beings, Benét depicts the war as the inevitable product of large forces beyond human comprehension, thereby mystifying the war's causes. Early in the poem both Jack Ellyat, the main Northern fictional character, and Clay Wingate, the main Southern fictional character, experience supernatural premonitions of an imminent upheaval, so the war is presented as something like an act of God, the product of fate or destiny rather than human decisions.

Benét's representation of the war as the inevitable shedding of blood necessary for redeeming the nation from the sin of slavery is similar not only to the rhetoric of John Brown, but also to Lincoln's language in the Second Inaugural: "... if God wills that it [the war] continue, until all the wealth piled by the bond-man's two hundred and fifty years of unrequited toil shall be sunk, and until every drop of blood drawn with the lash, shall be paid by another drawn with the sword, as was said three thousand years ago, so still it must be said 'the judgments of the Lord, are true and righteous altogether'" (Hollinger 477). For Lincoln the war is mandated by God as punishment for America's sin: "... American slavery is one of those offences which, ... having continued through His appointed time, He now wills to remove, and ... He gives to both North and South, this terrible war, as the woe due to those by whom the offence came..." (Hollinger 476–77). Such rhetoric, though it places responsibility for the sin on both North and South and is thus nonpartisan, also serves to remove the war's justification and its consequences from human responsibility. Lincoln had no choice, he claims, but to go to war and to continue the war—God has given this war to the United States as a just punishment for its sins, and God determines its duration and the suffering it causes. Benét picks up on Lincoln's mystification because it furthers his thematic goal (similar to Lincoln's political goal) of a nonpartisan depiction of the war's causes and a redemptive depiction of its results.

It is clear, however, that Lincoln did not go to war against the Confederacy in order to abolish slavery, but rather to preserve the Union, and the Emancipation Proclamation, as Garry Wills persuasively argues in *Lincoln at Gettysburg*, is a military rather than a political or moral document; i.e., abolition in the rebelling states is necessary and justifiable only in order to put down the insurrection and preserve the Union. For Benét, too, the preservation of the Union takes priority over the abolition of slavery as the ultimate purpose for which the war is fought. But why is the preservation of the Union so important? The poem offers no explicit answer, and elsewhere Benét offers only a vague notion of manifest destiny: "My sense of the union," writes Benét, "is of two majestic and continuing phases, the preservation of the Union and the continual restless movement of its people" (Fenton 344). The Civil War is essential to the fulfillment of that second phase, westward expansion, which is the subject of Benét's unfinished second epic, *Western Star*, the first volume of which won him a posthumous Pulitzer Prize in 1944. But Benét never explains why the preservation of the union and its overspreading the continent is necessary, or good, or worth 600,000 deaths. For most of his readers this may be a claim that needs no justification, a claim to be accepted without question; however, it is this kind of unexamined acceptance of conventional history that puts Benét at odds with the more iconoclastic poet-historians of his time.

If Benét is unclear on the war's causes, or more importantly its justification, he is able with his fictional storylines to tell coherent, meaningful tales associated with the war. His fictional characters, however, tend to be flat, and in some of them his Unionist bias seeps out. The Georgian Clay Wingate, for example, loves Sally Dupré, but the rigid class structure of the South drives him instead into the arms of the beautiful but vain and shallow Lucy Weatherby, a stereotypical Southern belle. The war is thus a good thing because it destroys the class system of the Old South, enabling the love of Clay and Sally to flower. Like the un–American Tories after the Revolutionary War, Lucy goes off to Canada, suggesting that the antebellum South was un–American in its Anglophilic, aristocratic pretensions. Jack Ellyat of Connecticut, who participates, somewhat unrealistically, in every major battle of the war, from Bull Run to Shiloh to Gettysburg, and is even incarcerated in the notorious Andersonville POW camp, falls in love with and impregnates Melora Vilas in Tennessee. After the war's end Melora, like Longfellow's Evangeline, travels the country in search of Ellyat, whom she finally finds and marries. Luke Breckinridge is a Southern Appalachian backwoodsman so stereotypically ignorant that he believes— literally, not figuratively—that the Yankees are the Redcoats, and the Civil War a reprise of the Revolutionary War. Cudjo, the slave who remains loyal to the Wingates even after Wingate Hall is burned by Sherman's troops, is counterbalanced by Spade, the runaway slave who makes the difficult journey north and eventually crosses the Potomac. He encounters racist taunts and exploitation even in the North, but eventually is hired

by the Pennsylvanian Jake Diefer, who has lost an arm in the war and can
no longer manage his farm by himself. With that image of racial harmony,
Benét ignores the very painful history of black Americans between 1865
and the poem's publication in 1928, and evades the question of the depth
of the nation's redemption from the sin of race-based slavery. The fictional
happy endings—Melora reunited with Ellyat, Sally Dupré winning Wingate
from Lucy, Spade working with Jake Diefer in an idyll of interracial harmony, Luke Breckinridge going home with the chambermaid Sophy—do
for Benét what history alone can not: they justify the suffering wrought by
the war, and turn the war into a Romantic tale of redemption. When Benét
turns to history itself for such justification, however, he cannot find it
because, to his credit, he is scrupulously faithful to the historical record,
in all its tangled complexity.

Benét is in control of his material and its meanings, either fictional
or historical, when he presents vignettes or images calculated to evoke a
particular emotional response. Indeed, his historical vignettes are especially powerful because they are not reduced to the often sentimental
meanings of the fictional storylines. When Benét moves away from
romance and emotion, however, he sometimes loses control of his material and its meanings. This is most clear in his treatment of the abolitionist
John Brown, whose presence hovers over the entire poem. Readers have
disagreed over the significance of Brown in the poem. John McWilliams
claims that Abraham Lincoln, and not "the murderous John Brown," is
the hero of the poem (61), while Henry Seidel Canby asserts that Brown,
not Lincoln, is the poem's protagonist (Benét, xii). Parry Stroud writes,
"The gigantic myth of the corporeal death and spiritual rebirth of Brown
… becomes an American version of the ancient Egyptian myth of Osiris
and the Greek myth of Dionysus" (70), the kind of exaggerated claim we
might expect from a critic careless enough to identify Spade as a Wingate
slave (54) when he is not. But if Brown is not Osiris or Dionysus, the
terms "protagonist" and "hero" are also misleading. Of all the poem's
critics, Allen Tate is the most perceptive on John Brown: "The symbol of
John Brown becomes an incentive to some misty writing, and instead of
sustaining the poem it evaporates in mixed rhetoric. Mr. Benét sees that
the meaning of the War is related to the meaning of Brown; yet what is
the meaning of Brown?" Because Benét never clearly answers that question, argues Tate, the war itself "has no meaning" in the poem.

Benét treats Brown ironically rather than romantically, but his irony
is inconsistent. In the Prelude, the words of a Negro spiritual ask for a
prophet or angel to free the slaves (12–13), and Brown sees himself as an
instrument of God: he calls himself "Jehovah's rod" (23) and refers to

himself and his followers as "pikes and guns / In God's advancing war" (25). Recalling his slaughter of five unarmed proslavery settlers in Kansas, Brown states, "Lord God, it was a work of Thine, / And how might I refrain?" (24). Although this language is quite similar to Lincoln's in the Second Inaugural, Benét is uncomfortable with Brown's fanaticism, and he notes the irony that the first man killed by Brown's Harper's Ferry raiders was the black baggagemaster, Shepherd Heyward. He notes also Brown's curious refusal, after seizing the armory's weapons, to retreat before the Virginia militia and federal troops could seize the Potomac Bridge and then surround him. Benét can be harsh in his depiction of Brown:

> He was a stone,
> A stone eroded to a cutting edge
> By obstinacy, failure and cold prayers.
> Discredited farmer, dubiously involved
> In lawsuit after lawsuit, Shubel Morgan [an alias Brown used]
> Fantastic bandit of the Kansas border,
> Red-handed murderer at Pottawattomie,
> Cloudy apostle, whooped along to death
> By those who do no violence themselves
> But only buy the guns to have it done,
> Sincere of course, as all fanatics are,
> And with a certain minor-prophet air,
> That fooled the world to thinking him half-great
> When all he did consistently was fail [47].

Then Benét's speaker corrects himself, returning to the image of John Brown as a "stone eroded to a cutting edge," and asserting that despite his unreasoning and destructive temperament, Brown was also "Heroic and devoted" (48) in a stonelike manner, and that he was a passive instrument of a large historical force beyond his comprehension: "Call it the *mores*, call it God or Fate, / Call it Mansoul or economic law, / That force exists and moves. And when it moves / It will employ a hard and actual stone" (48). These lines echo the supernatural premonitions that Wingate and Ellyat experience early in the book, as well as Lincoln's Second Inaugural, in their suggestion that the war is the product of something like fate or destiny rather than human decisions. However, they also seem to suggest that what we call "That force" is unimportant, which suggestion is arguable. If we call it "God," then history unfolds as Lincoln suggests in the Second Inaugural, or as Augustine suggests in *City of God*; if we call it "economic law," then history unfolds as Marx suggests it does. The difference is hardly insignificant, particularly with regard to the meaning of the Civil War. Yet Benét evades the question, largely, I think, because such a mystification of John Brown and the war's origins makes it easier to be nonpartisan (neither side is finally responsible for the war; destiny is responsible) and to effect the redemptive reconciliation between North and South that is, for Benét, the war's signal achievement.

In his failure and execution, John Brown becomes the catalyst that ignites the war, a "swift fire whose sparks fell like live coals / On every State in the Union" (48). Benét's dominant tone toward Brown, however, remains ironic, as in this description of contemporary accounts of the days before his execution:

> The North that had already now begun
> To mold his body into crucified Christ's,
> Hung fables about those hours—saw him move
> Symbolically, to kiss a negro child,
> Do this and that, say things he never said,
> To swell the sparse, hard outlines of the event
> With sentimental omen.
>   It was not so [51].

Was Brown successful? No, according to the poem's narrator at this point: "The slaves have forgotten his eyes. / ... / Cotton will grow next year, in spite of the skull. / Slaves will be slaves next year, in spite of the bones. / Nothing is changed, John Brown, nothing is changed" (52). But Brown's ghost replies, "There is a song in my bones" (52), "And God blows through them with a hollow sound" (53), and the poem's narrator admits, "I hear it" (53). That song, of course, faint as it is at first, will become "John Brown's Body," the tune of which will later be used for "The Battle Hymn of the Republic." Early in Book Two, which opens with the fall of Fort Sumter, Benét recalls Brown: "The stone falls in the pool, the ripples spread" (55).

At this point in the poem John Brown disappears, and the war takes center stage. He re-appears in 1862, at the end of Book Four, nearly three years after his execution, with the war in stalemate. The poem's narrator reports that certain Union soldiers claim to have seen him walking "in front of the armies" (183).

> A dead man saw him striding at Seven Pines,
> The bullets whistling through him like a torn flag,
> A madman saw him whetting a sword on a Bible,
> A cloud above Malvern Hill [183].

"But these are all lies" (183), insists the narrator. Brown is dead, his goals unrealized. "The South goes ever forward, the slave is not free, / The great stone gate of the Union crumbles and totters, / The cotton-blossoms are pushing the blocks apart" (184). Nonetheless, the narrator affirms for Brown a crucial role in the war, invigorating Union morale and providing a sanctifying purpose for the war effort: "His song is alive and throbs in the tramp of the columns" (183).

Yet Benét's discomfort with Brown persists. He is at pains to distinguish the man from the symbol. "But his song and he are two" (183), Benét insists, and addressing the man, he says, "You did not fight for the union or wish it well, / You fought for the single dream of a man unchained" (184). Benét aligns Brown with those radical abolitionists who would sooner dissolve the union than countenance slavery, whereas for Benét, the preservation of the union is the primary justification of the war. For Benét abolition, which has led to the South's secession, becomes at the nadir of Union morale the means to the end of the Union's preservation. Addressing Brown directly, Benét says, "You fought for a people you did not comprehend, / For a symbol chained by a symbol in your own mind, / But, unless you arise, that people will not be free" (184). So the man — failure, murderer, and fanatic — is transformed into and invoked as a symbol:

> Your song goes on, but the slave is still a slave,
> And all Egypt's land rides Northward while you moulder in the
>   grave!
> Rise up, John Brown,
> (A-mouldering in the grave.)
> Go down, John Brown,
> (Against all Egypt's land)
> Go down, John Brown,
> Go down, John Brown,
> Go down, John Brown, and set that people free! [185].

However, casting black slaves in the role of the captive Israelites, the American South as Egypt, and John Brown as the people's great deliverer, Moses, is an analogy that breaks down in several key respects. Moses was an Israelite, and their acknowledged leader, whereas Brown was not black; and far from being their acknowledged leader, his followers in the raid on Harper's Ferry included seventeen whites and only five blacks; Frederick Douglass, among others, had refused to join him. Finally, the Israelites eventually reached the Promised Land; whether American blacks have done the same, despite Benét's sunny depiction of Spade on Diefer's farm, is a far from settled question. Benét's attempt to separate, via irony, the man from the symbol remains problematic; Brown's moral intensity cannot be separated from his violence and fanaticism.

Brown indirectly accomplishes his goal—the Thirteenth Amendment abolishes slavery. But the means to that end—the Civil War—bring about much more than abolition and the preservation of the Union. Does the war effect the "new birth of freedom" that Lincoln prophesies at Gettysburg? Does it establish a nation committed to the moral ideals articulated by Jefferson in the Declaration of Independence? Having purged the nation of its sin (slavery), does it re-establish a covenantal relationship with God? Benét makes no such claims. In fact, on the consequences of the War he is remarkably close to Edmund Wilson, who describes

> the whole turbid blatant period that followed the Civil War—with its miseries of an industrial life that was reducing white factory workers to the slavery which George Fitzhugh had predicted, with its millionaires as arrogant and brutal as any Carolina planters, with the violent clashes between them as bloody as Nat Turner's rebellion or John Brown's raid upon Kansas, with its wars in Cuba and Europe that were our next uncontrollable moves after the war by which we had wrested California from the Mexicans and the war by which we had compelled the South to submit to the Washington government [794].

Similarly, Robert Penn Warren writes that the War's consequences include "not only the Union sanctified by blood, but also Gould and Cook and Brady and the Crédit Mobilier and the Homestead blood and the Haymarket riot ... the uncoiling powers of technology and finance capitalism, the new world of Big Organization" (153). At the end of his poem Benét makes remarkably similar points about what the war destroys, in addition to the institution of slavery and the agrarian values of the Old South, and what it brings about. Focusing on the irony inherent in the kind of nation the Civil War produced, Benét reminds us that Brown had been a shepherd and a farmer, not at home in towns or cities, and was a man more interested in the things of the spirit than in material prosperity. Yet ironically,

> Out of his body grows revolving steel,
> Out of his body grows the spinning wheel
> Made up of wheels, the new, mechanic birth,
> No longer bound by toil
> To the unsparing soil

Or the old furrow-line,
The great, metallic beast
Expanding West and East,
His heart a spinning coil,
His juices burning oil,
His body serpentine.
Out of John Brown's strong sinews the tall skyscrapers grow,
Out of his heart the chanting buildings rise,
Rivet and girder, motor and dynamo,
Pillar of smoke by day and fire by night,
The steel-faced cities reaching at the skies,
The whole enormous and rotating cage
Hung with hard jewels of electric light,
Smoky with sorrow, black with splendor, dyed
Whiter than damask for a crystal bride
With metal suns, the engine-handed Age,
The genie we have raised to rule the earth,
Obsequious to our will
But servant-master still,
The tireless serf already half a god—[335].

Benét sees the kind of society, the kind of nation, the Civil War gave birth to, but he refuses, finally, to judge or to evaluate those consequences. In "Ars poetica," Archibald MacLeish writes, "A poem should not mean / But be," summarizing what the New Critics called "the heresy of paraphrase," according to which a poem's meaning depends on its particular combination of formal literary elements. Any attempt to paraphrase the poem's meaning involves an inevitable reduction of that combination of elements, which only exists as the complete poem itself. Benét treats history as the New Critics treat poetry, and the "heresy of paraphrase" becomes for him the heresy of historical interpretation or judgment. In the poem's final lines, he warns his readers about "prophets," or overtly biased, partisan historians, who look at what America has become and either "Bawl out their strange despair / Or fall in worship there" (336). Cautioning his reader against either approach, he continues, in the poem's final four lines:

If you at last must have a word to say,
Say neither, in their [the prophets who either "bawl" or "wor-
    ship"] way,
"It is a deadly magic and accursed,"
Nor "It is blest," but only "It is here" [336].

For Benét, in interpreting the history of the Civil War and its consequences, our choices are limited to (1) the extreme reductivism of curse
or blessing, or (2) silent acceptance. He chooses the latter, and he advises
his reader to do so as well. One might argue that the choice is a version
of the either-or fallacy, and is thus a false choice: after all, we can imagine interpretations of the Civil War that are neither curse, blessing, nor
laconic acceptance. However, Benét is caught between his thematic goal—
to depict the war as a tragic yet redemptive reconciliation of North and
South that enables the reborn nation to fulfill its destiny—and his
admirable adherence to the historical record. He cannot deny what Wilson and Warren observe about the war's effects, and he is honest enough
to include such observations in his poem, yet he cannot bring himself to
the dangerous conclusion that such observations, at least implicitly, under-
mine his theme. In other words, the Civil War and its intractable, hugely
complicated history, its tangled mass of causes and effects, cannot be
reduced to the thematic meaning that Benét, like Lincoln, wants to give
it, and Benét is honest enough as a historian to concede implicitly this
point. That this point cannot be easily or neatly synthesized with the
poem's theme may be considered a weakness, but it also provides the kind
of unresolved tension that gives the poem much of its power and interest. Unlike such historian-poets as Pound, Eliot, and Olson, Benét is neither a revisionist nor a skeptic. He is in the political mainstream; he is of
the party of Lincoln, and *John Brown's Body* very effectively dramatizes
Lincoln's conception of the war. And Lincoln's conception, after all, has
become the nation's conception. It is certainly possible to take issue with
Lincoln's conception of the war, as Warren and Wilson have done, but to
criticize Benét for failing to do so is to criticize him for not having written a different poem, which is hardly fair.

Benét assumes the posture of the moderate antiextremist, the nonpartisan who simply and objectively recounts what happened, making the
war's significance clearer and more accessible in the themes of his fictional
storylines, and in so doing he presents a meaningful tale of suffering,
sacrifice, heroism, redemption, and reconciliation. Some of the hard,
intractable questions about the war are omitted, and these aporia, along
with the romantic emplotment of much of the narrative, are in part
responsible for the poem's having fallen into critical disfavor. *John Brown's
Body* rewards repeated reading, however, and along with such too often
neglected poems on history as Archibald MacLeish's *Conquistador* and
Robert Penn Warren's *Brother to Dragons*, Benét's poem stands as a major
work within the genre of American narrative poetry that takes history as
its subject.

WORKS CITED

Benét, Stephen Vincent. *The Selected Works of Stephen Vincent Benét Poetry and Prose.* New York: Farrar & Rinehart, Inc., 1942.

Fenton, Charles A. *Stephen Vincent Benét: The Life and Times of an American Man of Letters.* New Haven: Yale UP, 1958.

Griffith, John. "Stephen Vincent Benét," in *Dictionary of Literary Biography*, ed. Peter Quartermain, vol. 48, Detroit: Gale Research, 1985.

Hollinger, David A., and Charles Capper, eds. *The American Intellectual Tradition*, volume I. New York: Oxford UP, 1997.

Jackson, Frederick H. "Stephen Vincent Benét and American History." *The Historian* 17 (Autumn 1954): 67–75.

McWilliams, John. "The Epic in the Nineteenth Century." *The Columbia History of American Poetry*. New York: Columbia UP, 1993.

Monroe, Harriet. "A Cinema Epic." *Poetry* 33 (November 1928): 91–96.

Stroud, Parry. *Stephen Vincent Benét.* New York: Twayne, 1962.

Tate, Allen. "The Irrepressible Conflict." *The Nation* 127 (19 September 1928): 274.

Warren, Robert Penn. "Edmund Wilson's Civil War." *Commentary* 34 (August 1962): 151–58.

Wills, Garry. *Lincoln at Gettysburg: The Words That Remade America.* New York: Simon & Schuster, 1992.

Wilson, Edmund. *Patriotic Gore: Studies in the Literature of the American Civil War.* New York: Oxford UP, 1962.

7. American History in the Short Stories of Stephen Vincent Benét and Nathaniel Hawthorne

Nancy Bunge

Stephen Vincent Benét and Nathaniel Hawthorne's shared commitment to cultivating multiple perspectives makes the short story their natural form and history their natural subject. For they both recognize that history stretches one's imagination by encouraging one to acknowledge and understand not only events from other times, but the social and personal attitudes that shaped them. This knowledge inevitably forces one to conclude that the values of one's own time rest on and reflect limited cultural norms, not eternal truths.

Hawthorne saw the ability to accept and even revel in relativism that allows one to add "wisdom to wisdom, throughout Eternity" (Turner 210) as the quality that distinguishes human beings from animals. Consequently, obsessive characters who cannot accept and move beyond the limits of their perspectives, whether Puritans, scientists, or Merry Mounters, all travel towards doom in Hawthorne's tales. Benét affirms similar values in stories like "The Die-Hard" where Colonel Cappalow's commitment to his youthful standards leaves him stranded in a world of living death. Every day he reads old newspapers, freshly ironed to protect the illusion that he participates in the newness necessary to all vitality. The colonel's unnatural withdrawal from the world's complication helps explain his bitterness, especially towards those who have accommodated themselves to time's passage: "'There are many traitors. Men I held in the greatest esteem have betrayed their class and their system. They have accepted ruin and domination in the name of advancement'" (80).[1]

Thus, both Benét and Hawthorne create fictional worlds that carry the wisest characters and readers beyond the illusions of their time. Through the journey that constitutes the plot of Benét's "Johnny Pye and the Fool-Killer," Johnny Pye encounters those who embrace various truths such as cleverness, greed, war, or politics. Each time someone presents Johnny with a new philosophy, he embraces it for a time, comes to see its shortcomings and then moves on. Eventually, he meets the President of the United States who instantly recognizes Johnny's refreshing honesty and offers him the job of postmaster in Martinsville, Johnny's home town. Johnny eagerly accepts, "'for then I can marry Susie.'" The President responds, "'That's as good a reason as you'll find'" (103). So, after experimenting with a series of "truths," Johnny rejects them to follow his heart, return home and marry his sweetheart; he has come to understand the foolishness of ideology.

Many Hawthorne tales reflect the same rejection of absolute truths and a faith that those who truly love inevitably resist simpleminded explanations of life's complexities. Ernest, the central character in Hawthorne's story "The Great Stone Face," also considers and eliminates greed, war, and politics as adequate venues for approaching and appreciating life's richness. As Johnny Pye finds himself admiring most the old drunken fiddler who loved to play, Ernest believes the poet's perspective best captures life's richness. Ernest's story, like that of Johnny Pye, suggests that the truly wise person is one who has the courage to not only consider multiple possibilities, but also face and accept his or her limits, and move on to a deep acceptance of life's complication.

Those who achieve the understanding that moves beyond simple ideological explanation are freed from the hopeless attempt to order or control life, making it possible, even mandatory, for them to simply love it. Like Johnny, Ernest becomes the hero of his tale because he responds to the world with honesty and passion: "His words had power, because they accorded with his thoughts, and his thoughts had reality and depth, because they harmonized with the life which he had always lived. It was not mere breath that this preacher uttered; they were the words of life, because a life of good deeds and holy love was melted into them" [11: 47].[2]

Hawthorne and Benét both believed that only those like Johnny and Ernest who can accept that many things are true about the world simultaneously have the flexibility required to love others. Such people see richness everywhere, especially at home. Hawthorne's tale "The Threefold

Destiny" underlines this point with the story of Ralph Cranfield who, like Johnny Pye, travels the world in search of treasure, only to find it in the town where his journey began; he returns and marries his girlfriend, Faith Egerton: "Would all, who cherish such wild wishes, but look around them, they would oftenest find their sphere of duty, of prosperity, and happiness, within those precincts, and in that station where Providence itself has cast their lot. Happy they who read the riddle without a weary world search, or a lifetime spent in vain!" [9: 482].

That Ernest in "The Great Stone Face" takes nature as a role model suggests another theme shared by Benét's and Hawthorne's tales: nature's broad abundance can enrich the perspectives of those who open their hearts and minds to it. Benét presents this theme in "Jacob and the Indians" where Jacob's journey into the wilderness brings him in touch with larger dimensions of himself: "And as they sank deeper and deeper into the depths of the forest, and he saw pleasant streams and wild glades, untenanted but by the deer, strange thoughts came over him. It seemed to him that the Germany he had left was very small and crowded together; it seemed to him that he had not known there was so much width to the world" (11). Jacob emerges from the woods with a totally different value scheme than that which led him into it, just as a lifetime of contemplating the kindly face on the mountain near his home transforms Ernest. So Hawthorne and Benét agreed that, ideally, human beings cultivate the flexibility that leaves them open to the influence and understanding of history, nature and each other.

The conclusion of "Johnny Pye," however, also suggests a fundamental difference between the philosophy of Benét's history tales and Hawthorne's. As the story draws to a close, Johnny realizes that although all people are fools, history inevitably moves forward: "'There's the brave and the wise and the clever—and they're apt to roll it ahead as much as an inch. But it's all mixed in together. For, Lord, it's only some fool kind of creature that would have crawled out of the sea to dry land in the first place"(108).

Again and again, Benét uses history to affirm that, despite human frailty, the human race as a whole progresses. He cites the past to help sustain his readers' faith in the present's rich possibilities. Indeed, Benét sees this as the writer's obligation: he believes that readers "ask for faith and hope and goodness of spirit—for the succor and fortitude great work can bring to the troubled spirit in troubled and dissolving days. And this they are right in asking—we are all asking that from somewhere" (Fenton 382–3). Hawthorne, on the other hand, uses history primarily to coax his readers towards accepting the worst sides of their culture and themselves. Thus, he tells his countrymen tale after tale about their most embarrassing ancestors, the Puritans, hovering over the shameful details. Benét chooses to concentrate on periods of American history that lend themselves to more positive rendering: the American Revolution and the end of slavery. Even when they consider the same period, Hawthorne inevitably presents a more cynical version of it.

For instance, in "My Kinsman, Major Molineux," Hawthorne considers events leading to the American Revolution from the perspective of a boy named Robin. Robin Molineux has come to the city to rise in the world with the aid of his uncle, the British Representative; instead, he sees his uncle tarred and feathered by the townspeople not because he has done anything wrong, but because the villagers simply hate all those the British appoint to rule them. The narrator opens the story by making the irrationality and unfairness of the townspeople's reactions clear: "The people looked with most jealous scrutiny to the exercise of power, which did not emanate from themselves, and they usually rewarded their rulers with slender gratitude, for the compliances, by which, in softening their instructions from beyond the sea, they had incurred the reprehension of those who gave them" (11: 208). Similarly, the narrator's description of the revolutionaries suggests that rather than illustrating the birth of American democracy, this historical episode simply supplies an opportunity for the townspeople to act upon their inherent meanness: "On they went, like fiends that throng in mockery round some dead potentate, mighty no more, but majestic still in his agony. On they went, in counterfeited pomp, in senseless uproar, in frenzied merriment, trampling all on an old man's heart" (11: 230).

Stephen Vincent Benét's story "A Tooth for Paul Revere" also considers an event leading to the American Revolution from an unusual perspective. Benét tells the story of a man named Lige Butterwick whose concern for his crops leaves him little time or energy to invest in the political unrest surrounding him, like most people: "For now you take Lige Butterwick—and, before his tooth started aching, he was just like you and me.... It was troubled times in the American colonies. ... [B]ut Lige Butterwick, he worked his farm and didn't pay much attention. There's lots of people like that, even in troubled times" (18). A toothache forces him to set aside his job duties and travel to Boston so he can get a new tooth from Paul Revere. Lige's journey exposes him to events in the revolution, igniting his outrage at England's injustice and transforming him into an American revolutionary, so inspired by his cause that his tooth no longer bothers him: "'A tooth's a tooth.... But a country's a country. And, anyhow, it's stopped aching'" (31).

Both Benét and Hawthorne present fresh perspectives on the American Revolution, but while Hawthorne exposes the underside of sadism most would prefer to sweep under the rug of principle, Benét reminds his compatriots that the revolution depended upon the rare courage of multitudes of ordinary people who wanted only to make a decent living. These patriots who, like Lige, left their plows, risked their lives, and then were largely forgotten, constituted the revolution's heart. Benét symbolizes Butterwick's importance by having him smash a silver box belonging to Paul Revere although he knows that this act will start the revolution. So, Hawthorne and Benét both use the example of the American Revolution to reveal often overlooked dimensions of ordinary folk: Hawthorne emphasizes their cruelty while Benét stresses their idealism.

These different perspectives on the role of evil shape the treatment of the Devil in the stories of Benét and Hawthorne. Both Hawthorne's "Young Goodman Brown" and Benét's "The Devil and Daniel Webster" acknowledge the devil's role, or the importance of human evil, in shaping American history. In Hawthorne's story, the devil soothes Brown's fears that joining him will shame his family: "'I have been as well acquainted with your family as with ever a one among the Puritans; and that's no trifle to say. I helped your grandfather, the constable, when he lashed the Quaker woman so smartly through the streets of Salem. And it was I that brought your father a pitch-pine knot, kindled at my own hearth, to set fire to an Indian village, in King Philip's war'" (10: 77). In Benét's story, the Devil also boasts of his influence on American history: "'When the first wrong was done to the first Indian, I was there. When the first slaver put out for the Congo, I stood on her deck. Am I not in your books and stories and beliefs, from the first settlements on? Am I not spoken of, still, in every church in New England? 'Tis true the North claims me for a Southerner and the South for a Northerner, but I am neither. I am merely an honest American like yourself—and of the best descent'" (39).

Although Benét and Hawthorne agree on the Devil's importance, they offer differing evaluations of his strength. The Devil always wins in Hawthorne and those who will not accept him live the most miserably. In "Young Goodman Brown," the speaker at the witches' Sabbath in the forest declares, "'Evil is the nature of mankind'" (10: 88). All those present except Young Goodman Brown seem to accept this truth. Because Brown refuses to acknowledge his own evil, he spends the rest of his life projecting it on his community, making his life and death terminally grim: "A stern, a sad, a darkly meditative, a distrustful, if not a desperate man, did he become…. They carved no hopeful verse on his tomb-stone; for his dying hour was gloom" (10: 89–90).

On the other hand, in Benét's "The Devil and Daniel Webster," Daniel Webster defeats the Devil in a trial presided over by Hawthorne's ancestor, the witch-hanging Judge Hathorne selected, along with a jury of reprobates, by the Devil himself who agrees to a trial only on the condition that he choose the judge and jury. Daniel Webster insists only that they all be American.

Thomas Morton of Merry Mount, founder of the community in Hawthorne's tale "The May-Pole of Merry Mount," serves on this jury along with the likes of Simon Girty "who saw the white men burned at the stake and whopped with the Indians to see them burn. His eyes were green, like a catamount's, and the stains on his hunting shirt did not come from the blood of the deer" (40). By placing Morton on a jury composed primarily of cruel men, Benét sides with Hawthorne's view that all obsessive views, whether positive or negative, are fatally flawed. But while Benét's tale argues for the saving transformation of all the jurors, including Morton, Hawthorne's tale describes the obliteration of Morton's whole tribe: "As the moral gloom of the world overpowers all systematic gaiety, even so was their home of wild mirth made desolate amid the sad forest" (9: 66–67). Benét shows that Morton, along with the other jurors, can and will change if put in touch with his innate humanity.

How does this transformation take place? Daniel Webster simply tells the judge and jury Benét's favorite story: despite their flaws, human beings always progress and goodness always realizes itself, although slowly and clumsily, in time: "He was telling the story and the failures and the endless journey of mankind. They got tricked and trapped and bamboozled, but it was a great journey. And no demon that was ever foaled could know the inwardness of it—it took a man to do that"(43).

Webster's speech ignites the latent idealism of all his listeners. As he concludes, something softer has replaced the hardness they share: "He knew he'd done a miracle. For the glitter was gone from the eyes of judge and jury, and, for the moment, they were men again, and knew they were men" (43). For Hawthorne, "evil is the nature of mankind"; for Benét, goodness makes people human. While Hawthorne coaxes his readers to face their pettiness, Benét urges them to own their greatness. As a result, Hawthorne's characters, with rare exceptions, remain trapped in narrowness and obsession until the end of their tales; while, again and again, Benét shows characters moving beyond their limits towards freedom.

So Hawthorne's history tales are primarily stories of defeat, destruction and disillusion, whether it's Reuben Bourne shooting his own son in "Roger Malvin's Burial" or a family destroyed by both Quaker and Puritan fanaticism in "The Gentle Boy." Benét, on the other hand, presents history as a symbol of optimism and hope. The story of the slave who eventually achieves the freedom he seeks after a lifetime of obstacles and defeat detailed in "Freedom's a Hard-Bought Thing" seems a paradigm for Benét's view that history inevitably moves in a positive direction, although slowly and awkwardly.

With its portrayal of Hawthorne's contemporaries traveling to hell guided by their soothing ministers, Hawthorne's tale "The Celestial Railroad" suggests a nostalgia for the good old days when people took sin and guilt seriously, while Colonel Cappalow's affection for the past in Benét's "The Die-Hard" seems evil and perverse. The doctor-hero of the tale moralizes about Cappalow: "There's a Frenchman calls it a fixed idea. You let it get a hold of you ... and the way he was brought up. He got it in his head, you see—he couldn't stand it that he might have been wrong about anything. And the hate—well, it's not for a man" (87–88). Not accidentally, Benét makes a scientist a symbol of enlightened modernity here and the tale's spokesperson for truth, compassion and wisdom.

Hawthorne does not usually make scientists the heroes of his tales. Instead, his stories suggest that science's explosive growth has left its practitioners profoundly vulnerable to arrogance. In "The Birth-mark," Aylmer's faith in this own ability to perfectly control his environment with his scientific genius leads him to kill his wife. The same incapacity for frailty makes the title character of "Ethan Brand" kill himself rather than face the failure of his scientific investigations. So while Benét sees history moving in a positive direction with the aid of scientific development, Hawthorne notes the future's dangers, especially stressing the hidden risks of scientific progress.

Benét might well have traced these differing perspectives on history to the periods he and Hawthorne occupied. He believed the future belongs to the optimistic: "It is up to the writers, now, to see where they go next—what shapes they can summon from the ground. And the responsibility is not theirs alone. It is one that we all share. We all enjoyed the debunking and the disillusion. Now we are trying to go beyond that—we are trying hard, at long last, to find out what things have meaning, what things are worth keeping" (Fenton 383).

So while Benét and Hawthorne both link the study of history to flexibility, nature and love, their tales indicate opposing views about the direction of American history and the nature of the American character. Yet given their shared commitment to entertaining and exploring various perspectives, Benét and Hawthorne would probably have welcomed the other's rendition of the American story. For both men agreed that in a world where truth remains eternally elusive, one moves towards wisdom and love only by considering reality from as many angles as possible. Thus, it is finally not surprising that, despite his view that the American audience rightfully asks its authors for optimism, when asked to recommend books about American history, Benét writes, "Hawthorne's short stories (if they haven't been spoiled for you in class) give you a good deal of the Puritan and New England" (Fenton 216).

Works Cited

Benét, Stephen Vincent. *Selected Works of Stephen Vincent Benét. Poetry and Prose.* New York: Farrar & Rinehart, Inc., 1942.

Fenton, Charles A., ed. *Selected Letters of Stephen Vincent Benét.* New Haven: Yale University Press, 1960.

Hawthorne, Nathaniel. *The Centenary Edition of the Works of Nathaniel Hawthorne.* 21 Vols. Columbus, Ohio: Ohio State University Press, 1962.

Turner, Arlin, ed. *Hawthorne as Editor: Selections from his Writing in the American Magazine.* Baton Rouge: Louisiana State University Press, 1941.

Notes

1. All quotations of Benét are from *The Selected Works of Stephen Vincent Benét Poetry and Prose.* New York: Farrar & Rinehart, Inc., 1942.

2. All quotations of Hawthorne are from *The Centenary Edition of the Works of Nathaniel Hawthorne,* 21 Vols. Columbus, Ohio: Ohio State University Press, 1962.

8. Waking from Nightmares: Stephen Vincent Benét's Faustian America

Robert Combs

An understanding of Stephen Vincent Benét is incomplete without considering how his work embodies the Faust legend. "The Devil and Daniel Webster"—in its several incarnations as story, play, opera, and movie—has done more to keep Benét's name alive than his national epic of the Civil War, *John Brown's Body*, a bestseller in its day, and another, unfinished, large-scale work treating the western expansion of the United States, *Western Star*, both awarded Pulitzer prizes. Benét's fanciful Faust, Jabez Stone, a New England farmer who, as his name implies, suffers the hard luck of Job, mortgages his soul to the devil in exchange for seven— extended to ten—years of good luck, finally turning in desperation to Daniel Webster, famous orator and defender of the Union, to argue his case against Scratch, Benét's homespun Mephistopheles. In a happy ending rivaling Goethe's for audacity, Benét—like the great rhetorician he celebrates—wills a new moral beginning for his country into existence by the sheer magic of words. He convinces his audience, as does Daniel Webster his jury from hell, that it is possible—indeed necessary—always to be beginning again, starting over from scratch, so to speak. In this way Benét participates in the complex project of modernism. His patriotic Americana should be read not as mere chauvinism, but as a salute to freedom, which, as Goethe says, must be re-earned daily.

The "real" Dr. Johann Faust (1488–1541), a contemporary of Leonardo da Vinci, Columbus, Machiavelli, Erasmus, Copernicus, and, perhaps most importantly, Luther (1483–1546), was immortalized in the *Faustbuch* of 1587, translated into English in 1592 as *The Historie of the Damnable Life and Deserved Death of Doctor John Faustus* (Edinger, *Goethe's Faust* 13). The invention of the printing press is attributed to Dr. Faustus as well as all the aspirations and anxieties of Renaissance man at war with intellectual authority. As Heine says, "…with Faust ends the medieval religious era, and there begins the modern, critical era of science" (Heine 443). The sources of the Faust legend are part jestbook, part morality fable, complete with good and bad angels. Christopher Marlowe forged these elements into their first great literary treatment, *The Tragical History of Doctor Faustus*, including the conjuring of Helen of Troy ("Was this the face that launch'd a thousand ships…"). Faustus is a man in whom, in Hazlitt's words, " pride of will and eagerness of curiosity, sublimed beyond the reach of fear and remorse" (51). Marlowe's Faustus is psychologically interesting chiefly in his experience of the ironies of his success. Rather than making him happy, his newly gained magical powers merely intensify his painful loss of connection to God (Cole). And Mephistopheles seems to express the existential anguish of a whole world that will no longer know any certainties. He sincerely warns Faust to desist in his ungodly efforts:

> Why this is hell, nor am I out of it:
> Think'st thou that I, that saw the face of God,
> And tasted the eternal joys of heaven,
> Am not tormented with ten thousand hells,
> In being depriv'd of everlasting bliss?
> O, Faustus, leave these frivolous demands,
> Which strikes a terror in my fainting soul! [96].

In some sense, a profound sadness in the midst of life seems to lie at the heart of the Faust story, a longing that can never be satisfied, or that if satisfied only yields more longing.

It was for Goethe, who worked on his *Faust* I and II throughout his long life, to spell out this sadness by uniting two stories in one great work—those of Faust and Job. Indeed, it is possible to read Goethe's *Faust* as one long footnote to the Biblical Job. Goethe's "Prologue in Heaven" is an account of the Lord's conversation with Satan—here Goethe's roguish jester Mephistopheles—in which the Lord allows Satan to have his way with Faust. The drama's foregone conclusion is strongly implied by the Lord before the play begins: "Man ever errs the while he strives" (8), words which are echoed by Faust in his pact with the devil: "should ever I take ease upon a bed of leisure, / May that same moment mark my end!" (40). In other words, life is presented in Goethe's *Faust*, from the human as well as the divine perspectives, as an ongoing work in progress, full of error and disappointment, justified only by continuous "striving," never by completed accomplishment. The devil, too, has his role to play in such a conception of life. Mephistopheles defines himself to Faust as "Part of that force which would / Do ever evil, and does ever good" (33). The sadness out of which the Faust story grows, Goethe implies, is part of the enlightenment of Job.

C. G. Jung, Goethe's twentieth-century intellectual heir (Jung entertained the idea that he was actually descended from Goethe), must have been deeply influenced by *Faust* when he composed his great work *Answer to Job*. According to Jung, Job saw in his arbitrary suffering a revelation of the dark side of God and anticipated in that unspeakable insight the incarnation and sacrifice of Christ. As Jung puts it, "God wants to become man, but not quite. The conflict in his nature is so great that the incarnation can only be bought by an expiatory self-sacrifice offered up to the wrath of God's dark side" (456). Jung was appalled by the conclusion of Goethe's *Faust*, that is, by what it reveals about the Western world. In the last scenes, Faust sends his functionaries to dispose of Philemon and Baucis, the old couple who were the last on earth to honor the gods and who now stand in the way of Faust's last great project, the reclaiming of land from the sea. After they are murdered, Care creeps through the keyhole into Faust's heart and he dies. But his soul slips past Mephistopheles who is distracted momentarily by his lust for some of the angels hovering around, and Faust achieves heaven, just as the Lord predicted. Jung read the ending of *Faust* as suggesting that, for Goethe, the ethical contradictions of living a life measured by "striving" were unsolvable at this historical moment; the problems were projected into the beyond by Faust's death. But Jung saw the problems implied by the play as requiring more immediate attention. In *Memories, Dreams, Reflections*, Jung says, "I consciously linked my work to what Faust had passed over: respect for the eternal rights of man, recognition of 'the ancient,' and the continuity of culture and intellectual history" (235). The inscription Jung carved over the entrance to his Bollingen tower reads: *Philemonis Sacrum—Fausti Poenitentia* (Shrine of Philemon—Repentance of Faust).

No modern writer's relation to the Faust story is simply self-evident. In addition to examining Benét's treatment of this material in various forms, we need to place "The Devil and Daniel Webster" in a context that includes a nineteenth-century Romantic work which it echoes, Hawthorne's "Young Goodman Brown," and a twentieth-century high-modernist work, "To Brooklyn Bridge," by Hart Crane, which, incidentally, echoes a poem by Benét.

"The Devil and Daniel Webster" participates richly in the ethos of Romanticism. It employs an invented folktale for its narrative structure. No such story was ever told in "the border country, where Massachusetts joins Vermont and New Hampshire" (16). And its rhetoric of the tall tale seems to allude to folk heroes like Paul Bunyan. It invokes childhood remembrances as the narrator recalls the reputation of "Dan'l Webster" as it was passed on to him as a "youngster." It unites the historical and the supernatural, making the "real" glow with significance and the "fantastic" seem to have a plausible role to play in America's destiny. It fuses its characters with nature, giving them force and inevitability. Daniel Webster's voice is still heard in the thunderstorm long after his death, and the action itself takes place on a farm amidst plowing and other chores. Moreover, it has as its central figure a charismatic but interestingly flawed hero, in this case not ostensibly the Faust figure, but his defending attorney, a famous historical American politician, Daniel Webster.

The national anxieties at the heart of Benét's story were given definitive form by Hawthorne in his Faustian fable of 1835, "Young Goodman Brown." An innocent young man, married three months, has an appointment to keep with the devil. When he journeys into the dark forest, he meets a soberly dressed Mephistophelean stranger bearing a family resemblance to himself and discovers a host of trusted town elders eager to participate in a witches' Sabbath. Most shocking, though, is his discovery that his wife, named Faith, is among them. Just before he and Faith are initiated into this unholy communion—which consists of learning to see all hidden evil in others—Young Goodman Brown backs out, urges Faith to "resist the wicked one," and apparently awakes, still in the forest, but no longer able to enjoy human community. He remains married, fathers children, and attends worship services, but in an unalterably alienated, distrustful state. Hawthorne tells us, "his dying hour was gloom."

A vast critical commentary has attempted to sift through all the ambiguities of Hawthorne's allegory, witnessing to the story's engagement with themes that transcend historical, political, and theological categories. This nineteenth-century Romantic author is haunted by seventeenth-century Puritan scenarios not only because one of his ancestors (John Hathorne) was possibly involved in the witch trials, but because the dynamics of persecution, paranoia, and faith continually reassert themselves through the many social transformations of Hawthorne's America. Nancy Bunge convincingly argues that the story focuses upon the temptation every member of society faces to embrace conformist ideologies that ascribe fault to scapegoats and the difficulties such an individual faces if he or she refuses to do so. As Bunge states, "Societies encourage conformity because the assumption that this state, unlike all others, rests on a bedrock of truth, cannot survive examination" (12). Any society, almost by definition, becomes a jury of rogues. We could speculate that "faith" in Hawthorne's allegory, fairly innocent and abstract in youth, is easily transported into the domain of social privilege and condemnation when the bonds of marriage and earning a living begin to tighten. At the end of Hawthorne's story, Young Goodman Brown is suspended on the threshold of experience, imagining but not really seeing all the evil of the world, like a nervous, untested Job who can't stop worrying about what the Lord might let the devil do to him.

"The Devil and Daniel Webster" has obvious ties with Hawthorne's story. Justice Hathorne is the presiding magistrate among Jabez Stone's jury from hell. More significantly, Benét's devil, Scratch, identifies himself as Jabez's familiar and compatriot in rhetoric that echoes Hawthorne's devil:

> I have been as well acquainted with your family as with ever a one among the Puritans; and that's no trifle to say. I helped your grandfather, the constable, when he lashed the Quaker woman so smartly through the streets of Salem; and it was I that brought your father a pitch-pine knot, kindled at my own heart, to set fire to an Indian village, in King Philip's war. They were my good friends, both; and many a pleasant walk have we had along this path, and returned merrily after midnight. I would fain be friends with you for their sake" [Hawthorne 89].

> When the first wrong was done to the first Indian, I was there. When the first slaver put out for the Congo, I stood on her deck. Am I not in your books and stories and beliefs, from the first settlements on? Am I not spoken of, still, in every church in New England? 'Tis true the North claims me for a Southerner and the South for a Northerner, but I am neither. I am merely an honest American like yourself—and of the best descent—for, to tell the truth, Mr. Webster, though I don't like to boast of it, my name is older in this country than yours [Benét 22].

In each case, the devil argues eloquently for inclusion within the national history and identity, an argument as difficult to accept as to deny. He says, essentially, *we* (the devil and the United States) have disenfranchised Native Americans and enslaved African Americans. In addition, since *you*, Young Goodman Brown and Jabez Stone respectively, cannot successfully deny such a statement, you must continue in your bondage to evil. You must surrender your soul. Interestingly, in Hawthorne and in Benét, an individual—the devil—speaks for a group. Hawthorne's community of respected citizens at the witches' Sabbath and Benét's rogues' gallery jury— Simon Girty, King Philip (Metacomet), Governor Dale, Morton of Merry Mount, Teach the Pirate, and Reverend John Smeet—do not speak for themselves from within the multiple complexities of their life histories. They are spoken for as a group by the devil in each case. In both stories, the sense of evil relies upon collective representation. The devil's voice speaks with the voice of "we." For Hawthorne and for Benét, the literary task, the power of the literary representation of history, lies in restoring the individual voice. In a democracy, the royal "we" should not play very well. In Hawthorne's dark Romanticism, the ironies and ambiguities of the story enable the reader to grasp the possibility of individual freedom against the background of Young Goodman Brown's defeat. In Benét's stalwart tour de force, Jabez Stone's failure is recouped by an eloquent orator, Daniel Webster, as complex in himself as the nation he attempts to champion against the devil.

Benét clearly took his Daniel Webster from Van Wyck Brooks' *The Flowering of New England 1815–1865* (1936), from a chapter called "The New Age in Boston and Cambridge." Brooks discusses Webster and William Ellery Channing as the Representative Men—political and religious, respectively—of a time before Boston yielded intellectual renown to New York, when Boston was the Edinburgh of America. Webster was, according to Brooks, "the great political figure. A demon of a man, a full-blooded, exuberant Philistine, with a demiurgic brain and a bull's body, a Philistine in all but his devotion to the welfare of the State ..." (93). He fought both for the preservation of the Union and for the manufacturing interests of New England. His legendary persona was part farmer-fisherman, part Roman orator. He had little patience for traditional virtues like frugality or sobriety. Emerson reported Webster's three rules, by reputation, as being, "first, never to do today what he could defer till tomorrow; second, never to do himself what he could make another do for him; and thirdly, never to pay any debt today" (95). Webster embodied for the thousands that read his speeches at the fireside America as a symbol of liberty, America purged of colonialism, self-consciousness, and English manners. Noah Webster established American usage in language; "Dan'l" did the same in personality. Several details from Benét's story come right out of *The Flowering of New England*: Brooks' description of Webster in the language of nature—"The thunderclouds would gather on his brow and the lightning flash from his eye" (95). Moreover, we recognize several colorful details—the Ram named Goliath, the fishing rod called Killall. But the central theme associated with Webster in Brooks and Benét is the dignity and importance of history in a country and an age that understood itself in terms of oratory and history. For many, Webster seemed to summarize the whole age of the building of the Union up to the time of the Civil War.

Daniel Webster ultimately came to be seen, however, like Longfellow's Paul Revere, as a tarnished hero (Partenheimer 37). His early legal triumphs built up the legendary figure. The Supreme Court case *Dartmouth College v. Woodward* (1818) shaped the interpretation of contract law. *McCulloch v. Maryland* (1819) and *Gibbons v. Ogden* (1824) helped to put the country on a nationalistic course. He challenged John C. Calhoun of South Carolina and Henry Clay of Kentucky over states' rights. Webster was at the peak of his fame when he defended national sovereignty against Calhoun's fellow South Carolinian Senator Robert Hayne (Barber and Voss 10–11). In 1836 he was a Whig candidate for the presidency. But in 1850, in a desperate attempt to save the Union, he supported Henry Clay's Compromise of 1850, including the Fugitive Slave Law. Abolitionists were horrified. Emerson declared that the "fame of Webster ends in this nasty law" (Barber and Voss 11). John Greenleaf Whittier immortalized Webster's infamy in 1850 in his poem "Ichabod" (a Biblical name meaning "no glory"):

> Revile him not, the Tempter hath
> A snare for all;
> And pitying tears, not scorn and wrath,
> Befit his fall! [78].

Interestingly, Whittier places Black Dan, as he came to be called, in the company of the devil, just as, in a very different spirit Van Wyck Brooks calls Webster a "demon of a man." Whittier is implying that Webster has sold his soul, perhaps in his ongoing bid for president. Two years later, in 1852, Webster was dead.

Daniel Webster, then, is quite a Faustian figure in his own right. So we are justified, up to a point, in conflating the two figures Jabez Stone and Daniel Webster when interpreting Benét's story. Jabez Stone's temptation begins not with intellectual disillusionment but with a Joblike suffering of arbitrary disasters. "He had good enough land, but it didn't prosper him; he had a decent wife and children, but the more children he had, the less there was to feed them" (17). For two cents, he says, he would sell his soul to the devil, and the devil takes him up on it. Immediately his luck improves, he prospers, and he is elected to public office. But as the mortgage on his soul draws due, Jabez asks Daniel Webster to help him, which Webster agrees to do simply because the two New Hampshire men had once been neighbors in a sense. Webster fails to dissuade Scratch, who is a stickler for the letter of the law, opposed to all forms of compromise. So Webster addresses the jury from hell, not as the damned as such, nor as traitors, but simply as men. He restores their humanity by reminding them what it felt like to be human: "the freshness of a fine morning when you're young and the taste of food when you're hungry, and the new day that's every day when you're a child" (25). Webster affirms everything, the good and the bad, the suffering and the starvation because out of these "something new had come." He places his defendant with the jury in the same story, that of the "failures and endless journeys of mankind." No demon, he says, can ever know the "inwardness" (how like Goethe!) of this journey, only a free man. By finding against the defendant, the jury would be finding against themselves as demons. In the moment when they find in favor of Jabez Stone, they reaffirm the worth of life for everyone. But Daniel Webster's triumph is itself compromised. In a scene not in any of the Faust sources, the devil reads Webster's palm, finding that he will lose two sons in the Civil War and that his greatest desire, to be president, will never be fulfilled. Furthermore, Webster's last speech, the devil predicts, will turn many against him and he will be called Ichabod. Still, the Union will be saved.

Benét's story captures an undeniably Faustian pattern in the American imagination: a flawed hero willingly embraces failure and humiliation but ultimately contributes to a glory realized only after his passing. It is a variation on themes from the lives of Moses and Christ. A prophet leads his people to the promised land but cannot enter it himself. The savior is sacrificed so that his people may be saved. However, in the Faustian figure of Daniel Webster—and in the other American Faustian that Benét writes about so passionately, John Brown—there is a real association with darkness that cannot be resolved into a purely heroic image. It is worth thinking through Benét's story as an allegory of this pattern. Jabez Stone, American Everyman, suffering the accidents of misfortune and fears of poverty, sells his soul for two cents, that is, for short-sighted personal gains, the gains of factionalism or self-interest, a view of self as better than others. His immersion in *amour-propre* leads to despair, symbolically represented by Scratch's return to claim his soul. Jabez now appeals to a greater Self, with a more inclusive vision, Daniel Webster. The elder statesman helps him overcome his depression by showing him the Big Picture of American History, which includes figures far darker than himself who were part of America's destiny. Jabez Stone's humility and faith in himself are restored by terror—the vision that life or God requires arbitrary suffering and terrible sacrifice. Jabez Stone may even realize that he has perhaps been lucky compared to some of his jurors.

Benét's parable is not simply a rationalization of evil. It is a vision of the violence that history, politics, and religion involve, together with their attendant ironies. John Brown, Benét's hero of his epic of the Civil War, *John Brown's Body*, was no Childhood's Hero. He was a fanatic who succeeded only in getting a free black man shot and killed at Harper's Ferry. But John Brown's execution was possibly the spark that ignited the Civil War and ultimately freed the slaves. Nor was Benét's view of the Civil War a moralistic melodrama. Like Whitman, Benét champions freedom without demonizing the South. It is a question worthy of Job: who will weigh the justice of war? Scratch foretells that Webster will lose two sons in the Civil War, which he does, of course, but symbolically these sons surely stand for the losses on both sides.

Webster is a hero to Benét because he stands for inclusiveness. As Webster says to Scratch, "I'd go to the Pit itself to save the Union!" (28). "The Devil and Daniel Webster" is a defense of the great orator or what he means to Benét. Inclusiveness means a united front against the threat of fascism, or protofascist attitudes, coming from without or from within, that Benét continually affirms in editorial political works like "Nightmare at Noon" (368). It also means tolerance for and acceptance of differences. Ironically, the Civil War, which Webster tried to delay, has preserved a Union more factionally diverse, more full of challenges to equal rights than ever. It only makes sense to say, from Benét's point of view, that what we need now is a Daniel Webster to pull us together, remind us what it means to be human, and urge us to work together for the good of all. In Benét's work this patriotic sentiment is more complex, upon examination, than it might appear. Joblike terrors and Faustian deals with the devil energize a dialectic between separation and reunification, which is ongoing in a country as vast as America. Just as Mark Twain takes the national imagination back to a time before the Civil War in *Huckleberry Finn* in order to move it forward again with renewed conscience, humor, and humanity, so does Benét, in his now classic short story, make his audience look back and forward at the same time. In "The Devil and Daniel Webster," he has created a snapshot of that moment of terror and inspiration when a people torn by differences look for something deep they have in common.

It should not be surprising, then, that "The Devil and Daniel Webster" has enjoyed so long a life on stage and screen. A play, opera, or movie is a communal art form and must on some level unite its audience in a common understanding of the needs of its time. An operatic version of

Benét's short story, with music by Douglas Moore, was produced in New York in 1939, and Benét revised the script he wrote for the opera in 1938 for production later without music. The movie of 1941, a.k.a. *All That Money Can Buy*, with which Benét was involved, is a different breed of cat and very powerful in its way still today. In addition, there have been numerous adaptations for television.

The dramatic version creates a social context for the story by locating the devil's arrival to claim Jabez Stone's soul on his wedding day. It is a strong *mise en scène*, a country wedding with dancing and a Fiddler. Scratch arrives, usurps the Fiddler's position, and sings a song about a rake's progress, which ends with a dead husband and a sorrowing widow. The dramatic device of the interrupted wedding, which captures everyone's attention, gives a communal significance to what is occurring. It is as if life itself cannot move forward in its socially sanctioned forms until a deeper obligation is met, in this case a reconciliation with the nation's past. A solid spiritual foundation for the wedding must be laid in which the whole community participates. The national demons of the past must be exorcised and a renewed commitment to human freedom made before any meaningful marriage can occur. Webster's symbolic meaning is graphically asserted by Jabez Stone, who would rather die than let any harm come to the national symbol: "You're the whole United States ... Mr. Webster—he [the devil] musn't get you!" (24). The palm reading scene is omitted so that a strong curtain can follow Scratch's expulsion by Daniel Webster and a united crowd of wedding guests.

The opera, even more spectacular than the play, of course, allows Jabez Stone's wife, Mary, to take on the aura of Goethe's Gretchen in her association with nature and simple country life. Her aria, with its text from Ruth—"For thy people shall be my people"(54)—creates a typically operatic emotional tension to foreground Jabez Stone's predicament. The rogues from the jury are shrewdly led by Webster's questioning to identify themselves with the natural elements of their earthly existences, not the social distortions of their crimes. Webster asks Girty, "Have you forgotten the forest," and Teach the Pirate, "Have you forgotten the sea and the way of Ships," and King Philip, "Have you forgotten your lost nation" (76). The effect is to draw these characters into the opera's dramatic reclaiming of freedom as the only valid background for human endeavor. The crowd of wedding guests is very good as a populist chorus: "Neighbors, Neighbors, Neighbors all!—For the devil's sly and the devil's tough, But we've seen his cards and we've called his bluff!" (84). Both opera, with its published piano score, and the play script, readily available today at a low price, make the work accessible for amateur production.

The movie of 1941 "opens up" the play a good deal. We see Jabez Stone's Joblike suffering in the context of his home (he is already married), where his wife and mother depend upon him for survival. Most interesting is the dark, German-Expressionist cinematography, which makes the fascist threat—apparently the movie's theme—seem eminent, whether it is inside or outside the country. Daniel Webster here is working for reform legislation that would make it harder for loan sharks to take advantage of simple farm owners. Jabez Stone has betrayed his community by refusing to join the grange and by eventually becoming one of these loan sharks himself. He has a vaguely European housekeeper-mistress who threatens to usurp his wife's position and, by the end of his contractual period with the devil, a beastly spoiled brat son who shows what the country will come to if Daniel Webster doesn't intervene. Jabez Stone builds a mansion as a temple to himself and with the help of Scratch has turned all the local farmers into his employees. In one memorable surreal scene, the hellish neighbors of the European housekeeper from over the mountain invade Jabez's palace, grabbing food off his table. He is being treated—Scroogelike—to a vision of the world's starving classes and what his experience of them may be if he doesn't become more democratic. After Daniel Webster's victory, Jabez Stone's mansion burns to the ground—a scene Jabez now watches without regret—and he is restored to his humble humanity. The movie is utterly convincing in its sentiment, which is conveyed almost entirely by striking visual images.

It remains to reflect upon Benét as a "modern" author in a Faustian context. Although a highly regarded writer in his own day, Stephen Vincent Benét has not been canonized as a high modernist. Somewhat like the flawed heroes he wrote about, Benét has had an ironic literary fate. He worked hard to transform the National Institute of Arts and Letters, to which he was grudgingly admitted in 1929 by members like Hamlin Garlin and Robert Underwood Johnson, as a representative of the new generation (Fenton 323–330). When he was elected to a vice-presidency of the institute in 1936, he worked tirelessly, and to many objectionably, to bring new voices of American literature into what was a bastion of conservatism. Between 1937 and 1939, Thomas Wolfe, John Dos Passos, Ezra Pound, William Faulkner, and John Steinbeck, among others, were elected to membership. In addition Benét worked to begin giving sizeable grants to working writers. Between 1943 and 1946, thousand-dollar grants went to Carson McCullers, Karl Shapiro, Eudora Welty, Tennessee Williams, Marianne Moore, Robert Lowell, James Agee, Gwendolyn Brooks, and many others. But in spite of his two Pulitzer prizes, Benét's own fate in postwar America has been to appear old-fashioned. Identified, correctly, as an enthusiast for the Transcendentalists' optimism about American democracy, he is also sometimes grouped with Carl Sandburg, Vachel Lindsay, and Edgar Lee Masters as a writer who loved America's diversity, self-sufficiency, frankness, and innocence. Yet in all fairness, the great American Romantics Emerson and Whitman, as well as regionalists who find profound significance in the common man and Benét, whose "words recall the uncertainties and challenges of a forming nation, and probe into the quaint corners of our history—telling us what used to be, and has been lost, and must be found again" (Leslie 7), all have roles to play in the Faustian transformation of modern literature.

The Faust story, originally an imaginative response to challenges to intellectual authority in the early modern period, has since Goethe identified itself as the myth which expresses the struggles of all individuals willing to embrace the good and bad of critical scientific/political self-examination. Heine gives a very Faustian characterization of modernity in his essay on Goethe:

> ...we apprehend that men are called not only to a heavenly but also to an earthly equality; the political brotherhood preached to us by philosophy is more beneficial to us than the purely spiritual brotherhood which Christianity has procured for us; and knowledge becomes word, and the word becomes deed, and we can attain the Kingdom of God during our life on this earth; if on top of it we can still partake of that heavenly bliss after death which Christianity so specifically promises us, we shall be all the better pleased [Heine 443].

The cost of entering into a more or less permanent period of transition in pursuit of freedom is to suffer the anxieties of double consciousness and to experience the world's chaos without so many illusions of order. Goethe's Faust tells his assistant Wagner, "Two souls, alas, are dwelling in my breast"(27), the earthly and the heavenly, neither of which he is willing to surrender. And Faust expresses to Mephistopheles his desire to enter *fully* into life:

> Henceforth my soul, for knowledge sick no more,
> Against no kind of suffering shall be cautioned,
> And what to all of mankind is apportioned
> I mean to savor in my own self's core,
> Grasp with my mind both highest and most low,
> Weigh down my spirit with their weal and woe,
> And thus my selfhood to their own distend,
> And be, as they are, shattered in the end. (42)

The intellectual modernism that emerged in the early twentieth century shattered America's self-image, conventionally understood, scattering America across the world, and bringing all the world into America. However, Romantics and inclusive populists like Benét were still part of the conversation about the role of the writer's voice in the New World. A glance at Hart Crane, one of the highest of high modernists, establishes an unexpected connection to Benét and allows us to reflect on the range of Benét's modernity.

If one poem by Hart Crane had to be chosen to summarize his vision it might well be "To Brooklyn Bridge," the dedicatory introduction to his great work *The Bridge* (1930), which in some of its ambitions corresponds to Benét's *John Brown's Body*. Both are poems about the spiritual potentials of America. "To Brooklyn Bridge" actually seems to derive some of its most resonant initial images from a poem by Benét, "Lunch-Time along Broadway," published in 1920. Benét's poem begins,

> Twelve-thirty bells from a thousand clocks, the typewriter tacks
>   and stops,
> Gorged elevators slam and fall through the floors like water-
>   drops,
> From offices hung like sea-gulls' nests on a cliff the whirlwinds
>   beat,
> The octopus-crowd comes rolling out, his tentacles crawl for
>   meat [*Heavens and Earth* 41].

Arguably, Crane picks up from Benét's poem the scene of office workers high up in their skyscrapers (with sea gulls nesting and flying nearby), leaving their office machines, taking elevators down to the first floor, and going out to become part of the moving crowds in the streets of the vast metropolis. For Benét it is lunchtime, for Crane the end of the workday in the evening. These are Crane's magnificent lines that open "To Brooklyn Bridge":

> How many dawns, chill from his rippling rest
> The seagull's wings shall dip and pivot him,
> Shedding white rings of tumult, building high
> Over the chained bay waters Liberty—
>
> Then with inviolate curve, forsake our eyes
> As apparitional as sails that cross
> Some page of figures to be filed away;
> —Till elevators drop us from our day ...

For both poets, the scene is more than a realistic vignette; it is a vision, exciting and a little frightening, of New York as symbol of the human spirit set free to experience itself in all its glory and terror. Whether or not Crane actually used Benét's poem as a springboard, the similarities place Benét in the urban ethos of modernism. Moreover, looking more closely at Crane's poem, we recognize a number of common concerns.

The Bridge begins with what might be thought of as the provocation of the Faust situation: Satan's initial reply to the Lord's question to him, one of the sons of God. In Job, the Lord asks, "Whence comest thou?" Satan replies, "From going to and fro in the earth, and from walking up and down in it" (Job 1:7). *The Bridge* may be read in terms of all Satan sees, all he shows to Job, and as Job becomes Faust, actively involved with Mephistopheles, all Faust comes to know, including his marriage with Helen—all which the world teaches that transports as it breaks the heart. Crane had expressed this program in his first major poem of *White Buildings*, "For the Marriage of Faustus and Helen." It ends with a stanza that is simultaneously exaltation and cry, uniting the ecstasy of the jazz age and the terror of aerial warfare:

> Distinctly praise the years, whose volatile
> Blamed bleeding hands extend and thresh the heart
> The imagination spans beyond despair,
> Outpacing bargain, vocable and prayer.

The Brooklyn Bridge in Crane's dedicatory poem is a triumph of human effort and engineering that creates a hope, possibly a hopeless hope: that a continuity can be found in the midst of change, paradoxically perhaps *because* of change, which can connect if not unite the vast diversity of humanity. Perhaps the machine, which alienates man from nature and from God, will finally "lend a myth to God." Surely that phrase has an audacity worthy of Goethe and Daniel Webster.

The Faustian dare, growing out of but never completely away from despair, even as it is expressed in what Goethe called "a very serious jest," is Stephen Vincent Benét's great theme. In the New World of change, it is not possible, according to Faust, to hold back from experience. One must move through it, into nightmares that are and are not of one's own making, believing in the Romantic dawn of awakening. A dramatic treatment of four stories by Benét done by F. Andrew Leslie, *Stephen Vincent Benét's Stories of America* (1971), expresses Benét's faith in the ability of humanity to survive its Faustian ordeal with grace. This stage adaptation uses no sets or scenery, but relies on lighting, mime, and music to create an abstract treatment of Benét's themes. The actors remain on stage throughout the performance with open scripts. The dramatic readings interpret "Jacob and the Indians," "A Tooth for Paul Revere," "O'Halloran's Luck," and "Johnny Pye and the Fool-Killer." The first three express the trials of underdogs of various ethnic extractions surviving and even, to their surprise, thriving in strange new worlds. "Johnny Pye and the Fool-Killer" is a Faustian fairy-tale parable that expresses Benét's love for America. Johnny Pye is an orphan who runs through a series of adventures fleeing the "Fool-Killer." Whenever he succeeds at anything (when he is tempted to cease from striving), whether it is being clever, rich, or heroic, he hears the footsteps of the Fool-Killer and moves on. After he has had his Job experiences of losing his wife and then his son to drowning, he confronts the Fool-Killer. He knows the answer now to his riddle, When is man not a Fool? The answer is when he is dead and gone. Now Johnny believes only a fool would wish not to die when life has been as richly completed as his has been. So he goes to meet the Fool-Killer without fear. The view of America Benét expresses at the conclusion of this work is exactly the view of the world expressed by Faust at the conclusion of Goethe's drama. The survivors of Johnny Pye declare,

> There is a country of hope, there is a country of freedom.... It is not an earthly paradise, a Garden of Eden, or a perfect state. It does not pretend to be any of those things.... It has not solved every problem of how men and women should live. It has made mistakes in its own affairs, mistakes in the affairs of the world.... But it looks to the future always—to a future of free men and women, where there shall be bread and work, security and liberty for the children of mankind [53].

How like the last words Faust speaks as he dies:

> Yes—this I hold to with devout insistence,
> Wisdom's last verdict goes to say:
> He only earns both freedom and existence
> Who must reconquer them each day.
> And so, ringed all about by perils, here
> Youth, manhood, age will spend their strenuous year.
> Such teeming would I see upon this land,
> On acres free among free people stand.
> I might entreat the fleeting minute:
> Oh tarry yet, thou art so far!
> My path on earth, the trace I leave within it
> Eons untold cannot impair.
> Foretasting such high happiness to come,
> I savor now my striving's crown and sum [294].

The partnership or collusion implied by the title of Benét's story "The Devil *and* Daniel Webster," in addition to reiterating some of the conventional wisdom about politicians, suggests something about the power of accumulated experience to enlighten and liberate. Goethe and Benét testify that once free oneself, one will naturally desire to stand upon the earth among all free people.

WORKS CITED AND CONSULTED

Barber, James, and Frederick Voss. *The Godlike Black Dan: A Selection of Portraits From Life in Commemoration of the Two Hundredth Anniversary of the Birth of Daniel Webster.* Washington: Smithsonian Press, 1982.

Benét, Stephen Vincent. "The Author is Pleased." *New York Times* 28 Sept. 1941: x4.

_____. "The Devil and Daniel Webster." In *The Devil and Daniel Webster and Other Writings.* New York: Penguin, 1999.

_____. *The Devil and Daniel Webster.* Play in One Act. 1938. New York: Dramatists Play Service, 1966.

_____. *John Brown's Body.* 1927. Chicago: Ivan R. Dee, 1990.

_____. "Lunch-Time along Broadway," S4N, 9 (July 1920). Reprinted in *Heavens and Earth.* New York: Henry Holt, 1920.

Benét, Stephen Vincent, and Douglas Moore. *The Devil and Daniel Webster.* Opera, first performed in New York at the Martin Beck Theatre, May 18, 1939. New York: Farrar & Rinehart, 1939.

Benét, Stephen Vincent, and Dan Totheroh. *The Devil and Daniel Webster.* Movie, a.k.a. *All That Money Can Buy,* Dir. William Dieterle. RKO, 1941.

Brooks, Van Wyck. *The Flowering of New England.* New York: Dutton, 1952.

Brown, Jane K. *Goethe's Faust: The German Tragedy.* Ithaca: Cornell UP, 1986.

Bunge, Nancy. *Nathaniel Hawthorne: A Study of the Short Fiction.* New York: Twayne, 1993.

Butler, E. M. *The Fortunes of Faust.* Cambridge: Cambridge UP, 1952.

Cole, Douglas. *Suffering and Evil in the Plays of Christopher Marlowe.* Princeton: Princeton UP, 1962.

Combs, Robert. *Vision of the Voyage: Hart Crane and the Psychology of Romanticism.* Memphis: Memphis State UP, 1978.

Crane, Hart. "For the Marriage of Faustus and Helen." In *The Complete Poems and Selected Letters of Hart Crane.* Ed. Brom Weber. New York: Doubleday, 1966.

_____. "To Brooklyn Bridge." In *Complete Poems.*

Edinger, Edward. *Encounter with the Self: A Jungian Commentary on William Blake's Illustrations of the Book of Job.* Toronto: Inner City Books, 1986.

_____. *Goethe's Faust Notes for a Jungian Commentary.* Toronto: Inner City Books, 1990.

Fenton, Charles A. *Stephen Vincent Benét: The Life and Times of an American Man of Letters 1898–1943.* New Haven: Yale UP, 1958.

Fuess, Chaude M. *Daniel Webster*. 2nd ed. 2 vols. 1930. New York: Da Capo, 1968.

Goethe, Johann Wolfgang von. *Faust*. Trans. Walter Arndt. Ed. Cyrus Hamlin. New York: Norton, 1976.

Haile, H. G. "Faust als Nationales Symbol bei Stephen Vincent Benét und Thomas Mann." *Zeitschrift für Deutsche Philologie*. 111.4 (1992): 608–24.

Hawthorne, Nathaniel. "Young Goodman Brown." In *The Celestial Railroad and Other Stories*. New York: Penguin, 1980.

Hazlitt, William. *Lectures on the Literature of the Age of Elizabeth and Characters of Shakespeare's Plays*. London: Bell & Daldy, 1870.

Heine, Heinrich. "Faust." From *The Romantic School*. 1833. Trans. Dolores Signori, with the assistance of Walter Arndt. In *Faust*. Ed. Cyrus Hamlin. 1976. Pp. 442–4.

Jung, C. G. *Answer to Job*. 1952. In *Psychology and Religion: West and East*. Vol. 11 of the *Collected Works of C. G. Jung*. Princeton: Princeton UP, 1975.

Leslie, F. Andrew. "Adaptor." *Stephen Vincent Benét's Stories of America*. New York: Dramatists Play Service, 1971.

Marlowe, Christopher. *Dr. Faustus*. In *Christopher Marlowe's Dr. Faustus: Text and Major Criticism*. Ed. Irving Ribner. New York: Odyssey, 1966.

Mason, Eudo C. *Goethe's Faust: Its Genesis and Purport*. Berkeley: U of California UP, 1967.

Nathans, Sydney. *Daniel Webster and Jacksonian Democracy*. Baltimore: Johns Hopkins UP, 1973.

Partenheimer, David. "Benét's 'The Devil and Daniel Webster'" *The Explicator* 55:1 (Fall 1996): 37-40.

Paul, Sherman. *Hart's Bridge*. Urbana: U of Illinois P, 1972.

Singer, Robert. "One Against All: The New England Past and Present—Responsibilities in *The Devil and Daniel Webster*." *Literature Film Quarterly* 22:4 (1994): 265–7.

Whittier, John Greenleaf. "Ichabod." In *Songs of Labor and Other Poems*. 1850. In *The Poetical Works of John Greenleaf Whittier*. New York: Houghton, 1975.

9. American Reincarnations: "The Devil and Daniel Webster" from Fiction to Drama to Film

Lincoln Konkle

Whether discussing a film adaptation of last year's best-selling novel or an earlier adaptation of a timeless work of literature, the inevitable questions are, "Was it faithful to the book? Did it capture the essence of the original?" The most common if not inevitable answer is, "The book was better." In the age of poststructural theory and criticism, this subject, at least from a scholarly point of view, is itself rife with ontological and epistemological issues: What is the essence of a work of literature? How is that essence knowable so that it can be, if you will, *reincarnated* by the adaptation? Is not an adaptation always an interpretation of the original, since works of literature are inherently ambiguous because language itself is inherently ambiguous?

Between 1936 and 1941 Stephen Vincent Benét wrote three versions of "The Devil and Daniel Webster": the original short story published by the *Saturday Evening Post* in 1936, an opera libretto (almost immediately revised as a one-act play by cutting the songs) produced by the American Lyric Theatre in 1939, and the screenplay for a feature film produced by RKO Pictures under the title *All That Money Can Buy* in 1941. Even in this rare instance of the author adapting his own original, there are still factors that make the task of analyzing and assessing the adaptations problematic. For one, Benét was not the only artist involved in adapting his story: he collaborated with composer Douglas Moore on the opera, and with producer-director William Dieterle and co-screenwriter Dan Totheroh on the film. Then there is the assumption of reviewers and critics that even Benét's original short story is itself an adaptation of the Faust legend; but which version of it? Christopher Marlowe's play *The Tragical History of Dr. Faustus?* Goethe's epic *Faust?* Gounod's opera?[1] The issue of Benét's sources or inspiration for the story is itself a complicated one, involving other literary, cultural, historical, and autobiographical factors. Whatever other issues arise in comparing the reincarnations to the original, in the process of adapting "The Devil and Daniel Webster" from fiction to drama to film, Benét shifts the emphasis away from Daniel Webster as an American hero in the genre of the tall tale, to Jabez Stone as an everyman figure in the morality play tradition. This brings "The Devil and Daniel Webster" full circle back to the Faust legend, which somewhat diminishes the affirmative American theme of the original story.

Although it is quite likely that Benét was, on some level, thinking of the Faust legend, there are other significant sources—literary, historical, and autobiographical—that may have contributed to the creation of "The Devil and Daniel Webster." Stroud considers the Book of Job in the Bible to have partly inspired the story. In addition to the superficial similarity of the protagonists enduring a hard life, Stroud cites the similar sounds of the names Job and Jabez (117). However, Job was a "perfect and upright man, one that feared God, eschewed evil" (Job 1:1 KJV) while Jabez is not "a bad man to start with, but an unlucky man."[2] The name of Benét's protagonist may indeed have been derived from the Bible, but not from the Book of Job. In 1 Chronicles 2:55, "Jabez" is a village or region. In 1 Chronicles 4: 9–10, "Jabez" is a man: "Jabez was more honorable than his brothers. His mother had named him Jabez, saying, 'I gave birth to him in pain.' Jabez cried out to the God of Israel, 'Oh, that you would bless me and enlarge my territory! Let your hand be with me, and keep me from harm so that I will be free from pain.' And God granted his request."[3] Another correspondence to the Book of Job is the metaphysical conflict: "The soul of Jabez is contested for, not by God and the Devil, but by an American demigod and Mr. Scratch" (Stroud 118). That is, the devil and Daniel Webster fighting for Jabez's soul parallels Satan and God disputing over Job's faithfulness at the beginning of the Book of Job.

In his source study James A. S. McPeek makes a compelling case that Benét unconsciously followed the plot of a fable in Lewis B. Monroe's *Fourth Reader*, which was widely used in grade schools at the time of Benét and McPeek's childhood. According to McPeek, the two major similarities of "The Captive Woodchuck" to "The Devil and Daniel Webster" are the action of having two boys contest the fate of a woodchuck they caught in a trap, and the boy who successfully argues that the woodchuck should be freed is named Daniel. A possible textual corroboration of McPeek's claim of unconscious influence is that Benét does use the word *woodchuck* in "The Devil and Daniel Webster" where the devil has implied that Miser Stevens is dead, to which Jabez responds, "You can't tell me he is! He was just as spry and mean as a woodchuck, Tuesday!" (35). Further evidence for this is that in the play version of "The Devil and Daniel Webster" there is another speech that uses woodchuck: "—if I planted gardentruck, the woodchucks ate it" (19).

Canonical works of literature may also have influenced Benét in the writing of "The Devil and Daniel Webster." In "As We Remember Him," a collection of tributes published in the *Saturday Review of Literature* after Benét's death, John Berdan recognizes an affinity Benét has with Nathaniel Hawthorne (see Bunge in this volume); certainly Hawthorne's tale "Young Goodman Brown" employs something of the same scenario as "The Devil and Daniel Webster." Other possible American literary influences include Washington Irving's "The Devil and Tom Walker," Edgar Allan Poe's "The Bargain Lost," which he revised as "Bon-Bon," and Mark Twain's "The Mysterious Stranger." While all of these are possible models for the story, Benét himself cited the major source: "Then Van Wyck Brooks' *Flowering of New England* gave me the clue to Webster" ("Words and Music"). Although both Stroud and Fenton acknowledge this statement, they did not examine Brooks' portrayal of Daniel Webster in comparison to Benét's. Given their strikingly similar treatment of Daniel Webster, a more in-depth consideration of the influence of Brooks upon Benét is warranted.

Webster is described in *The Flowering of New England* as a man of the people, a farmer as well as a statesman:

> They knew all of his ways and the names of his guns and animals, as the Jews of old knew the weapons of Nimrod, or Abraham's flocks and herds,—his great ram Goliath, his shot-guns, "Mrs. Patrick" and "Wilmot Proviso," his trout-rod "Old Killall." They knew he had written the Bunker Hill oration, composed it word by word, with Old Killall in his hand, wading in the Marshfield River. They had heard of his tens of thousands of swine and sheep, his herds of Peruvian llamas and blooded cattle, the hundreds of thousands of trees he had raised from seed [Brooks 95].

As Brooks paints him, Webster was a legend in his own time: every boy and girl had seen a picture of Webster displaying "the dark brow that looked like Monadnock" (94–5). It is evident from these passages that Benét relied heavily on Brooks' characterization of Daniel Webster, using some of the same details and language.[4]

Apart from these literary and historical sources for "The Devil and Daniel Webster," Singer makes a reasonable case that Benét's film adaptation was influenced by the cultural climate of America in 1941, but what Singer says is valid at the time Benét wrote the original short story as well: "Benét's sentimentalized tale of this misguided farmer ... personalizes the socioeconomic Depression-era plight of the New England farmer" (268). Singer subsequently broadens the scope of his point: "Benét's contexture of sociohistorical developments involving the faith and fortunes of late 1930–40s America employs the economic crisis and ensuing world war as an external conflict in which farmers represent the human side of the political dilemma" (269). Singer could have expanded his reading of the cultural context of Benét's film to say it was also a response to threats to American ideology, such as the agitation of leftist members of the intelligentsia in the United States during the 1920s and 1930s. David Garrett Izzo, in his play *The American World of Stephen Vincent Benét*, has Benét-as-character interpret the story in the context of its times: "As a parable, Jabez represented the average American down on his luck during the depression; the judge and jury represented the fascists; and Scratch—well Ol' Scratch is the devil, and it's up to Daniel, as the U.S., to come to the rescue" (20).

A final possible inspiration for "The Devil and Daniel Webster," which was written during the summer and published in the fall of 1936, is the dire financial straights Benét was in and had been in since losing most of his earnings from *John Brown's Body* in the stock market crash of 1929. Despite the multitude of magazines to which his agent sold his short stories, Benét had difficulty consistently making a living with his writing. It seems that Benét may have thought he was selling out, if not literally selling his soul to the devil, first with learning to write formula fiction for slick magazines, and then when he went to Hollywood.[5] The hardship and subsequent moral dilemma Jabez Stone faces, especially in the film adaptation, were not solely part of an act of literary borrowing, but were, rather, an aspect of the timeless human condition which Benét himself was grappling with, which many Americans were grappling with during the Great Depression, as Fenton suggests: "The hero of 'The Devil and Daniel Webster' was the New England statesman, but the author's kinship was with Jabez Stone, the bedeviled farmer who worked a rocky strip of New Hampshire land" (293). It was, perhaps, Benét's identification with Jabez and his empathy for the American populace that account for his impetus to reach a broader audience through adaptation first to the theatre and then to the screen, and the evolution of the narrative that shifts away from Daniel Webster to focus on the American Everyman character, Jabez.

The complexities of the origin of "The Devil and Daniel Webster" make the story itself more challenging to study as the source for the adaptations. Thus, it is necessary to analyze the story itself for its essential narrative components that Benét would later attempt to reproduce in a different genre or medium.

The Story

There are five distinctive characteristics of "The Devil and Daniel Webster": the mythic-heroic portrait of Webster; the scene between Jabez Stone and the devil in which Miser Stevens' soul tries to escape; the portrayal of the devil as Mr. Scratch, "a home-grown devil" (Benét "Author is Pleased"); the climactic trial scene, with especial attention given to Webster's speech that moves the jury of the damned to side with the defense by affirming America and its values; and, finally, the tall tale tone.

In Sickels' discussion of Benét's balancing of romanticism and realism (445), she suggests that his folk-tale rendition of Daniel Webster is closer to a Paul Bunyan story than a historical or realistic description. In fact, the character sketch that opens the story raises Daniel Webster to the level of the supernatural:

> Yes, Dan'l Webster's dead—or, at least, they buried him. But every time there's a thunderstorm around Marshfield, they say you can hear his rolling voice in the hollows of the sky. And they say that if you go to his grave and speak loud and clear, "Dan'l Webster— Dan'l Webster!" the ground'll begin to shiver and the trees begin to shake ... [and] he's liable to rear right out of the ground [33].

As with tales of Paul Bunyan, "The Devil and Daniel Webster" emphasizes size, mostly by a verbal motif of the word *big* and variations of it, beginning with the second paragraph of the story: "You see, for a while, he was the biggest man in the country. He never got to be President, but he was the biggest man" (32). Obviously Daniel Webster's bigness is metaphorical as opposed to Paul Bunyan's literally being a giant, but Benét does describe Daniel Webster with superlatives related to the bigness of his voice, his strength, his farm, and his taste for Medford rum. During the trial scene, the narrator says that Webster's "voice got like a big bell" (42). Even his soul is of impressive size, according to the devil: "Now, a man like Dan'l Webster, of course—well, we'd have to build a special box for him, and even at that, I imagine the wing spread would astonish you" (36). In fact, the narrator of the story tells the audience that they are about to hear the tallest of the tales about Daniel Webster: "And the biggest case he argued never got written down in the books, for he argued it against the devil, nip and tuck and no holds barred" (32). Exaggerations are inherent to tall tales and folk tales, but the myth of America itself also manifests the theme of bigness. The geographical size of the United States, the New World, and its resources, the Land of Plenty are important features of American culture even today.

Besides the abstract quality of size, Benét heightens his depiction of Daniel Webster as a character in a more concrete, specific way. Although Webster's fame was made as a lawyer and statesman, the story combines his oratorical powers with a physical prowess like a Daniel Boone or Davy Crockett, but in the exaggerated mode of legends or tall tales:

> They said, when he stood up to speak, stars and stripes came right out in the sky, and once he spoke against a river and made it sink into the ground. They said, when he walked the woods with his fishing rod, Killall, the trout would jump out of the streams right into his pockets, for they knew it was no use putting up a fight against him; and, when he argued a case, he could turn on the harps of the blessed and the shaking of the earth underground [32].

Benét continues this more earthy characterization: "It was early in the morning when he got to Marshfield, but Dan'l was up already, talking Latin to the farm hands and wrestling with the ram, Goliath" (36), who the narrator earlier described as having "horns with a curl like a morning-glory vine and could butt through an iron door" (32). Furthermore, the allusion to the biblical Goliath, who literally was a giant, further elevates the heroic character sketch of Webster. Even his horses are of extraordinary speed and of noble name: "he told 'em to hitch up Constitution and Constellation to the carriage. They were matched grays with one white forefoot, and they stepped like greased lightning.... Jabez Stone had lost his hat on the way, blown off when they overtook a wind" (37). These Herculean powers and feats are described with an implicit nudge and a wink as Benét signifies the tall tale genre from the beginning of the story to the end by putting Daniel Webster's powers and deeds in the oral tradition, which suggests the idea of a legend, a "whopper," a folk or even a fairy tale. For example, the first paragraph of the story ends with the disclaimer, "At least, that's what I was told when I was a youngster" (32).

The second essential narrative element in "The Devil and Daniel Webster" that Benét tries to re-create in both the play and film is the scene where the devil drops by Jabez Stone's farm to remind him that his contracted period of prosperity expires in a year, at which time Jabez will have to surrender his soul. Despite the tongue-in-cheek tone of the opening pages, this episode is chilling in its dramatization of the ultimate loss of liberty: a damned soul. Following a narrative summary of how Jabez's misfortunes have been replaced by making a fortune, Benét has him express to the devil "considerable doubts as to that mortgage holding in court," his "always having been a religious man" and "[t]his being the U.S.A." (34). The devil responds by examining Jabez's contract in a "big black pocketbook, full of papers," flipping by "Sherwin, Slater, Stevens" (35) before he finds Stone, suggesting that he has lured many ordinary persons like Jabez into selling their souls. Benét dramatically confirms this by having Jabez see something "flutter out of the black pocketbook. It was something like a moth, but it wasn't a moth. And as Jabez Stone stared at it, it seemed to speak to him in a small sort of piping voice, terrible small and thin, but terrible human. 'Neighbor Stone! Help me! For God's sake help me!" (35). Jabez recognizes the voice of Miser Stevens, who he insists is still alive, but when he hears the church bell toll, he realizes the truth. This scene is essential to the story because it effectively brings home to the reader or viewer that just like a common, ordinary person such as Jabez Stone, we all may be tempted to sell our souls.

The third essential element of "The Devil and Daniel Webster" is its characterization of the devil. Benét wanted to create an American devil: "I couldn't help trying to show [Daniel Webster] in terms of American legend; I couldn't help wondering what would happen if a man like that ever came to grips with the Devil—and not an imported Devil, either, but a genuine, homegrown product, Mr. Scratch" ("The Author is Pleased"). This suggests that a fundamental factor in Benét's creative process was to reincarnate the Faust legend, or more generally the devil, in specifically American terms, ideals, and actions. The most explicit manifestation of Benét's intention occurs in the scene before the trial when Daniel Webster tries to free Jabez by employing various legal maneuvers. When he says, "Mr. Stone is an American citizen, and no American citizen may be forced into the service of a foreign prince!" the devil replies, "And who calls me a foreigner?" He continues with the best speech in the story:

> When the first wrong was done to the first Indian, I was there. When the first slaver put out for the Congo, I stood on her deck. Am I not in your books and stories and beliefs, from the first settlements on? Am I not spoken of, still, in every church in New England? ... I am merely an honest American citizen like yourself—and of the best descent—for to tell the truth, Mr. Webster, though I don't like to boast of it, my name is older in this country than yours [39].

In other speeches the devil employs terms of business and the law, which are not exclusively American institutions, of course, though they are essential to the American system of democratic capitalism. In the pretrial scene, which one might even call a hearing, the devil says to Daniel Webster, "I shall call upon you, as a law-abiding citizen, to assist me in taking possession of my property" (38). Unmoved by any of the great lawyer's attempts to find a loophole in the contract, the devil sticks "to the letter of the law" (39) and begins himself to talk more like a lawyer: "if you have no more arguments to adduce" (39); Benét even has the narrator define the devil as "the King of Lawyers, as the Good Book tells us" (39), again, tongue firmly in cheek.

Another aspect of Benét's homegrown devil has precedent in American literature. He is referred to by the narrator as "the stranger," but offers an actual name when queried by Daniel Webster: "'I've gone by a good many [names],' said the stranger carelessly. 'Perhaps Scratch will do for the evening. I'm often called that in these regions'" (38). The devil is referred to as "the stranger" in Edgar Allan Poe's "The Bargain Lost," a story which also has as its premise a conversation with the devil who carries a "pocket book" stuffed with many papers that he calls "agreements" (93).[6] In Washington Irving's tale "The Devil and Tom Walker," which, according to Fenton (294), Benét did not read until after his story had been published, the devil character gives a very similar response to Benét's Scratch: "Oh, I go by various names.... In this neighborhood I am known by the name of the black woodsman," to which Irving's Faust character, Tom Walker, replies, "You are he commonly called Old Scratch" (396). The name Scratch is particularly appropriate for an *American devil*, since the word also means money, struggling to make a living, and hasty, as in scratch paper or a scratch crew (*Slang Partridge's English* 387).

The fourth crucial attribute of the story is a technical tour de force by Benét. If there is one image from "The Devil and Daniel Webster" that stays in the reader's mind, it has to be the trial scene in which Daniel Webster represents the defendant, Jabez Stone, before a jury of damned souls, historical figures who were all in some way traitors to America. This is the scene readers have been waiting for since the beginning of the story, Daniel Webster's "biggest case," the one in which he argues against the devil himself. As Benét explained to an interviewer, "Webster's strong point was oratory ... so naturally he'd have to meet the devil in an oratorical contest and win" (Fenton 295). However, the only *mano a mano* action between the devil and Daniel Webster occurs immediately before and after the trial. In fact, during the trial itself they hardly interact at all. Benét merely summarizes the devil presenting his case, so that we never do see him living up to the narrator's sobriquet for the devil, "the King of Lawyers."

The climax of the trial and the story is Daniel Webster's speech to the jury; however, if readers remember this speech, it is a testament to Benét's skill as a fiction writer that he makes them think they have read a great speech by the American master of oratory, when only a summary is given. To present the actual speech would have required that its content and style be as masterful and as eloquent as the historical Webster's. It would have had to be so good that the reader could believe the speech really would move a jury of damned souls to find for the defense, which is no easy task, even for a jury of damned *American* souls. But that is precisely what Benét has Webster use to make his case: the fact that the members of the jury are all Americans, though it is doubtful that very many readers would recognize the seven members of the jury who are actually named (for example, Walter Butler, Simon Girty, and Teach).

It could also be argued that what saves Jabez from the devil is not Daniel Webster's oratorical greatness, but rather the greatness of America itself, the ideas and values associated with America that would be manifest in an American folk tale, in an American myth. Rather than having Webster win Jabez's release through legal tricks, Benét has him draw on the patriotism supposedly inherent in every American, and certainly inherent in the historical Daniel Webster. A significant portion of Benét's paraphrase of the speech sounds the American theme:

> He was talking about the things that make a country a country, and a man a man.... They were good things for any man. But without freedom, they sickened.... He talked of the early days of America and the men who had made those days.... But he showed how, out of all the wrong and the right, the suffering and the starvations, something new had come. And everybody had played a part in it, even the traitors [42].

Clearly the story as a whole reads as a fictional anthem to America itself, as well as to one of its significant historical figures, Daniel Webster. References to the Salem witch trials, the Revolutionary War, Benedict Arnold, the Constitution, Indians, slavery, the War of 1812, John C. Calhoun, the Missouri Compromise, the Civil War, all permeate the story so that the reader is almost constantly encountering one or more signifiers of America and its history.

If Benét did write "The Devil and Daniel Webster" as an American adaptation of the Faust legend, then his emphasis was not on the Faust character, but rather on the character who is an incarnation of America that can save Faust, perhaps reflecting an inherent American optimism. Daniel Webster represents America, but not as an American everyman, not an average, common, ordinary American; rather, as a larger-than-life American, a representation of America at its best. Jabez is merely the catalyst that provides the opportunity for Daniel Webster to reaffirm America's heroic status in world history and American democratic values. This is also what distinguishes "The Devil and Daniel Webster" from other adaptations of the Faust legend, its nationalist theme and tone, which are parts of Benét's works as a whole.[7]

The essential aspects of the story discussed above—heroic portrait of Daniel Webster, the Miser Stevens scene, Mr. Scratch as an American devil, the trial before a jury of the damned and Daniel Webster's patriotic speech—would have to be included in any faithful adaptation of "The Devil and Daniel Webster." When examining Benét's adaptation of his story as drama, one wonders how he would translate these elements to the stage, which does not normally include the device of a narrator to tell the audience what to think about a character or events but must, instead, show them. Additionally, without the narrator how could Benét maintain the tall tale tone that makes possible the hyperbole in describing Daniel Webster, and how could he make the supernatural qualities of the narrative work on stage? With respect to these and other issues, Benét's play adaptation of "The Devil and Daniel Webster" is only moderately successful in translating his story to the stage. The play begins to diminish Daniel Webster's role and emphasize Jabez's; in fact, Benét makes little attempt to elevate Daniel Webster's stature to demigod as he did in the story. The tall tale tone is completely absent. Indeed, the opening of the play in many ways is conventional realistic drama; only with the appearance of a rather conventionally villainous Mr. Scratch does realism begin to be replaced by the supernatural dramatized by theatrical special effects. Finally, although the Miser Stevens soul scene and the trial are theatrically effective, Benét does not successfully dramatize Daniel Webster's oratorical defense of Jabez and America.

The Play

Benét's earlier foray into the theater had been unsuccessful on all counts,[8] but he had collaborated with composer Douglas Moore on an American-subject opera, *The Headless Horseman*, an adaptation of Washington Irving's "The Legend of Sleepy Hollow," in 1937 with some success. He and Moore both wanted to use American folk material as the subject for another collaboration, and so their opera of "The Devil and Daniel Webster," with Moore's music and Benét's libretto produced by the American Lyric Theatre and directed by John Houseman, opened May 18, 1939, at the Martin Beck Theatre for a limited run. The production was successful, according to Fenton (352); yet, reviews were mixed and a letter from Benét to Moore seems to be an attempt to cheer Moore up after a poor reception (*Selected Letters* 322-23). Whatever its merits as opera, as an adaptation of his story Benét's libretto is strikingly different in ways that change the essential nature of the story. These differences are amplified even more in the one-act play version that Benét created mainly by cutting out the songs or rewriting a song or two originally written in verse as a prose speech. Apart from this, the differences between the libretto and the one-act play of "The Devil and Daniel Webster" are so minute that the two scripts are virtually one and the same text.[9]

Upon reading the one-act play of "The Devil and Daniel Webster" one notices the change of the story to follow a more Aristotelian notion of plot (the unity of time). Benét commented, "The plot [of the story] covered a good many years—they had to be compressed to hours" ("Words and Music"). Although it is common for plays to begin as near to the climax of the action as possible, many playwrights have chosen to skip over large periods of time between scenes or acts, as did Benét's Yale classmate and friend Thornton Wilder in *Our Town* (see Shea in this volume). In order to avoid this, Benét has the play begin on the evening on which the devil will come to collect Jabez's soul. It is also Jabez's wedding day, with the opening action depicting the wedding reception attended by a number of men and women from the community, and takes place in "a New Hampshire farmhouse" in 1841. Since Jabez already sold his soul to the devil ten years prior, the play presents him as the prosperous farmer and state senator that the narrator of the story merely tells the reader Jabez later becomes. During the dance, a number of Jabez's neighbors wonder how he came by his prosperity, which apparently was Benét's attempt to create a mystery for the audience until the real conflict of the play begins with the arrival of the stranger, Mr. Scratch. This does not occur until page twelve, only two pages after Daniel Webster makes his entrance. Webster is not even mentioned until page eight of the play. Benét employs the story action of Miser Stevens's soul escaping from the devil's collection box as the catalyst for revealing that Jabez sold his soul, which also serves to clear the stage of Jabez's neighbors and sets up the confrontation between Daniel Webster and Mr. Scratch in the trial scene. Here, the play follows the story as written, dramatizing the pretrial legal maneuvering, the summoning of a judge and jury of the damned, and the trial won by

Webster. Benét greatly reduced the after-trial scene as it appeared in the story, cutting out where Scratch predicts Daniel Webster's future. The play closes, rather awkwardly, with Webster hoping there will be pie for breakfast, a line near the end of the story, but not having the same effect as the narrator's concluding statement: "But they say that whenever the devil comes near Marshfield, even now, he gives it a wide berth. And he hasn't even been seen in the state of New Hampshire from that day to this. I'm not talking about Massachusetts or Vermont" (46). As Stroud says, this ending "returns the story to the register of Yankee humor and state pride and saves it from over-serious moralizing" (117). However, the play *The Devil and Daniel Webster* is not saved from "over-serious moralizing."

One result of the changes Benét made in the plot is that it switches the emphasis from Daniel Webster as an American legend and folk hero to Jabez Stone as a corrupt American success story. The original story did have Jabez undergo a rags-to-riches transformation, which is suitable for a folktale of America as the land of opportunity with a Protestant work ethic, but this transformation was merely reported to the reader by the narrator. The initial and dominant image of Jabez in the story is as a down-on-his-luck farmer, a Joblike sufferer, to be pitied and even empathized with. In the play Jabez is no longer like Job; he has acquired wealth and fame through corrupt means, which would hardly engage the audience's sympathy, even when he explains to Mary, his bride of a few hours, why he sold his soul to the devil. The stage directions describe Jabez and his wedding celebration thus: "he looks important" (5) and "There is an air of prosperity and hearty country mirth about the whole affair" (6), definitely a change in mood from the narrator's introduction of Jabez as not "a bad man to start with, but an unlucky man. If he planted corn, he got borers; if he planted potatoes, he got blight. He had good enough land, but it didn't prosper him" (33). In the story there is an entire paragraph illustrating that Jabez was unlucky; in the play there are repeated references to Jabez being lucky, even by Daniel Webster himself (11). In the story Jabez gets "sick of the whole business" (33) of bad luck after breaking his plow, the proverbial "last straw" (33) that causes him to say in desperation, "I vow it's enough to make a man want to sell his soul to the devil! And I would, too, for two cents!" (33). In the play Jabez describes himself as "A youngster with a lot of ambitions and no way in the world to get there. I wanted city clothes and a big white house—I wanted to be State Senator and have people look up to me" (19). Making him a man of ambition who achieves his goals by selling his soul takes the character back to Dr. Faustus, the great overreacher. This is a fundamental transformation of Jabez's character.

Benét also makes the play in part a love story with the separation of the newlyweds seeming as much the crisis as the imminent damnation of Jabez's soul. In the opera version Jabez and Mary sing beautiful love songs to each other before the arrival of the devil (libretto 12–14); these are briefly reprised after Mr. Scratch is dispatched (libretto 73–4). At the end of the play before his concluding inquiry about pie, Webster intones, as he joins Jabez's and Mary's hands, "And whom God hath joined let no man put asunder" (36). Adding a love story does not in itself distort the essence of the original; Jabez was married in the story, and since Benét collapsed the story's events leading up to the trial into exposition, he needed something to lengthen the action leading up to the trial in the play. However, since the love story culminates subsequent to Jabez selling his soul (in the story he was already married with children when the devil appears), it is tainted with the possibility that Jabez acquired not only wealth and power by contracting with the devil, but also love. He says to Mary, "It was all for you" (10), and later he tells her that before he sold his soul, before his farm had become prosperous, he would "lie awake nights and try to figure out how to get somewhere—but there wasn't any way. And all the time you were growing up in the town. I couldn't ask you to marry me and take you to a place like that" (19). Then, after telling Mary about the day he made the bargain and the transformation in his fortunes it wrought, he despairs, saying, "And it's all come true and he's kept his part of the bargain. I got the riches and I've married you" (20). Jabez's love for Mary appears even more corrupt if one realizes that he marries her knowing they will not even have one night together—the day after her wedding she will be a widow. Again, in making these changes Benét has brought his story back to the Faust legend and undermined the affirmation of America with this corruption of the American dream.

A further deviation from the story is that the play manifests not the fantasy and humor of the tall tale genre, but a conventional theatrical realism at times quite somber. The realism is established by the concrete setting of the interior farmhouse, the specified date of 1841, and the ordinariness of the action in the first half of the play before the demonic trial. The only nonrealistic element of the play's style is having Jabez's neighbors and later the jury of the damned speak in chorus, a vestige of the opera origin of the play. This minor aspect of stylization is not enough to overcome the overall realistic mode of the mundane action in the first part of the play. In the story the only action written in scenic mode involves the supernatural; the rest is narrated. Extended realistic action to begin the play obscures the fantasy nature and tall tale tone of the story.

The play's somberness stems also from the characterization of Mary as a devoutly religious woman. In this she is reminiscent of the Faust inspiration of the story, paralleling the good angel of the morality play. In the story the imminent damnation of Jabez's soul does not have the serious tone that it does in the play because of the tongue-in-cheek narration. For example, Benét follows Jabez's oath to sell his soul with one of several jokes on Yankee stubbornness: "Then he felt a kind of queerness come over him at having said what he'd said; though, naturally, being a New Hampshireman, he wouldn't take it back" (33). Another running joke is on the teeth of the stranger, hinting at a more conventional image of the devil: "They were white teeth and plentiful—some say they were filed to a point, but I wouldn't vouch for that" (33). The narrator's allusion to the oral tradition reminds readers not to take the story too seriously. The one place in the play where the tone approximates the tall tale hyperbole occurs in a speech of Daniel Webster's while he and Jabez wait for the clock to toll midnight, when the devil will come for Jabez's soul: "Ten-year-old Medford. There's nothing like it. I saw an inch-worm take a drop of it once and he stood right up on his hind legs and bit a bee" (23). Webster's next line in response to Jabez's refusal of a drink also resurrects the story's humor: "Oh, come, man, come! Just because you've sold your soul to the devil, that needn't make you a teetotaler" (23–4). Still the lighter moments are too few in the play.[10]

In the story, Jabez and his predicament function to set up what is of real importance: the heroic portrayal of Daniel Webster. This is where the stage adaptation fails, not only in Webster's delayed entry, but also in his diminished stature due to the lack of a narrator to elevate his accomplishments and abilities. In the story, Daniel Webster is practically the first thing mentioned; in the play, he is referred to in a contrived speech when the wedding guests are saluting Jabez and then one shouts, "Hooray for Daniel Webster!" (8) This is not as effective as the story's tribute to Daniel Webster:

> You see, for a while, he was the biggest man in the country. He never got to be President, but he was the biggest man. There were thousands that trusted in him right next to God Almighty, and they told stories about him that were like the stories of patriarchs and such...; and when he argued a case, he could turn on the harps of the blessed and the shaking of the earth underground.... A man with a mouth like a mastiff, a brow like a mountain and eyes like burning anthracite—that was Dan'l Webster in his prime [32].

Nowhere in the play is mentioned Webster's Herculean strength in being able to wrestle his ram Goliath (32), or how "when he walked the woods with his fishing rod, Killall, the trout would jump out of the streams right into his pockets, for they knew it was no use putting up a fight against him" (32), nor does the play refer to Webster's great oratorical powers.[11] It could have been quite effective theatrically if Benét had used a narrator or at least a character to state the line from early in the story, "They said, when he stood up to speak, stars and stripes came right out in the sky" (32), with Webster in a spotlight center stage and the American flag projected on a cyclorama behind him or on a scrim in front of him. Except for a line Jabez addresses to Webster, "But you're the whole United States!" (24), the play does not attempt to associate Webster with America as its defender and champion. Benét made this explicit in the story in the post-trial scene in which the devil tells Webster his future: "'One question,' he said. 'I have fought for the Union all my life. Will I see that fight won against those who would tear it apart?'" (45). In the play Webster's historical role is not featured.

This leads to a question that may be asked of all adaptations: to what extent does Benét rely upon the audience being familiar with the original? Since the play's opening has the wedding guests concerned with the mystery of Jabez's prosperity, it would seem that Benét did not assume the audience knew the story. Even if he did count on the audience remembering the story, it is unlikely that they would recall the device by which he elevated Webster to mythic proportions, the opening paragraphs written in the tall–tale mode of hyperbole. Perhaps Benét did not feel that any actor could live up to the expectations created by the story's build-up; however, in the opera version a great singing voice could have helped heighten the stage presence of Webster. Without the build-up, Webster does not seem an equal contestant to the devil. In the play, Webster is no longer the focus and purpose of the narrative; rather, he is reduced to his role in the plot as the savior of Jabez's soul.

Mr. Scratch fares somewhat better than Daniel Webster onstage because Benét did not cut anything from the story that established his character; for the most part he lifted Scratch's dialogue from the trial scene word for word. A nice touch in the play is to have Scratch play the fiddle "in a horrible discord" (14), which ties into folk stories about the devil as a fiddler. However, Scratch seems more of a conventional stage villain of nineteenth-century melodrama when he advances on Jabez and the crowd, rushes toward Mary (14–15), and shouts at the wedding fiddler, "Idiot! What are you doing with my collecting-box?" (15–16). After Miser Stevens' soul escapes and Jabez says that Stevens is still alive, Benét's stage direction describes Scratch as "dominating them" (16). That is the genius of the characterization of Scratch in the story: he is anything but a cliched or conventional portrait of the devil. In the story Scratch is ever polite, never physically or even verbally aggressive. He is a "home-grown devil" who abides by the rule of law, enters openly into a contract with Jabez and others, and relishes a good legal contest. The portrait of the devil in the story is essentially a comic one, which keeps the tone from becoming too serious. For example, in reference to the death of Miser Stevens, Scratch says,

> "In the midst of life—" said the stranger, kind of pious.... "These long-standing accounts," said the stranger with a sigh; "one really hates to close them. But business is business" [35].

To reproduce this comic characterization of Scratch in the play version, an inventive stage comedian would have been needed since the lines in the story are often made funnier by the comments of the narrator. For example, the devil is described during the trial in a way that brings him down to a human register quite comically: "He was a great lawyer, Dan'l Webster, but we know who's the King of Lawyers, as the Good Book tells us, and it seemed as if, for the first time, Dan'l Webster had met his match" (39). The contrast of the narrator's reference to the Bible as "the Good Book" with Mary's straightforward quoting from the Bible in the play also illustrates a difference in tone between the story and the play.

The final essential element of the story that is crucial to a successful adaptation of it is Webster's climactic closing statement that wins over the jury of the damned and frees Jabez from his contract with the devil. This speech is important for its resolution of the plot, its support of Benét's portrait of Webster as American hero, and its affirmation of America as a nation founded upon the right of individual liberty. Since the portrait of Webster is diminished within the play overall, the speech is also diminished in its effect. In the story Benét identifies Daniel Webster with the nation, portraying him as the champion of the union right from the start:

> ... if you go to his grave and speak loud and clear, "Dan'l Webster—Dan'l Webster!" ... after a while you'll hear a deep voice saying, "Neighbor, how stands the Union?" Then you better answer the Union stands as she stood, rock-bottomed and copper-sheathed, one and indivisible, or he's liable to rear right out of the ground [32].

(This image of a grave-bound voice asking how the Union stands was also used by Benét in his 1936 poem "An Ode to Walt Whitman.") Then, when Webster delivers the speech in the trial, he is not only defending Jabez, but himself and the United States against the charge of having sold out for material gain. This is what makes the speech moving, even in the tall-tale context, and makes "The Devil and Daniel Webster" not just a great story, but a great *American* story.[12]

To write a great patriotic speech for the play that would move a jury of the damned was no easy task. Benét had recognized this when he wrote the original: "For, in the story, I had carefully avoided writing Webster's speech to the jury of the damned who tried the case of the Devil versus Jabez Stone. I had done so deliberately and even, it seemed to me, with some ingenuity. But I couldn't possibly avoid it in a trial-scene to be played on the stage. There would have to be words for an actor to say or sing" ("Words and Music"). For the opera Benét chose not to have Webster sing the speech, but to have it "spoken against music, not delivered as an aria" ("Words and Music"). Thus, Benét was counting on the music to heighten the action and the characters: "For the librettist, too, there is something very fascinating in watching what music can do to words—to heighten or soften them, to amplify or develop them" ("Words and Music"). In the play version Benét does not mention music to back the speech; it would have to stand on the quality of the writing and the talent of the actor playing Webster.

The play speech is effective where it hews closely to the paraphrase of the speech in the story. For example, in the story the narrator tells us,

> And he began with the simple things that everybody's known and felt—the freshness of a fine morning when you're young, and the taste of food when you're hungry, and the new day that's every day when you're a child. He took them up and turned them in his hands. They were good things for any man. But without freedom, they sickened [42].

In the play, Webster says, "Of common things I shall speak, of small things and common. The freshness of morning to the young, the taste of food to the hungry, the day's toil, the rest by the fire, the quiet sleep. These are good things. But without freedom they sicken, without freedom they are nothing" (33). Benét also uses in the play these effective sentences from the story: "There was sadness in being a man but it was a proud thing too" (34 play, 42 story) and "No demon that was ever foaled could know the inwardness of it" (34 play, 43 story). But where the speech in the story merely summarized the things that Webster said at length, the play version omits them altogether. There is no reference to "the sorrows of slavery" and "the early days of America and the men who had made those days" (42), the parts of the speech that would have presumably moved the jury of the damned, all of whom "had all played a part in America" (40). This is also the aspect of the speech that would have supported the speech's affirmation of America despite all the wrongs.

Benét does try to duplicate the overall design of the speech, though inverting the order of the sections on Jabez Stone and "the one spot of land that each man loves and clings to" (43). The difficulty lies in that much of the story's passage about the speech describes the effect of Webster's words rather than summarizing the content of the words. For example, the conclusion of the speech in the story is moving not because of what the narrator reports Webster as saying, but how he says it and its effect upon the jury: "And when Dan'l Webster finished he didn't know whether or not he'd saved Jabez Stone. But he knew he'd done a miracle. For the glitter was gone from the eyes of judge and jury, and, for the moment, they were men again, and knew they were men. 'The defense rests,' said Dan'l Webster, and stood there like a mountain" (43). The narrator allows the readers to think they have read a great speech, as these descriptions of Webster speaking illustrate: "And when he talked of those enslaved, and the sorrows of slavery, his voice got like a big bell" (42), "It wasn't a spread-eagle speech, but he made you see it" (42), "his voice rang like an organ" (43), and "For his voice could search the heart, and that was his gift and his strength" (43). Even if Benét had employed a narrator for his play, he could not well have had him deliver these lines in the midst of Webster's speech, for that would disrupt the willing suspension of disbelief and negate the speech's emotional impact. The only alternative was for Benét to write a great speech for the actor to deliver.

Benét was only partially successful in composing new lines for Webster's closing remarks to add to what he took directly from his story's summary of the speech. Where the narrator says that Webster's voice "was like the forest and its secrecy, and to another like the sea and the storms of the sea; and one heard the cry of his lost nation in it, and another saw a little harmless scene he hadn't remembered for years. But each saw something" (43), in the play Benét has Webster address individual members of the jury who were identified by Mr. Scratch when he summoned them, and then has them respond. This is a bit of theatrical genius: Webster gets to vary his mode of delivery to specific characters while the jury members responding individually and in unison show the audience the effect that Webster is having upon them. For example, he speaks directly to the pirate:

WEBSTER: *[to Teach]* Have you forgotten the sea and the way of ships?
TEACH: The sea—and the swift ships sailing—the blue sea.

JURY: Forgotten—remembered—forgotten yet remembered.
WEBSTER: You were men once. Have you forgotten?
JURY: We were men once. We have not thought of it nor re-
          membered. But we were men [34].

The audience *and* the jury are moved enough to believe that Jabez should
be let out of his contract. The speech also succeeds where Benét makes
the theme of freedom and liberty explicit: "When the whips of the oppressors are broken and their names forgotten and destroyed / I see you,
mighty, shining, liberty, liberty! I see free men walking and talking under
a free star./ God save the United States and the men who have made her
free" (34).

Some of the other new lines Benét composed for the play speech do
not follow the logic of this supernatural situation. Benét has Webster say,
"We stumble into the pit—but, out of the pit, we rise again" (34), but the
damned members of the jury would have no hope of rising out of the pit.
If anything, this line would remind them of their own eternal condemnation and harden their hearts toward Jabez. Earlier in the speech, Benét
has Webster try to manipulate the jury into identifying with Jabez, but
then makes a statement that could get the audience thinking a little too
literally about salvation and damnation: "Now here is this man with good
and evil in his heart. Do you know him? He is your brother. Will you take
the law of the oppressor and bind him down?" (34). While the language
may be effective by echoing Revolutionary War rhetoric, it nonetheless
alludes to the law that would condemn Jabez to an eternity in hell; the
source of that law is God, not the devil. Given the earlier straightforward
religious speeches by Mary, this speech could jar the audience out of the
fantasy of the play and start them thinking about actual beliefs about God
and the devil, heaven and hell, which is, again, too heavy in contrast to
the lighter tone of the original story.

Another problem with the speech Benét wrote for the play is its
brevity. On the page, it is about the same length as the paragraphs describing the speech in the story, but since the narrator summarized parts of it
that would have taken some time to utter, it would have been a substan-
tially longer speech than what appears in the play. In the story the narrator reports on the passage of time to give the impression of a long speech:
"The fire began to die on the hearth and the wind before morning to
blow. The light was getting gray in the room when Dan'l Webster finished"
(43). Reading the speech in the play, it seems that Webster is just getting
going when he rests, leaving the impression that the speech is of less stature
than one would expect it to be for its purpose: the closing remarks of the

attorney for the defendant in a trial. Benét could not have made Webster's closing remarks as long as they seem to have been in the story; he couldn't possibly sustain the audience's interest no matter how good the writing. Yet, the entire speech, including where Webster interacts with the members of the jury, is only two pages of the acting edition, which would take approximately three minutes to deliver on stage. Benét could have elaborated more on the theme of freedom and of individual liberty, on the history of the United States in which the members of the jury had played a part, and on Jabez Stone's common humanity. With the short speech he did compose, the action—persuading the jury of the damned to find in favor of Jabez—is unconvincing.

Despite Webster's climactic speech falling short of what it needed to be, Benét did succeed overall in adapting the major scene of the story, the confrontation between Daniel Webster and the Devil. From Scratch's arrival at midnight to "take possession of [his] property" (25) to his departure after the jury finds for the defendant, Jabez Stone, Benét follows his story at times word for word. He fleshes out the pretrial legal maneuvering effectively, writing convincing speeches that occasionally provoke laughter, for example the following exchange:

> WEBSTER: ... This precious document isn't worth the paper it's written on. The law permits no traffic in human flesh.
> SCRATCH: Oh, my dear Mr. Webster! Courts in every State in the Union have held that human flesh is property and recoverable. Read your Fugitive Slave Act. Or, shall I cite Brander versus McRae?
> WEBSTER: But, in the case of the State of Maryland versus Four Barrels of Bourbon—
> SCRATCH: That was overruled, as you know, sir. North Carolina versus Jenkins and Co.
> WEBSTER: [unwillingly] You seem to have an excellent acquaintance with the law, sir.
> SCRATCH: Sir, that is no fault of mine. Where I come from, we have always gotten the pick of the Bar [25].

Another good addition to the play from the trial scene in the story is having the clerk announce, "The World, the Flesh and the Devil versus Jabez Stone" (29). This heightens the contest as well as lifting the play out of the mundane realistic narrative that began it.

Where Benét most succeeded in reincarnating his story as a play is in staging the supernatural events and characters in the climactic trial; in fact, he even improved upon the story in this regard. The best example is in the entrance of the jury of the damned. In the story the narrator tells the reader, "And with that, and all of a sudden, there was a rushing of wind outside and a noise of footsteps. They came, clear and distinct, through the night. And yet, they were not like the footsteps of living men.... And with that the fire burned blue and the door blew open and twelve men entered, one by one" (40). This seems an all too mortal way for immortal souls from hell to appear. In contrast, in the play Mr. Scratch summons the damned jurors with an incantation supported by theatrical effects:

> He points his finger where the jury is to appear. There is a clap of thunder and a flash of light. The stage blacks out completely. All that can be seen is the face of SCRATCH, lit with a ghastly green light as he recites the invocation that summons the JURY. As, one by one, the important JURYMEN are mentioned, they appear.

> > I summon the jury Mr. Webster demands.
> > From churchyard mould and gallows grave,
> > Brimstone pit and burning gulf,
> > I summon them!
> > Dastard, liar, scoundrel, knave,
> > I summon them! Appear! ... [27].

Benét's skills as a poet served him well as he has Scratch go on to name seven of the notorious figures from early American history and describe each one's crimes in verse. This scene has the same charm as the supernatural action of the story.

Furthermore, the jury is theatrically conceived in such a manner as to evoke the supernatural: "*They are eerily lit and so made-up as to suggest the unearthly. They sit stiffly in their box. At first, when one moves, all move, in stylized gestures. It is not until WEBSTER's speech that they begin to show any trace of humanity. They speak rhythmically, and, at first, in low, eerie voices*" (28). Benét also wrote a couple of speeches for the jury that are chilling; for example, when they say of Jabez, "He'll fry like a batter-cake, once we get him where we want him" (30) or a bit later, "A farmer—he'll farm in hell—we'll see that he farms in hell" (31). Thus, the members of the jury, like the wedding guests earlier, act as a chorus as they did in the opera, but in the straight play version their speaking and moving together sets them off from the mortal characters on stage. The effect would probably work even better if the wedding guests earlier, and briefly later when they return at the end to chase the devil away, did not speak in chorus.

The other scene of the play in which Benét theatricalizes the supernatural aspects of the story is when Miser Stevens's soul momentarily escapes Scratch. In the story this took place in a meeting between Jabez and the devil a year before Jabez's soul was to be taken possession of. When the stranger opens his collecting box to check the contract,

> he saw something else flutter out of the black pocketbook. It was something that looked like a moth, but it wasn't a moth. And as Jabez Stone stared at it, it seemed to speak to him in a small sort of piping voice, terrible small and thin, but terrible human. "Neighbor Stone! Help me! For God's sake, help me!" But before Jabez could stir hand or foot, the stranger whipped out a big bandanna handkerchief, caught the creature in it, just like a butterfly, and started tying up the ends of the bandanna [35].

Although this is a quaint imagining of the manifestation of a human soul and the devil's possession of it, what makes the scene work is Jabez's emotionally genuine response; for him, it is a very real demonstration of the moral danger he is in. Here a more serious tone is necessary in order for the trial scene to have real dramatic importance.

In the play, Benét employs the escape of Miser Stevens's soul for the same purposes, as well as the means of the wedding guests discovering that Jabez has sold his soul to the devil. In this, too, Benét was fairly successful in reimagining the scene for the stage, if one remembers that it was 1939 when special effects were not as technologically sophisticated. Two notes at the end of the acting edition explain how Benét envisioned the scene on stage:

> NOTE B. As a practical moth-effect would be difficult, the whole business of the moth can be suggested by the Crowd turning, staring and pointing, first up, then right, then left, following the flight of an imaginary moth. The stage begins to darken at the first letting of the moth out of the box, and the following scene is played in dim light.
>
> NOTE C. The speeches of the Moth should come, in a high, shrill voice from somebody concealed among the crowd where he will not be seen by the audience. If desired, the speeches can be spoken from off stage [37].

If well-choreographed and if the actor speaking Miser Stevens' speeches had the appropriate voice, this bit of supernatural action could work well on stage. The wedding guests' reaction would cue the audience's own confusion and then fear when the fiddler says, "It ain't no common moth! I seen it! And it's got a death's head on it!" (16). After the "moth" cries out for help, Daniel Webster says, "It wails like a lost soul," and the others reply, "A lost soul—lost—lost in darkness—in the darkness" (16). Having the wedding guests function not just as surrogates of the audience response but, in lieu of the narrator in the story, to help stimulate audience response, was an astute invention upon Benét's part.

Benét's dramatic adaptation of "The Devil and Daniel Webster" exhibits theatrical genius in recreating the supernatural aspects of his brilliant story for the stage. Still, the first part of the play is too mundane and realistic, dispelling the tall-tale tone of the story. The plot of the stage version of the story de-emphasizes the central figure of Daniel Webster and diminishes the affirmation of America. Recasting Jabez as a corrupted American success story fails to make him a character with whom the audience would want to identify because they only see the corrupt "after" rather than the sympathetic "before" of the story. Perhaps if Benét had employed a narrator to build up Daniel Webster to the heroic level the story did, and had shown Jabez as the poor farmer with terrible luck and after a blackout leapt over the years that he grew in wealth and fame and shown him as a lost soul who seeks out the help of a larger-than-life Webster, then the play would have re-created the brilliance and charm of the story for theatregoers.

The Film

The 1941 film adaptation of "The Devil and Daniel Webster" proved to be more successful in dramatizing Benét's original story than the play version. The plot of the film is more faithful, though it too adds Jabez's wife, Mary, as a devout woman. Furthermore, the overall tone, while not as light as the tall-tale tone of the story, does avoid the heavy, somber mood of the play, due mainly to the delightful comic performance of Walter Huston as Scratch. The film also does a much better job than the play of depicting Daniel Webster as a heroic figure, and the speech Webster delivers to the jury of the damned is more powerful than in the play, though not quite what one would hope could have been achieved had all the elements of the film medium been utilized. Finally, while the title characters of the story are given their due, the film follows the play in emphasizing Jabez more than the story. That is, the film presents Jabez as an American everyman, though he is still saved by the American hero, Daniel Webster.

How much Benét is responsible for the content of the film version of "The Devil and Daniel Webster" is impossible to determine. He is listed as one of two screenwriters, his name appearing below Dan Totheroh's in the end credits, though it comes before Totheroh's in the beginning credits. He did contribute to the screenplay from the beginning of the project, as is evident from a letter he wrote to the producer and director of the film, William Dieterle, in 1940: "It makes me very happy to think you like so much of what I have done and I know the story could be in no better hands than yours" (*Selected Letters* 357). Fenton's note on the same page says that Benét wrote a preliminary scenario. Benét, however, did not have the final say on the screenplay, as is suggested by a letter he wrote to Dieterle after viewing a cut of the film. In the letter he objects to the title change (it was released as *All That Money Can Buy*, a line from the film), a drinking contest between Webster and the devil, and to Jabez going fox hunting; all of these remained in the film.

Establishing a definitive text of the film adaptation of "The Devil and Daniel Webster" is even more problematic than it was for the libretto-converted-into-a-play. According to *Cinemania 95*, the original print *of All That Money Can Buy* was 112 minutes long. The Home Vision Cinema videocassette titled *The Devil and Daniel Webster*, despite the claim on the cover of being "unabridged and restored" and the assertion that "This acclaimed restoration has been pieced together from various existing prints to provide the most complete version available," is only 106 minutes in running time. The shooting script published originally in *Twenty Best Film Plays* (1943) contains lines of dialogue and brief scenes that do not appear in the videotape; however, because it is a shooting script, some of the content would not have been in the final cut of the film as John Gassner, one of the collection's editors, says in his preface about all of the scripts (vi, vii). The nature of the differences between the shooting script and the videocassette—not just deletions but additional material—would suggest that, as with any film, dialogue was revised and new shots and scenes were improvised during the process of filming.[13]

Viewing the film *The Devil and Daniel Webster* it is immediately apparent that the plot is more faithful to the story than the play was in that it begins with Jabez as a poor farmer. Unlike the play, the film shows both the "before" and the "after" of Jabez Stone. The film effectively establishes Jabez, played by James Craig, as a down-on-his-luck, common man. Shortly after the opening credits the camera shows us a page from Scratch's book with Jabez's name and beneath it an assessment of his accomplishments: "children: none credit: none" (videocassette). The first line of dialogue by Ma Stone, Jabez's mother, a strong supporting character added to the plot, immediately makes him sympathetic: "Now, son. Cheer up" (952). The opening minutes of the film establish how difficult the Stones have it. In fact, it is not merely breaking his plow, as in the story, that prompts Jabez's oath leading to the pact with the devil. In the film their pig has broken its leg; they are about to lose the farm to Miser Stevens; Mary has fallen off the wagon and hit her head, knocking her unconscious; a fox carries off two of their hens; and, finally, carrying a sack of seed that he was going to offer to Miser Stevens as payment, Jabez spills it in a mud puddle, making it worthless. All of this allows the audience to identify and sympathize with Jabez before he sells his soul. Even after he bargains for "money and all that money can buy" (959), Jabez remains mostly sympathetic due to the film's depiction of his basic humanity. The film associates Jabez with Job by having Ma Stone read from the Book of Job in the opening scene; then Jabez compares himself with the biblical symbol of human suffering:

> JABEZ: This man, Job, he had troubles, didn't he? Hard luck—
>   like me.
> MA STONE: Now, Jabez Stone, as for what you're calling hard luck,
>   we made New England out of it—that and codfish
>   [953].

Having Ma say Jabez's name allows the audience to hear the auditory similarity between the two names. Furthermore, the Jabez-Job association is subtly reinforced in the casting of Jane Darwell as Ma Stone; just one year earlier she had won an Academy Award for best supporting actress as Ma Joad in *The Grapes of Wrath* (1940), which is also a modern Job story.

Another improvement of the film plot over the play is that it has Jabez already married, as in the story; thus, there is no suggestion that Mary was part of the bargain with the devil.[14] As in the play, Mary, played by a wholesome-looking Anne Shirley, is a religious woman, along with Ma Stone, and is devoted to her husband. She quotes scripture to Jabez, prays for him in a scene in church, and she is the one who goes to Daniel Webster for help, though not because she knows Jabez has literally sold his soul but because he has changed so much toward her and their neighbors, many of whom are now in debt to him as he was once in debt to Miser Stevens. None of this was in the story, of course, but it was necessary in a film adaptation for Benét to show something of Jabez's life before and after the deal with the devil. A feature film has to be longer than the content of the short story in which the intervening years between the selling of Jabez's soul and the night Scratch comes to collect it were merely summarized.

Mary and Ma Stone were also necessary for dramatic and moral balance once the decision was made to add the character Belle, a *femme fatale* played by French actress Simone Simon. She tempts Jabez away from Mary and serves as Scratch's surrogate when he is not present (he tells Jabez he will send "a friend" of his to the christening of Jabez's son, and she appears as the new maid). Mary and Belle correspond to Marguerite (from Goethe's *Faust*) and Helen of Troy (Marlowe's *Dr. Faustus* and Goethe) respectively, as Singer points out in his study of the film (266, 267). In addition, although Belle's character of "the other woman" is pure Hollywood, she adds to the supernatural element of the film that prevents too strong a sense of realism being established, which was one of the flaws of the play adaptation. When Belle first appears and again at Jabez's party, she is shot in a very prominent soft focus, and the same eerie background music that accompanied Scratch's entrance also plays in the background of her first scene. Thus, the film has doubled the moral agents vying for Jabez's soul: two religious figures, Mary and Ma Stone, versus two evil figures, Scratch and Belle. Daniel Webster in the trial scene tips the balance in favor of the good side.

The plot of the screenplay of *The Devil and Daniel Webster* becomes a battle for Jabez's soul. Once a simple farmer struggling to pay his bills, he becomes a greedy, powerful miser. The audience can see Jabez begin to change almost immediately after he has made the deal with the devil. After Jabez shows Mary and Ma Stone the gold coins, they sit down to dinner and he begins to ravenously eat his food and then looks up at Ma and Mary who are saying grace; he stops eating and stares, seeming to realize himself that his behavior has already changed. As his fortunes increase, Jabez goes from sympathizing and empathizing with other farmers' bad luck to relishing in his fields being spared from a hailstorm that destroys his neighbors' fields, thanks to Scratch's intervention. Throughout the film other characters comment on Jabez's transformation, which is signaled visually by his costume changing from farmer's work clothes to a new suit with tall, shiny black boots to a foxhunting outfit to a tailor-made tuxedo for his party. A final example of how the film effectively depicts Jabez's transformation occurs following a poker game. Having won big, Jabez stands on his porch looking satisfied and smoking a cigar, corresponding to Scratch's smoking; when one of the departing players refers to the village, Jabez, puffing away, says contemptuously, "The village—humph" (videocassette).

Although Daniel Webster and the devil are presented as equal combatants, the film places a great deal of emphasis on Jabez as an American Faust character. While one might attribute this to the influence of German director and producer William Dieterle, who had filmed a screen adaptation of *Faust* in 1926,[15] it must be remembered that Benét had already moved the story in that direction in the stage version. Further-more, Jabez is more of an everyman character than a tragic hero, as the title character is in both Marlowe's and Goethe's versions of the Faust leg-end. The film underscores the universality of Jabez's story by implicating the audience at the beginning and ending. At the start of the film a writ-ten preface reads, "But it could happen anytime—anywhere—to any-body.... Yes—it could even happen to you" (videocassette). At the end of the film, Scratch, after perusing his book of accounts, looks directly at the camera and points to the audience, implying that they are next on his list. The story as filmed ties into the morality-play tradition, which strives for a greater universality than Benét's original story.

Yet Jabez does not dominate the film, nor is the tone overly somber as it was in the play. Unlike the play, the film introduces Daniel Webster early on. He is mentioned in a conversation between Jabez and other farm-ers down on their luck in the first scene, and then the film cuts to Daniel Webster writing a speech in Washington, D.C.; in a montage of shots the speech is read aloud by Webster, two farmers, and Jabez, presumably from the newspaper. After Jabez has made his bargain with Scratch, he meets Webster when the famous statesman is traveling through Cross Corners; they play a game of horseshoes, the townspeople toast Webster, and Jabez makes a short speech in his honor. After this, Webster is mentioned throughout the film until we see him later when Mary goes to his farm in Massachusetts to ask for his help; he listens and gives her words of encour-agement. On his way to Jabez's party, Webster offers a buggy ride to "Lit-tle Daniel," tells him about the greatness of the United States, and spanks the boy for hitting the horses with a stone from his slingshot. Then the other farmers of Cross Corners ask Webster for help in dealing with Jabez and the hard contracts they have signed with him. Webster comes to Jabez's mansion and gives him a good dressing down. Finally, there is the trial and the brief breakfast scene afterward. Thus, in the film Daniel Web-ster is "onstage" much longer than he was in the play.

Similarly, Scratch appears at the beginning and end and throughout the film, so much so, in fact, that if any character dominates, it is he, and the film might well have been called "Scratch."[16] He opens the film, walk-ing toward the village of Cross Corners when he stops to check his book for prospective clients. Next his shadow appears on the wall beside Web-ster when he is writing the speech in defense of farmers, and we hear Scratch whispering about Webster's ambition for the presidency. After he tempts Jabez into selling his soul, Scratch appears extensively in the scene in which Webster comes to Cross Corners. Scratch is also present through-out the series of scenes showing the rise of Jabez's fortunes. Following

Scratch's walking by the Stone farm on the night little Daniel is conceived, Jabez momentarily repents of the deal and starts to chop down the tree that bears the date when the contract expires; Scratch causes a hailstorm that stops him and then he appears to warn Jabez that he is in danger of breaching their contract. The audience then sees Scratch's head in a huge closeup blurred by soft focus looking down upon the ruined crops of Jabez's neighbors and laughing, suggesting his omnipotence in matters of fortune. In the next scene Scratch comes into the tavern and offers those farmers money to work in Jabez's fields. Recalling the stage adaptation, Scratch plays the fiddle at the harvest dance when Belle is dancing, tempting Jabez. At the housewarming party for Jabez's new mansion, Scratch appears when Jabez calls for a fire, and the escape of Miser Stevens' soul is played out in revised form. Scratch then tries to bargain with Jabez, offering him an extension in exchange for his son. Scratch's penultimate appearance is in the trial. Finally, at the end of the film Scratch is back on the country road, appears to see the audience, and points his finger at them. So the film ends where it began, with Scratch looking for another victim.

As for the tone, like in the story, the comic characterization of Scratch prevents the film from becoming too heavy. In the film Scratch seems everpresent, along with the mischievous grin and laugh that actor Walter Huston employed in his portrayal of Scratch as Benét's "home grown" devil. Huston's performance, which earned an Academy Award nomination, is the most praised aspect of the film in reviews: *Time* says, "Walter Huston plays the Devil with demoniacal glee.... [H]e is a puckish tempter.... [H]e seems to be hugely enjoying his part. He is the kind of Devil most people would like to know" (98); the *New York Times* says of Huston, "He gives the devil his due, and makes the old boy a wily, smooth, genial and thoroughly charming old rogue." He smiles even after he has lost the trial. The devil could not be conceived in a less threatening way; in fact, he comes across as a merry trickster, like Puck in *A Midsummer Night's Dream*, rather than as a predator of souls. Huston's wry portrayal of the devil keeps the film from becoming too serious.

In addition to Huston's performance as Scratch, there are other vestiges of the tall tale from the short story. The film begins with the opening paragraph of the story: "It's a story they tell in the border country, where Massachusetts joins Vermont and New Hampshire. It happened, so they say, a long time ago ... " (videocassette). This prepares the audience to hear some whoppers, such as when the farmers are talking to Jabez about joining the Grange, a farmer's association. One describes a hailstorm they had in June: "Hailstones so mighty chickens sat on 'em thinking they was eggs" (955). The film also uses the only tall-tale line from the play, when Webster tells Jabez about an inchworm who had a sip of Medford rum and then bit a bumble bee (989). There are a few times when the film employs the Yankee humor and state rivalry as in the story; for example, Ma Stone says she was never fond of Job because he "took on too much," sounding "as if he came from Massachusetts" (954). Humor is injected into the screenplay in other ways. The satirical jabs against lawyers in the story and play have been replaced in the film with jokes on politicians. When Scratch and Webster run into each other in Cross Corners, Scratch offers his help in the upcoming election. Webster says, "I'd rather see you on the side of the opposition"; Scratch replies, "I'll be there, too" (963). The film still takes the moral aspects of the story seriously, sometimes with dramatic music played on the soundtrack to underscore the gravity of the situation. But the mixture of melodrama and comedy in the film, while not as tongue in cheek as the original story, is much lighter than the play adaptation.

The film's greatest improvement over the play is in its depiction of Daniel Webster as a larger-than-life American hero. In addition to being on-screen or referred to throughout the film as in the story, Webster's moral stature is elevated by his fighting the devil from the beginning. In the scene that shows him writing a speech in support of a bill that will help the farmers, the shadow of the devil whispers to him, "You're wasting your time writing speeches like that. Why worry about the people and their problems? Start thinking of your own. You want to be president of this country, don't you? ... Don't be a fool. Stop bothering with that speech and get busy promoting yourself" (956). Edward Arnold, the actor playing Webster, uses facial expressions in response to Scratch's words to show that he is tempted, but he finally silences Scratch by shouting "Be still!" The sentiments of the speech he is writing make Webster appear to be the great orator and champion of American values he is alleged to be, as suggested by this passage read by the farmer: "We talk much and talk warmly of political liberty, but who can enjoy political liberty if he is deprived permanently of *personal* liberty? To those individuals doomed to the everlasting bondage of debt, what is it that we have free institutions of government?" (videocassette). Webster is portrayed as a populist, a politician for the people; wearing a stovepipe hat even makes him appear Lincolnesque.

Still, the film employs little of the story's tall-tale hyperbole that portrayed Webster as a Paul Bunyan-like figure of physical prowess as well as oratorical greatness. In cutting the majority of the tall-tale build-up of Webster as a legendary figure, Benét—or Dieterle—may simply have been bowing to the realism inherent in the photographic medium of film. That detriment also became a benefit in the performance of Edward Arnold as Webster. He was a large man with a noble face and baritone voice suitable for impersonating the great statesman. Movie audiences would have been familiar with Arnold's previous performances as a powerful political figure from the films *Mr. Smith Goes to Washington* (1939), *Meet John Doe* (1941), and *Cardinal Richelieu* (1935); he also played the president in a radio series titled "Mr. President" ("Edward Arnold" *Cinemania 95*). Arnold's performance is praised in most of the reviews; for example, "But the gusty spirit of the fantasy derives chiefly from Edward Arnold's characterization of the almost legendary Webster ..." ("The Devil in a Legal Knot" *Newsweek*), and a contemporary assessment says that Arnold "is riveting as the noble Webster" (Martin and Porter 455). Arnold's delivery, not only of the climactic speech in the trial but also of the patriotic speech to Little Daniel in the buggy, is genuinely moving. In another speech, Benét's words and Arnold's delivery of them combine to elevate Daniel Webster and the affirmation of America theme. Taking the narrator's lines in the story about Webster giving his horses patriotic names, Benét turns this into an allegorical speech instructing little Daniel and the audience about the American form of government: "No, Daniel—they are not race horses. They are good old friends of mine. I call 'em Constitution and Bill of Rights; the most dependable pair for long journeys. I've got one called Missouri Compromise, too, and then there's a Supreme Court—fine, dignified horse, though you do have to push him now and then" (983). Arnold speaks the lines with pride and wisdom, reassuring the audience, perhaps, that America was still working.[17] Benét himself wrote of the performances in the film, "I don't see how Huston and Arnold could have done better" (*Selected Letters* 379).

One way in which Huston and Arnold—and Benét—could have done better is at the beginning of the trial scene. In the play Benét had realistically and entertainingly developed the pretrial legal maneuvering between Scratch and Webster that is only summarized in the story, but all of that was cut in the film; thus, when Scratch says his line, "If you have no more arguments to adduce" (990), we have not actually seen Webster adduce any arguments. The only attempt he made to "settle out of court" was to offer monetary compensation. Furthermore, when Webster calls for a trial, it is not a dramatic moment as it is in the story and the play; in those versions, Webster hits upon the idea of a trial in response to Scratch's speech about being an American: "'Aha!' said Dan'l Webster, with the veins standing out in his forehead. 'Then I stand on the Constitution! I demand a trial for my client!'" (39). In the film Arnold makes this demand calmly, and just as calmly offers his own soul as incentive for the devil to allow the trial: "If I can't win this case with a jury, you shall have *me*, too" (991). Huston's only response to that is to raise his eyebrows and expel his breath in a "Whew" (videocassette); rather than heightening the drama of this moment, the film lets it fall flat.[18]

Webster's closing speech in the trial functions as the climax of the plot of the film as it did of the plots of the story and play, and Benét did improve upon the play version of the speech overall. While Webster speaks to individual members of the jury, the film does not retain their collective responses that in the play dramatized the effect his words were having upon them. Benedict Arnold does bow his head in shame when Webster recounts his treachery, but this is not the same as the members of the jury feeling like men again in a collective chorus, which justifies their defiance of Scratch in finding for the defense.[19] Additionally, H. B. Warner, the actor playing Justice Hathorne (who is an actual historical figure, Nathaniel Hawthorne's great-grandfather whom Hawthorne alludes to in his story "Young Goodman Brown"), looks moved after Webster finishes his speech, but it is the jury, not he, who must be persuaded to find for the defendant. For some reason Benét did not carry over from the play version of the speech one of the best lines of the story description of the speech: "No demon that was ever foaled can know the inwardness of that—only men—bewildered men" (34).

These deficiencies notwithstanding, Benét did add powerful new lines to Webster's closing remarks. He strengthened the sense of the jury being damned Americans with these lines: "Mr. Scratch was right—you were Americans all! Oh, what a heritage you were born to share! Gentlemen of the jury, I envy you! For you were there at the *birth* of a mighty Union" (993). By having the living Webster say he envies the dead and damned members of the jury, this also expresses the affirmative tone toward America in the story's rendering of the speech. Furthermore, Benét does a better job of having Webster force the jury to identify with Jabez: "Tonight, you are called upon to judge a man named Jabez Stone. What is his case? He is accused of breach of contract—He made a deal to find a short cut in his life—to get rich quickly…. The same deal all of you once made" (993). He drives home that Jabez's enemy was—*is*—their own enemy as well:

> All of you were fooled like Jabez Stone—fooled and trapped in your desire to rebel against your fate. Gentlemen of the jury—it's the eternal right of man to raise his fist against his fate, but every time he does he stands at crossroads. You took the wrong turn and so did Jabez Stone…. Mr. Scratch told you that your soul is

nothing and you believed him.... Now—here is this man—*He is your brother!* You are Americans all, you cannot (*pointing at the devil*)—take his side—the side of the oppressor [993].

With this patriotic command, Webster implores them, "Gentlemen of the jury—don't let this country go to the devil! *Free Jabez Stone!* God save the United States and the men who made her free!" (993). This speech correlates the defense of the microcosm—Jabez Stone—with the macrocosm of America, which was the symbolic action of the story speech.

The freedom theme is stressed even more in the film version of the speech than in the play, as Benét repeats this effective line, "When the whips of the oppressors are broken, and their names forgotten and destroyed, free men will be walking and talking under a free star," and then follows it with new words that bring together the agricultural symbols from earlier in the film with the national and spiritual themes: "Yes, we have planted freedom here in this earth like wheat. We have said to the sky above us, 'A man shall own his own soul'" (993). The film speech is about twice as long as in the play, which somewhat mitigates the sense of it being too short for closing remarks and for the persuasive effect that it is supposed to have upon the jury of the damned. However, it does not give the sense of a marathon speech that goes on through the early morning hours, culminating right before dawn, as in the story. This could have easily been achieved in the film with the use of dissolves to convey the passage of time. Nevertheless, the requirements of filming the trial scene did inspire Benét to write a speech that is eloquent and powerful enough to move the audience and a jury of the damned.[20]

Although the speech was well written by Benét and delivered movingly by Arnold, Dieterle did not take advantage of available cinematic effects to heighten the speech, apart from shooting Arnold in close up through much of it so that he would have appeared gigantic on the screen of a movie theater. Dieterle could have shot Arnold from a low angle, giving him the appearance of an even larger stature and employed music to back the speech, as Benét and Moore had done in the opera version. Arnold also could have moved more rather than remaining in front of the jury for the entire speech. Dieterle or the cinematographer, Joseph August, did shoot Arnold against a dark background and brightly lit his face and the sleeves and collar of his white shirt to create a dramatic black and white contrast. But more stylization would have been appropriate, especially since it is the climax of the plot.

The entire trial scene is dramatized less effectively than it was in the play. Neither the script as published nor the film as recorded on video-cassette show the disappearance of the jury and Justice Hathorne once the verdict is rendered; they are not accounted for at all, unlike in the story and the play, where they are made to disappear simultaneously with the crowing of a rooster. To make characters instantly vanish was a standard film effect, even in 1941. Furthermore, the entrance of the jury is filmed in a manner that would have been quite appropriate for the stage—they walk up through a trapdoor in the floor of Jabez's barn—but seems unimaginative for film. Somewhat more cinematic, the jury and Justice Hathorne are shot in a blurry soft focus, the same camera effect used for Belle and her ghostly friends "from over the mountain" in the party scene. However, rather than having the jury speak in unison, as in the play, the film employs a metallic, echoing sound for the response of the jury that is even difficult to identify as coming from them. Justice Hathorne's voice seems electronically altered when he speaks, which is effective, but the jury does not speak except for when Webster is feeling the pressure of the situation; then we hear them chanting, "Drag him down with us" and "Lost and gone" (992). These lines are difficult to hear in the film and are not as good as the lines in the play. Furthermore, the film does not have Scratch summon the jury with an incantation in verse, which was quite effective in the play; instead, in a prose speech he merely identifies all twelve members of the jury, as they climb up through the trapdoor. A more imaginative dramatization of the supernatural, which is a large part of the charm and overall success of the story and the play, would have enhanced the film.[21]

Even worse was the film's handling of the escape of Miser Stevens' soul. As a character who appears only in the one scene in both the story and the play, Miser Stevens' role in the film is cleverly expanded. Seeing Stevens count his gold coins before Jabez pays off his mortgage to him, thanks to Scratch, establishes Stevens as a warning of the consequences of having "money and all that money can buy." When Scratch enters the tavern to recruit workers for Jabez after the hailstorm has destroyed other farmers' fields, Miser Stevens leaves without a word. He knows who Scratch is because he has made the same deal with Scratch that Jabez has.[22] The film makes effective dramatic use of the character when right before his death Stevens is obviously worried about his soul and tries to warn Jabez:

STEVENS: You are afraid!
JABEZ: Afraid ... of what?
STEVENS: —of what happens after we die!

JABEZ: Are you plumb crazy, man! What do you *think* hap-
          pens? We're buried—that's all.
STEVENS: But what becomes of our souls?
JABEZ: Why do you fret about something that isn't there?
STEVENS: *[With a frantic note in his voice]* Don't say that—I *know*
          it is—[985].

This is a frightening moment, especially when Belle forces Stevens to dance with her and he is afraid because it is a dance of death.

Here the film incorporates the action of Miser Stevens's soul escaping and being recaptured by Scratch, which was done effectively in the play and is one of the best parts of the story. The literalism of film, however, does not support this story element. Dieterle films an actual moth, seen briefly when Scratch opens his book to check Jabez's contract; then it is immediately captured in Scratch's handkerchief without any flying about or struggle. Jabez asks what it is, and unlike in the story, Scratch tells him explicitly that it is Miser Stevens's soul (987). The subsequent dialogue more or less follows the story in having Scratch make comparative comments about the size of souls, especially Daniel Webster's, and then we hear a sound that is meant to be Miser Stevens crying for help, as in the story and play. The line as uttered is distorted, perhaps mechanically as it sounds like a kazoo. Presumably, the purpose of distorting the line is to signify the different state of a disembodied soul, but the words are nearly unintelligible, and it was only with repeated viewing of the videocassette that one could discern the words, "Help me, Neighbor Stone! Help me!" Jabez then sees Stevens' body in the empty ballroom of his mansion, the other party guests and Belle having left. This is a fairly effective moment, the melodramatic music on the soundtrack notwithstanding, but reconceptualizing the scene this way loses the story's effect of Jabez hearing the church bells toll, seeing something *like* a moth fly about and struggle against Scratch's imprisonment of it, and Jabez's—and the reader's—horrified epiphany that Miser Stevens had also entered into a contract for his soul with the devil and it has just come due. The escape of Miser Stevens' soul appears very late in the film, rather than midway as in the story and the play. Thus, one of the best scenes of the original was detrimentally altered in the adaptation.

Finally, the film rushes the denouement of the plot unnecessarily. This was not the result of inartistic editing; the shooting script itself provides very little action and dialogue after Webster defeats the devil. As in the play, the story's post-trial scene in which Webster threatens Scratch with a battering from his ram Goliath and forces the devil to sign a promise to steer clear of Jabez and the entire state of New Hampshire, and the devil's telling Webster his future, all of that is reduced in the film to Scratch, after Webster has kicked him out the door, leaning back in the window to say, "You'll never be *president*—I'll see to that!" (994). The film ends with a hug between Mary and Jabez, the announcement that Jabez's new mansion is burning down, and a number of farmers joining the Stones and Webster for a huge breakfast at an enormous dining table set up in the yard, which has had no dramatic explanation for its being there. Granted, the end of the film is successful in returning to the lighter tone associated with Scratch throughout: Ma Stone presents Webster with a pie but when the cover is removed it is missing and she says "What the D—" (994); the camera cuts to Scratch out on the country road eating the pie, then back to Ma Stone bringing an even larger pie out from the house, saying, "Well, who laughs last … " The final shot is the aforementioned one of Scratch looking for another victim and pointing to the audience. Signifying the tongue-in-cheek tone, the music on the soundtrack is at first merry and playful and then becomes exaggeratedly dramatic. This was quite effective, but the film would have benefited from a slower wrapping up of the plot.

The major features in comparison to the story and play versions of "The Devil and Daniel Webster" show that, overall, the film adaptation is in many ways a successful reincarnation of the short story for the cinematic medium. Benét effectively lengthened the plot with extended roles for Scratch, Webster, Jabez, Mary, and even Miser Stevens. He returned to the before-and-after structure of the story's plot, depicting Jabez as a sympathetic farmer struggling to provide for his family before he gives in to temptation and becomes rich and corrupt. With the aid of Walter Huston's delightful comic performance, Benét was able to keep the tone of the film from becoming too heavy, as was the case with the play, and additional references to Webster and Edward Arnold's portrayal elevated the figure of Daniel Webster to a heroic stature similar to that in the story, though not with the same tall-tale hyperbole of a folk hero. The film treatment of the story's supernatural elements was not as successful as it might have been, but the affirmation-of-America theme was better expressed than in the play.

Since Benét played a major role in the creation of both adaptations, it seems that he grew as a dramatist in correcting some of the errors of the play version when he wrote the screenplay. One wonders, had it been as common then for a screenwriter to also direct his script as it is today, if Benét's directing would have even more faithfully reincarnated one of the great American short stories.

WORKS CITED

Adams, Samuel Hopkins. *The Godlike Daniel*. New York: Sears Publishing Co., 1930.

"As We Remember Him." *Saturday Review of Literature* 26 (27 March 1943): 7–11.

Beale, Paul (ed.). *A Concise Dictionary of Slang and Unconventional English; from A Dictionary of Slang and Unconventional English by Eric Partridge*. New York: Macmillan Publishing Company, 1990.

Benét, Stephen Vincent. "The Author is Pleased." *New York Times* (Sept. 28, 1941), 4.

_____. "Daniel Webster and the Ides of March." *Saturday Evening Post* 212 (28 October 1939): 18–19, 40–7.

_____. "The Devil and Daniel Webster." *The Selected Works of Stephen Vincent Benét Volume Two: Prose*. New York: Farrar & Rinehart, Inc., 1942, 32–46; reprt. from the *Saturday Evening Post* 209 (24 October 1936): 8-9, 68–74.

_____. *The Devil and Daniel Webster: An Opera in One Act*. (Libretto.) New York: Farrar & Rinehart, Inc., 1939.

_____. *The Devil and Daniel Webster*. (One-act play.) New York: Dramatists Play Service Inc., 1939.

_____. *Selected Letters of Stephen Vincent Benét 1898–1943*. Ed. Charles A. Fenton. New Haven: Yale UP, 1960.

_____. "Words and Music: Inside Story of 'The Devil and Daniel Webster.'" *Saturday Review of Literature* 20:10 (20 May 1939), 10.

Benét, Stephen Vincent, and Dan Totheroh. *All That Money Can Buy*. (Screenplay.) *Twenty Best Film Plays*. Ed. John Gassner and Dudley Nichols. New York: Crown Publishers, Inc., 1943, 951–994.

Bible Gateway. Gospel Communications Network Online Christian Resources, A Ministry of Gospel Films, Inc.

Cinemania 95: The Entertaining Guide to Movies and the Moviemakers. Microsoft Home, Microsoft Corporation, 1992–1994.

Cohen, Arthur. Liner notes for *Stephen Vincent Benét's* The Devil and Daniel Webster *read by Pat Hingle*. New York: Caedmon Studios, 1982.

Connors, Martin, and Jim Craddock (eds). *Videohound's Golden Movie Retriever 1998*. Detroit: Visible Ink Press, 1998.

"The Devil in a Legal Knot." *Newsweek* 20 October 1941, 75.

Fenton, Charles A. *Stephen Vincent Benét: The Life and Times of an American Man of Letters, 1898–1943*. New Haven: Yale UP, 1958.

Harvey, Peter. *Remincenses and Anecdotes of Daniel Webster*. Boston: Little, Brown & Co., 1877.

Irving, Washington. "The Devil and Tom Walker." *Tales of a Traveller*. New York: G. P. Putnam's Sons, 1849, 391–409.

Izzo, David Garrett. *The American World of Stephen Vincent Benét*. Orem, UT: Encore Performance Publishing, 1999.

Jackson, Frederick H. "Stephen Vincent Benét and American History." *The Historian* 17 (Autumn 1954): 67–75.

Kimbel, Bobby Ellen (ed.). "Stephen Vincent Benét" in *The Dictionary of Literary Biography*, vol. 102, American Short Story Writers 1910–1945. Second Series. Detroit, London: Broccoli Clark Layman Gale Research Inc., 11–19.

Maddocks, Gladys Louise. "Stephen Vincent Benét: A Bibliography." *Bulletin of Bibliography and Dramatic Index* 20 (1951–52): 142–6, 158–60.

MacLeish, Archibald. *Scratch*. Boston: Houghton Mifflin Company, 1971.

Martin, Mick, and Marsha Porter (eds.). *Video Movie Guide 1992*. New York: Ballantine Books 1991.

Partenheimer, David. "Benét's 'The Devil and Daniel Webster.'" *The Explicator* 55:1 (Fall 1996): 37–40.

Poe, Edgar Allan. "The Bargain Lost." *Collected Works of Edgar Allan Poe: Tales and Sketches 1831–1842*. Ed. Thomas Ollive Mabbott. Cambridge: The Belknap P of Harvard UP, 1978, 85–95.

_____. "Bon-Bon." *Collected Works of Edgar Allan Poe: Tales and Sketches 1831–1842*. Ed. Thomas Ollive Mabbott. Cambridge: The Belknap P of Harvard UP, 1978, 96–117.

Remini, Robert V. *Daniel Webster: The Man and His Time*. New York: W. W. Norton & Co., 1997.

Sickels, Eleanor M. "Stephen Vincent Benét." *College English* 14 (1953): 440–446.

Singer, Robert. "One against All: The New England Past and Present Responsibilities in *The Devil and Daniel Webster*." *Literature-Film-Quarterly* 22: 4 (1994): 265–71.

Stroud, Parry. *Stephen Vincent Benét*. New York: Twayne Publishers, Inc., 1962.

Van Gelder, Robert. "Mr. Benét's Work in Progress." *New York Times Book Review*, 6 (April 21, 1940), 20.

Walsh, Thomas F. "The 'Noon Wine' Devils." *The Georgia Review* 22 (1968) 90–96.

NOTES

1. Stroud cites the Faust legend as one of the inspirations for Benét's story (117), and both Walsh and Singer discuss "The Devil and Daniel Webster" at length as an adaptation of the Faust legend.

2. This and all subsequent quotations are taken from *The Selected Works of Stephen Vincent Benét* 2 vols. Introduction by Basil Davenport. New York: Rinehart and Co., Inc., 1942, and will be cited parenthetically in the text.

3. "Jabez sounds like the word for pain," according to the note provided by *Bible Gateway* Gospel Communications Network. It is also possible that Benét came upon the name in *The Godlike Daniel* (1930) where Samuel Hopkins Adams mentions that one of Daniel Webster's college acquaintances was named "Jabez Whitaker" (18).

4. Interestingly, there is something resembling the Faust legend in the life (or, at least, the biographies) of the historical Daniel Webster: "He might be the 'Godlike' to many, but to others he remained 'Black Dan,' one of the greatest intellects 'God ever let the devil buy'" (quoted in Remini 29). The nickname "Black Daniel," which Benét uses in his story, stems not only from Webster's black eyes, but also his dark complexion. Adams explains that he was a "black Celt, deriving his beauty and his dark distinction from a Welsh grandmother" (75). Webster was famous not only for his voice and eloquence, but also for his stare or "black look" (Remini 27).

5. Benét first responded to the allure of Hollywood to work with director D. W. Griffith on a movie about Abraham Lincoln, a noble artistic project in Benét's mind. However, his letters home to Rosemary reveal his disgust with the lack of integrity in the movie business. See Fenton 115, *Selected Letters* 201, 202–3, and Izzo and Konkle's article "Benét as Dramatist" in this volume.

6. In a revised version of "The Bargain Lost," retitled "Bon-Bon," Poe gives the stranger "a set of jagged and fang-like teeth" (105), similar to Mr. Scratch's teeth "that were filed to a point" (33).

7. Jabez's plight and subsequent contract distinguish the story from European incarnations of Faust because, as Stroud says, he trades his immortal soul "not for power, like the German, but for the American Dream of prosperity" (118).

8. See Fenton 135–41 for a summary of Benét's collaboration with John Farrar on two plays in the early 1920's, and also Izzo and Konkle's essay "Benét as Dramatist for Stage, Screen, and Radio" in this volume.

9. All references will be to the Dramatists Play Service acting edition unless otherwise noted.

10. The play's origin as opera may have influenced the somber tone. One line from the libretto indicates just how heavy the dialogue was to match the music: "But the man who has sold his soul away / Must burn in flame till the Judgment Day" (31). Perhaps if Moore and Benét had adapted the story as a Broadway musical rather than as an opera the tone would have been lighter.

11. In the opera Benét did give Webster a song that attempted to heighten him with his daily routine of wrestling his ram Goliath (42–3). However, it comes so late in the plot—right before the trial scene—that it is not as effective in elevating Daniel Webster's stature as it would have been earlier.

12. As Sickels noted, "Most of [Benét's] best short stories have the quality of legend or myth. The most famous of them, 'The Devil and Daniel Webster,' has all but become an actual American legend" (445).

13. References to plot and character will be to the videocassette; when a line of dialogue is quoted it will be from the published script unless otherwise noted.

14. However, one could interpret the film to imply that Jabez's and Mary's son, "little Daniel," named after Daniel Webster, is the product of Scratch's machinations. Before the pact, Jabez had no children despite being married for two years. While this may appear similar to the problem in the play with Jabez's marriage to Mary being part of what he longed for before selling his soul, here the audience sees that there is no explicit bargain made for a son.

15. In addition, before *The Devil and Daniel Webster* Dieterle had directed two Hollywood films with titles suggesting similar subject matter: *The Devil's in Love* (1933) and *Satan Met a Lady* (1936) (*Cinemania* 95).

16. Archibald MacLeish used that as the title of his play "suggested by Stephen Vincent Benét's 'The Devil and Daniel Webster,'" which is a much more intellectual and grave telling of the broad outlines of the story. In fact, it is much closer in tone and theme to MacLeish's earlier Pulitzer Prize–winning play in verse *J.B.*, a modern retelling of the book of Job.

17. In his study of the film, Singer makes several references to how it is a

response to the contemporary crisis, despite its historical subject: "Webster appeals for relief and compassion for these farmers, reflecting a New Deal platform. Webster thus represents on-screen the positive powers that protect the impoverished and errant from sinister, antidemocratic forces. This is a positive affirmation of the powers of government, and any parallels between the characters of Webster and FDR would not be too exaggerated" (269).

18. Strangely, when Webster demands to be heard during the trial, Justice Hathorne tells him, "You may speak, if you like, but be brief. And let me warn you, Mr. Webster—if you speak and fail to convince us, then you, too, are doomed!" (992). Following this line there is dramatic music and the camera cuts to a closeup of Webster's face, heightening the moment. The film seems to have forgotten that Webster had already offered himself up as collateral for the chance to defend Jabez before the trial even began.

19. By including Benedict Arnold, the film sacrifices the joke from the story, of Webster noting the absence of Benedict Arnold, the most famous American of ill repute, when Scratch summons the jury (40–1).

20. Perhaps the excellence of the patriotic speeches in the film contributed to Benét's going on to write wartime propaganda for radio. A commentator in the *New York Times* referred to the words of one of Benét's pieces for radio as "Lincoln-like" (Fenton 361).

21. Admittedly, reviews and Benét himself praise the film's handling of the supernatural overall; see *Selected Letters* (379–80). Nevertheless, when one compares the film's treatment of the trial scene to the story's and the play's, it is clearly underplayed.

22. The shooting script contains a scene not in the videocassette that made this even more explicit. After Jabez pays him and Miser Stevens realizes where the gold has come from by comparing his coins with Jabez's, he goes to a church with his gold, intending to donate it, but Scratch intervenes, offering him an extension on his contract if he will "forget this stupid repentance idea" (962). Stevens then says it isn't the money he cares about now but the fact that he is so lonely; Scratch tells him he can talk to Jabez Stone. Dramatically it might have been better to have kept this scene, if indeed it was cut from the original print of the film, for it prepares the audience for when Stevens does talk to Jabez in the party scene, and it does suggest there is hope for Jabez and for all of us through free will choice of good over evil.

10. Stephen Vincent Benét in the Twilight Zone: Fantasy and Science Fiction

Toby Johnson

Sacred scriptures are still being written today. In spite of the widely proclaimed notions in the religions of the Book—Judaism, Christianity, and Islam—that Truth was revealed once and for all, in the distant past, by their God, new religious myths and sacred writings are being produced all the time.

According to the major Western traditions, all of which trace their foundations to Abraham the Patriarch and the basis of their Scriptures to Moses the Liberator, the Bible and Koran represent the final written word of God.

In fact, though, religion has kept changing all through history. The-ologians and Church officials have reinterpreted the details of the revela-tion, emphasizing different ideas at different times, usually to respond to changing political, cultural and moral circumstances. New ideas were introduced by spiritual writers, mystics, and poets.What characterizes this whole notion of Revelation in the past is an idea of authority that has dominated human culture until quite recently.

Today we no longer hold the argument from ancient authority to be exclusively convincing. We no longer look to the ancients for the only ver-sion of truth. So while religion still prevails as the proclaimer of cherished beliefs and stories that are passed down to influence human culture and behavior, much of the discussion of how to think about the meaning of life has shifted to anthropology, literature, poetry, and modern mythopoeism.

Curiously in our modern "demythologized" world, we are probably bombarded by more mythic stories than any human beings before us. Every night on TV we are offered story after story of heroes dealing with problems, overcoming obstacles and saving the world with every click of the remote and every turn of the hour. Of course, most of these stories aren't referenced to the meaning of life (though even a crime drama about the police capturing a criminal demonstrates the notion of the cosmic battle between good and evil).

Renowned comparative religions scholar and mythographer Joseph Campbell observed that virtually all the stories that interest human beings from poetic epics to religious mythology to the modern novel follow the same basic pattern—what he called the hero cycle.

One of the areas of literature and modern popular culture, however, that does often explicitly deal with issues of meaning and metaphysical significance is what is loosely called science fiction. In a way, this flows right out of the modern rejection of the argument from authority. What makes a novel or a movie "science fiction" is usually that it is set in the future and it is in the future that the issues of meaning will be resolved.

Within the genre of science fiction is a subgenre that deals specifically with spiritual and metaphysical issues that is perhaps best identified by its manifestation in 1950s television in the phrase coined by writer-producer Rod Serling: The Twilight Zone. Indeed what made a story fit in this category is that it dealt with a slightly alternative reality in order to make a salient or poignant observation about commonly shared reality, often by means of an ironic or surprising ending.

Stephen Vincent Benét preceded Rod Serling by some twenty years, but one can clearly find in his work precursors of the Twilight Zone. Benét's most famous story, "The Devil and Daniel Webster," demonstrates this kind of modern myth creation following the ancient pattern of pseudepigrapy and interestingly twisting the notions of religious authority. The Faustian story is told by an anonymous narrator about an event in mythic time about characters from the indeterminate American past.

The story goes that the patriot, statesman and smooth-talking attorney Daniel Webster is called upon to defend one Jabez Stone in a trial contesting a contract with the Devil for Stone's soul. Webster argues democratic, American principles and humanistic values against the Devil's letter-of-the-law claim on Stone. While all this is told in the form of a tall tale, Webster's victory demonstrates the conquest of American humanism over traditional religion. The twist is that the Devil, Mr. Scratch, stacked the case in his own favor by populating the jury with denizens of Hell, all notorious murderers, pirates, renegades, or stiff-necked inquisitors in early American history. But Webster was able to change them back to compassionate men and so influence their verdict by his eloquence and by the beauty of the American dream of opportunity, even for the damned.

The legal basis of the defense is that Jabez Stone is an American citizen and so cannot be forced into the service of any foreign prince, even the Devil himself. It is noteworthy that the defense never calls for mercy or forgiveness based on Christian sentiments. Webster never calls upon religion to save his client. Rather his claim is based in the nobility and rightness of the American dream, even when it contains wrongs, for they too have played a part in the creation of America. In Benét's *Selected Works* (1942), this story is listed in the section called, "Stories of American History." This is misdirection. The story is not history at all but a fantasy cast with historical figures. Hence, it should have been placed in the section with other stories of its type collected under the rubric "Fantasies and Prophecies" which further demonstrate how modern wisdom is communicated in brief detours through the Twilight Zone.

The initial stories in this section are lighter fare to amuse and entertain; the latter were written as warnings of the rise of fascism. The first story in "Fantasies and Prophecies" sets the stage for the others in this section. It offers us—readers of Stephen Vincent Benét's some 60 years after his death at age 44 in 1943—a curious perspective on the writer's life and influence. "The Curfew Tolls" is couched in a series of letters written by an Englishman in the late 1780s to his sister back in England while he is convalescing at a spa on the French Riviera called St. Phillipe.

The epistler reports that he has made the acquaintance of a strange little man in the village who demonstrates great knowledge of war and military strategy. The little man's own life seems shoddy and banal. He is a ne'er-do-well major who by twist of bad fortune has ended up on half-pay stationed in the little health resort with no promise of military accomplishment left to him.

The Englishman is fascinated by the little man's bravado and partly sorry for him because his life has come to so little. So he befriends him just at the time the major is dying. In reward, he is left the man's voluminous writings on military strategy and the obligation of writing the soldier's epitaph.

During the time of his final illness, the major asks the Englishman to read to him—not from the Bible, as one might have thought, but from the poem by Thomas Gray "Elegy Written in a Country Churchyard." The poem concerns the irony that death ends all ambition, and greatness—or the lack of it—may be but a mere fluke of fortune. The poet muses that in the graves of the country churchyard may lie souls who but for a simple twist of fate might have been world leaders or famous artists or poets.

> My friend the major's malady approaches its term—the last few days find him fearfully enfeebled. He knows that the end draws nigh; indeed, he speaks of it often, with remarkable calmness. I had thought it might turn his mind toward religion, but while he accepted the ministrations of the church, I fear it is without the sincere repentance of a Christian. When the priest had left him, yesterday, he summoned me, remarking, "well, all that is over with," rather more in the tone of a man who has just reserved a place in the coach than one who will shortly meet his maker.
>
> "It does no harm," he said reflectively. "And, after all, it might be true. Why not?" and he chuckled in a way that repelled me. Then he asked me to read to him—not from the Bible, as I would have expected, but some verses from Gray. He listened attentively, and when I came to the passage, "Hands that the rod of empire might have swayed," and its successor, "Some mute inglorious Miltons," he asked me to repeat them. When I had done so, he said, "Yes, yes. That is true, very true. I did not think so in boyhood—I thought genius must force its own way. But your poet is right about it...."
>
> "Come Major," I said soothingly, "we cannot all be great men, you know. And you have no need to repine" [396].

Here the story shifts into the Twilight Zone—and establishes the context for the other "Fantasies and Prophecies"—with a surprise ending as the Englishman's epitaph for the little major reveals that all this has been happening in an alternative reality. For the ne'er-do-well soldier turns out to have been one "Napoleone Buonaparte." When the Englishman finally thinks of a conventional epitaph for the major's stone, he admits that he thought of "excerpting the lines of Gray's—the only ones that are still ringing in my head. But on reflection, though they suit well enough, they yet seemed too cruel to the dust" (398). The secular here gives way to the traditional even though the former is herein thought more appropriate.

The fantasy tale "The King of the Cats" is a comedy about the appearance of a greatly acclaimed orchestra director whose talent is based on his wielding his baton with a feline-like tail that is in itself a source of amazement. While most of the characters in the story are actual human beings, they all have names that sound like cat names while the conductor is a cat in a man's disguise. The ruse of M. Tibault, the cat in director's clothing, is foiled when the cat imposter is led to expose himself when he is told an old and magical story of the funeral of a cat on whose coffin was placed a small crown. Whenever the tale is told, it incites any real cats hearing it to exclaim, "Then I'm the King of the Cats," which M. Tibault proclaims precipitously and suddenly disappears forever.

While the wisdom of the story is light, there is a cute message about cat psychology—and its implications for human psychology; namely, that every cat seems to think itself King of the Cats, which is to say, ego leaps to self-aggrandizing conclusions—supposedly to its own downfall. It must be noted that the trap didn't work as expected for the Princess Vivraka-narda (herself described as convincingly feline), whose suitor it was who set the trap of the retold tale in hopes of getting the princess for himself. Instead, at story's end, she appears to have run off with Tibault to be his queen in the mysterious kingdom of the cats.

"Doc Mellhorn and the Pearly Gates" is a wonderful example of the Twilight Zone story. An old-time country doctor—the kind who does card tricks to calm youthful patients—dies and goes to Heaven, but because he is so obsessed with his profession and committed to helping his patients, he has no time for Heaven. Partly out of denial that he's really dead and partly out of his dedication to his practice—his religion is serving others—he quickly leaves Heaven and proceeds, through a backroads entrance, into Hell, noting, "Well, I can't see that it's so different than other places…. Warmish, though" (421). There, he sets up practice easing the suffering of the damned *and* of their demon torturers as well. Of course, he is ruining Hell by making it too comfortable and is soon forced back to Heaven, though even then he refuses to take it seriously. The story ends with him playing a sleight-of-hand trick on the Father of Medicine, old Aesculapius himself.

As in "The Devil and Daniel Webster," Benét makes fun of conventional Christian metaphysics and morals by offering the example of the scrappy, but kindly and plucky old American country doctor as the meaningful saint for today. The modern myth demonstrates virtue based on humanism and nonchalance, not religious purity and sanctimoniousness.

The first story of warning, "The Last of the Legions," is an account in the first person of a Roman centurion of the withdrawal of Roman forces who conquered and occupied Britain, a withdrawal that is precipitated by the threats of Alaric on Rome itself. The gimmick of the story in great part is anachronism—a mainstay of the Twilight Zone style of storytelling. For example, the soldier says, "We'd have blocked up half those windows where I come from—once they start shooting fire arrows, big windows are a nuisance, even in a fortified town" (435). The allusion is to windows with glass. The centurion speaks with surprisingly modern sophistication, and world weariness, as he muses on the place in history the Roman occupation of Britain will ultimately play. Benét echoes his military childhood when the centurion notes: "I'm a child of the camp— I was brought up in the legion. The tale is that the first of us came with Caesar—I don't put much stock in that—and of course we've married British ever since" (431). Indeed, he has less faith in legend and more in what he can actually see. As he observes the decline of Roman power, only half understanding that that is what is happening, he mourns the loss of discipline and authority, saying, "I don't care for torture myself—it leaves a bad taste in your mouth—but there are times when you have to use a firm hand" (432). He wistfully envies one of his soldiers who has deserted the legion to stay with a woman he's fallen in love with and thereby to "go native," giving up Roman civilization and power for personal happiness. He also knows what he'll do to the young man if he catches him, even though he likes him: "I have my orders" (440). He is a soldier; he does his duty. In the end, the Centurion longs to call out to the British barbarians to whom Rome has brought culture and civilization to remember the legion, but he sees, poignantly, that there is nobody to say it to who will understand, let alone care. Besides, as a soldier, he has no time for such personal things.

The next two stories have more emphatic warnings of, first, the coming danger, and, second, the possible aftermath. "The Blood of the Martyrs" and "Into Egypt" partake in what has become a sort of subgenre of its own within the category of speculative fiction and political commentary, the impending dystopia of totalitarianism. The stories, written in 1936 and 1939 respectively, describe a kind of Russian/German-like Orwellian dictatorship in which truth and humanity are sacrificed for power and efficiency. The two stories are surprisingly prophetic, written as they were a little before most Americans understood what had actually been going on in Nazi Germany. They were also, of course, antitotalitarian propaganda inspired by Benét's strong faith in Americanism at a time such propaganda was needed.

"The Blood of the Martyrs" tells of a Nobel prize–winning biochemist, Professor Gregor Malzius, who has been imprisoned, tortured and condemned to be shot in a purge of intellectuals in a fictional cultural revolution called the "cleansing." As the story opens, instead of being executed, Malzius, to his surprise, is being freed. The dictator himself has come to the prison to emancipate the professor and, indeed, to proclaim him new president of the National Academy of Science. As the emancipation proceeds, Malzius realizes the dictator is not interested in his research or in the truth that his science can uncover, but in having him, a respected and distinguished scholar, openly declare his allegiance to the dictator—and thereby to quash opposition to the regime beginning to appear in such places as the British Parliament. Because Malzius is terrified of being tortured further, he sees that his only real choice is to give in and be a pawn to the lies of the regime or to so egregiously offend the dictator as to finally provoke his long-threatened execution. He chooses not to betray his former students, to whom giving truth was paramount. Thus, after promising to sign a loyalty oath, he instead throws the inkwell at the dictator, splashing his face and uniform with ink. As the ploy succeeds and the professor is about to be shot by firing squad, he thinks,

> There had been a girl called Anna once; he had almost forgotten her. And his rooms had smelt a certain way and he had had a dog.... He raised his head and looked once more at the gray foggy sky. In a moment there would be no thought, but while there was thought, one must remember and note. His pulse rate was lower than he would have expected and his breathing oddly even, but those were not the important things. The important thing was beyond, in the gray sky that had no country, in the stones of the earth and the feeble human spirit. The important thing was the truth.
> "Ready!" called the officer. "Aim! Fire!" But Professor Malzius did not hear the three commands of the officer. He was thinking about the young men [460].

"Into Egypt" is about the expulsion of the "Accursed People" from the homeland, an obvious parallel to the Jews under Nazi Germany, though that is never said explicitly as such. The last of the Accursed People to pass through a checkpoint are a man and woman with a young child riding on a donkey. Livestock is specifically forbidden on this tortured march of expulsion, so the lieutenant at the checkpoint should confiscate the animal and will, but for one small thing. As he is questioning the father, he notices the child's hands. Because of that he allows the struggling little family to pass and to keep their donkey. But he is deeply disturbed. The punch line of the story is the lieutenant's explaining about the child: "Its hands had been hurt ... In the middle. Right through. I saw them" (471). The family is, of course, Joseph and Mary bringing poor little Jesus, already showing the wounds of his suffering—a poignant twist of the Christian myth, taking it out of its ancient, but distant and otherworldly context, and applying it to modern day politics with a message about ethnic tolerance.

The last of the stories Benét included in his "Fantasies and Prophecies" is one of his most famous because it is often considered a forerunner to the modern science-fiction story. "By the Waters of Babylon," published in 1937, is set in a future world after a terrible holocaust called the Great Burning has devastated the Earth. The narrator and protagonist is the son of a priest. He has been trained in the law; he knows the chants and the spells. He knows it is his place to continue the teaching that there are certain "Dead Places" divinely forbidden to people. But also because he is the son of a priest, he knows he must follow the intuition of his dreams. In his dreams he has seen the gods walking and knows he must go to the Place of the Gods.

In obedience to the classic Campbellian hero-cycle, the young protagonist must risk the danger of the Dead Places to journey to the Place of the Gods. During the journey he remembers the legends he has learned about the gods. He expects it will kill him, but he must seek out the truth.

In a conclusion, now familiar to science-fiction fans from such movie classics as *The Planet of the Apes*, the young hero comes first to Washington DC and then to New York City. As he explores the strange ruins where he has been taught the Gods lived, in a sealed room he comes upon a semimummified corpse. He makes the great discovery that the Gods were men. He has achieved an enlightenment. From it he realizes that it was not gods or demons who caused the world to be as it is, but just men, like him: "They were men who were here before us. We must build again" (483).

On the surface, Benét's story is a warning about the potential of modern warfare to cast us all back to the Stone Age, as the cliché goes. But it is also a critique of religious myth. For the hero's discovery is that what he learned in the legends of his tribe as truth was really a mistaken view of history. The dangers of the Dead Places were based on toxic poisons left by the war, not on mysterious taboo violations divinely revealed by gods. That same critique, the Twilight Zone–style story of science fiction, can be applied to the myths of current religion. Though Benét doesn't say it, isn't it the obvious corollary that the Bible and various sacred scriptures were written by men, not gods? Moreover the discovery—or rediscovery—of this truth offers the possibility for continuing human evolution.

Reading his stories with hindsight, one has to wonder what would have become of Stephen Vincent Benét had his life not ended so early. As it was, of course, he did achieve significant fame. His stories are part of the canon of American literature and he has become a minor mythmaker for the American vision. At any rate, stories like "By the Waters of Babylon" and "The Blood of Martyrs" demonstrate his prophetic vision and his grasp of the nature of myth and storytelling. He indeed is one of the mythopoeists of the sacred scriptures of humankind.

WORK CITED

The Selected Works of Stephen Vincent Benét, Volume Two: Prose. New York: Farrar & Rinehart, 1942.

11. Benét as Dramatist for Stage, Screen, and Radio

David Garrett Izzo and Lincoln Konkle

Stephen Vincent Benét is best known as the author of the classic Civil War verse epic *John Brown's Body* and the much-anthologized short story "The Devil and Daniel Webster." Yet Benét was once the most popular writer in America who also wrote many more stories, novels, poems, *and* dramatic works. The fact that Benét wrote plays, opera libretti, and screenplays has largely been forgotten even though millions of Americans heard his radio scripts in the late 1930s and early 1940s. For those familiar with Benét's work in any form, his visceral approach in poems and prose emphasized the spoken word and, in fact, many of his short stories have been adapted as plays by other writers because of their inherent stage-worthy narratives. (For example: *Stephen Vincent Benét's Stories of America*, adapted for the stage by F. Andrew Leslie, Dramatists Play Service Inc., 1971.)

Benét had a colorful childhood that was augmented by a lively imagination and the doting attentions of his parents and his brother and sister. In a 1976 memoir of her brother's childhood, Laura Benét recalls nine-year-old Stephen's facility for storytelling once he got his first type-writer, and quotes this early piece in its entirety:

Mr. Progg's Conversion

Mr. Progg reeled home from the saloon, singing as he drew near his house. His wife looked out of the window as he approached. "I will fix him," said she. Next day she went downtown and bought a cat, the duplicate of their pet cat. She also bought a can of green

215

paint. That night when Mr. Progg again made his way home, singing "We won't go home until morning," a pair of fierce green eyes glared at him from the window of his little home.

An hour later a badly frightened man handed the pledge to his wife—and the cat understood.

The End [Qtd. in L. Benét 101].

Benét's flair for the dramatic began early and Benét's family was a ready and willing audience for his stories. His parents were open-minded and progressive. Family friend and poet Leonard Bacon said of Colonel Benét, "He knew more about English poetry than most poets and all professors.... Such a man deserved to have all three of his children become poets" (qtd. in Fenton 11). In 1915 William Rose helped his younger brother to get his first book published. *Five Men and Pompey: A Series of Dramatic Portraits,* while certainly verse, is verse drama in the form of six orations.[1] The third portrait is "The Forlorn Campaign (Crassus in Parthia. B.C. 53)":

> Go then, Valerius. Let the legions know,
> That I will answer this new embassy
> Within the hour...They will mutiny,
> If I refuse these terms...What shall I do?
> *What shall I do?* The trap is plain enough
> To me; but they, they only see the rough,
> Long road and the red, ever-circling cloud
> Of horsemen, raining arrows on them there.
> Gods! And the mountains are so near, so near!
> Scarce three days march...that we shall never make [23].

This eloquent monologue reminds one of a soliloquy or heroic speech from one of Shakespeare's tragedies or history plays. Benét's inclination towards the dramatic and dramatic monologues would serve him well for the rest of his writing career.

When Benét entered Yale in 1915, he was already considered a *wunderkind* by such notables as F. Scott Fitzgerald, who esteemed Benét's poetry better than that of his good friend and Princeton classmate John Peale Bishop, who he thought was very good. Critic Malcolm Cowley remembers that "Benét was the bright star not only of Yale but of all the Eastern colleges" (qtd. in Fenton 57). At Yale, Benét concentrated on getting published in the Yale literary magazines and enjoying his friendships with Thornton Wilder, poets H. Phelps Putnam and John Farrar (who would later create the publishing firm of Farrar & Rinehart in 1929, which Benét would join in 1936), novelist Hervey Allen, and playwright Phillip Barry.

Tappan Wilder, the nephew of Thornton Wilder, recalls his uncle telling him about the Yale days when he and Benét would read their plays to each other. Wilder and Benét, along with Richard Bassett, John F. Carter, Arthur Dallin, Norman Fitts, Ramon Guthrie, William Hanway, Quincy Porter, and Roger Sessions, founded in November 1919, a small literary magazine that lasted four years, the *S4N* ("space for name"), a title that anticipates postmodern reflexivity. They called it an "idea exchange."

At Yale Benét and Wilder met with and saw a recital by poet-performance artist Vachel Lindsay who wrote poems meant to be dramatized; he had a profound impact on the two undergraduates. Wilder wrote about meeting the poet in his diary entry of 18 March 1918: "Wednesday aft. met Mr. Nicholas Vachel Lindsay at the [Elizabethan] club and Dr. Seymour asked me to dinner that evening to meet him.... Steve [Benét] came in afterward at table: [drawing of table by Wilder]. Afterward Mr. Lindsay read Congo, Gen. Booth enters Heaven, Lincoln and many others! He reads dramatically with shreeks [*sic*], intonings and chantings" (qtd. in Izzo 227). Wilder and Benét never forgot Lindsay's dynamic performance.[2] For Benét, Lindsay proved that poetry could be potent dramatic oratory and it was to Lindsay that Benét's poems were very often compared. Many of Benét's poems were written as dramatic monologues with an eye as well as an ear to potential performance.

John Farrar, Benét's classmate, recalled that at Yale his friend's "first play ... was a farce concerning the Greek Gods and heroes called *Poor Old Medusa*. It was produced under Monty [Montillion] Woolley's direction along with a satire ... by Philip Barry and a war number of mine, in the ballroom of the Taft Hotel at New Haven before the 'Pump and Slipper Dance' in the spring of 1919. It was ... pungent and certainly, before that exacting audience, successful" (Farrar 17). Woolley, who would later become a stage and screen actor, was a professor during the time Benét was at Yale. In the same year he and Benét would also collaborate on an acting version of Christopher Marlowe's *Tamburlaine the Great*.

In 1924, Benét and his friend John Farrar collaborated on two Broadway plays. The first was a long version of Farrar's "war number" from their Yale days called *Nerves*; the second was *That Awful Mrs. Eaton*. They wrote these plays virtually simultaneously, their first efforts as professional dramatists. Farrar recalled that during the rehearsals of *Nerves* they managed to convince an unknown, Humphrey Bogart, that he could be a natural on the stage. Bogart did, in fact, become a stage and screen star, receiving his first good review in this play. *Nerves* was a World War I melodrama about an American officer who is falsely labeled as being afraid in training camp but later proves his courage in battle and wins the girl. *That*

Awful Mrs. Eaton is about the wife of President Andrew Jackson's Secretary of War. Mrs. Eaton, having been a tavern keeper, is looked down upon by the wives of the Washington establishment. Jackson champions her attributes and she ultimately wins over her detractors by hosting a successful party at the White House. *Nerves* opened on 1 September 1924 and *That Awful Mrs. Eaton* on 24 September 1924. Reviews for both ranged from mixed to poor. Critics recognized youthful talent but also faulted the young writers for trying to say and do too much. Later Benét would consider these plays as object lessons teaching him what not to do. His future screenplays, librettos, and radio scripts would emphasize a lean rather than an overstuffed approach.

In October of 1929 Benét lost all of his earnings from the enormously successful *John Brown's Body* in the stock market crash that started the Great Depression; he was almost broke. Relief came from California where the acclaim for his American *Iliad* had reached all the way to Hollywood. In 1929 the most esteemed American filmmaker of the silent era, D. W. Griffith, decided it was time to do his first "talkie." He sought out the author of the noble portrait of President Lincoln in *John Brown's Body* to write the screenplay for the cinema biography, *Abraham Lincoln.* Benét traveled to Hollywood and quickly learned that screenwriting was a frustrating process due to interference from studio executives and requiring on-the-fly rewrites to accommodate the day-to-day changes that evolved as Griffith directed the film. Griffith was often not sure of what he wanted for a scene until it was actually being shot and Benét would have to write dialogue on the spot. The task was arduous and at times exasperating to Benét, who recorded his dismay at the backstage intrigue typical of Hollywood in a letter to his agent Carl Brandt:

> Nowhere have I seen such shining waste, stupidity and conceit as in the business and managing end of this industry. Since arriving, I have written four versions of *Abraham Lincoln,* including a good one, playable in the required time. That, of course, is out. Seven people, including myself, are now working in conferences on a 5th one.... If I don't get out of here soon I'm going crazy [Fenton 236].

After seeing some particularly egregious behind-the-scenes machinations Benét said to a friend: "Aren't there any men of principle in this town?" The answer he got was "No!" Nonetheless, the film was made and released in 1930 to generally good reviews.

Given the circumstances of the making of the film as Benét himself described in the above-quoted letter, it is impossible to view *Abraham*

Lincoln and determine with certainty which aspects of the film were created by Benét. However, he was given principal credit for the screenplay, as the opening credits state, "Adapted for the Screen by Stephen Vincent Benét" and "continuity and dialogue Stephen Vincent Benét and Gerrit Lloyd."[3] Some features of *Abraham Lincoln* do resemble either Benét's earlier works or works he would write after the screenplay. For example, in the Civil War sequence of the film the crosscutting between scenes showing the Northern leaders and troops and the Southern leaders and troops parallels the structure of *John Brown's Body* in which Benét alternated between the two storylines of the North and South. Similarly, the film represents both the Northern and the Southern points of view on the issues leading to the Civil War, as did *John Brown's Body*. Thus, Robert E. Lee is depicted sympathetically, showing how greatly he feels the defeat for the sake of his soldiers, just as Lincoln is shown having great concern for the Union troops. Also, both Lincoln and Lee are shown overturning an officer's order to execute a deserter and spy, respectively.

The major focus of the film, as it belongs to the "biopic" genre, is on the portrait of Abraham Lincoln from young adulthood to assassination after the war is over. The film begins with the same tall-tale heightening of character as Benét later employed in his story "The Devil and Daniel Webster." As a strapping young man, Lincoln offers to join his newfound friends in a toast if any of them can drink straight from the barrel as he can. One man replies, "Ain't no man living can do that," but Lincoln precedes to lift a barrel and put the spout to his lips, suggesting he has amazing strength. In another early scene he is called "the best rail splitter in the country" by his employer. It is even insinuated that Lincoln has mystical powers when he claims to have a "vision of a ship with white sails" before every victory during the war.

Also like the character of Daniel Webster in the story, the film holds up Abraham Lincoln as a martyr for preserving the Union. Time and time again he says that the Union must be saved at all costs, even when his advisors are urging him to let the South secede because the price in northern blood is too high. By the last third of the film Lincoln has reached the status of American icon. As the film has progressed, Walter Huston, the actor who plays the president, has come to resemble more and more the figure we know from famous photographs. In one scene he is even shown in a close up with his head in profile so that he looks like the image of Lincoln on the penny. At the very end of the film after Lincoln has been assassinated, the log cabin in which he was born is again shown and then the camera dissolves to the Lincoln Memorial, and gradually the camera zooms in to reveal a halo of light encircling the statue. Along with his visions and beatific smiles after the war is won, the final images suggest that Lincoln has been elevated to the level of an American saint. The biopic has become hagiography, as with Benét's depiction of John Brown and Daniel Webster in the earlier and later works.

Although much of the above representation of Abraham Lincoln might be attributed to D. W. Griffith or collaborators on the screenplay, there is one final aspect of the portrait of Lincoln that almost certainly came from Benét. From the beginning of the film to the end Lincoln is shown to be a common man with great humility and a down-to-earth personality. Through much of the early part of the film Lincoln is seen in a reclining pose, whether he is talking with friends or courting Ann Rutledge. Even when he is president he occasionally lies on the floor or scratches his leg with his other stockinged foot, much to first lady Mary Todd Lincoln's chagrin. Benét would employ the same balanced, almost paradoxical characterization of Daniel Webster in the story and film versions of "The Devil and Daniel Webster." The great orator was shown to be just as content sipping from a jug of Medford rum or taking a catnap, as he was delivering a speech. Throughout his career, whether writing in poetry, fiction, or drama, Benét showed the greatest respect in his characterizations for men and women of humility, compassion, and tolerance; nowhere to be found was the elitism or admiration for the upper class as in the work of such contemporaries as T. S. Eliot and F. Scott Fitzgerald. The earthiness of his characters in *Abraham Lincoln* as well as in the film version of *The Devil and Daniel Webster* and his radio scripts in the forties demonstrate that Benét could write realistic drama that constituted an aesthetic suitable for his democratic vision.

Benét, however, while learning the film business and sharpening his skills as a dramatist, would never work in Hollywood again. He did contribute to two films in the future but remained in New York.[4] The Hollywood scene was too unreal for Benét, who in 1930 was more concerned with the bitter reality of business failures and mass unemployment caused by the Depression.

In 1937, perhaps inspired by his children, Benét wrote a libretto aimed at young audiences. He adapted Washington Irving's folk story "The Legend of Sleepy Hollow" as a light opera with composition by another old Yale friend, Douglas Moore; they called it *The Headless Horseman*.[5] Written specifically for the theater department of Bronxville High School in New York City where Moore's children were students, *The Headless Horseman* was staged by the school on 17 March 1937. This was followed by a radio performance over NBC on 22 April 1937. An acting version was published as well, and other high schools mounted productions of *The*

Headless Horseman. Neither Benét nor Moore knew in 1937 that this venture would be a prelude to a major opera they would create two years later.

Benét did not so much adapt "The Legend of Sleepy Hollow" as use it as the inspiration for his own story. That is, the libretto for *The Headless Horseman* is virtually an original work in that Benét borrowed only the barest outline of characters and action from Irving's tale: Ichabod Crane, the schoolmaster who has his eye on Katrina Van Tassel and her father's fortune, is run off by the ghost known as the Headless Horseman, who in reality is Crane's rival suitor, Brom Bones, dressed up as the legendary apparition. Although Ichabod's characterization is consistent with the story, Benét wholly invents the characterizations for Katrina, her father, and Brom Bones. Dramatically the opera is fairly sound: the central conflict lies between Katrina and Brom, who want to marry, and her father and Ichabod, who prevent it because the Van Tassels follow a family tradition of marrying the eldest daughter to a schoolmaster. To do otherwise is met with the fate of being carried off by a ghost. This plot of superstition-crossed lovers resembles not that of "The Legend of Sleepy Hollow" but rather that of *Romeo and Juliet* or, even better, *A Midsummer Night's Dream* since it resolves happily with Ichabod fleeing Sleepy Hollow and Brom announcing that he has secretly been studying to become a schoolmaster and so he can marry Katrina with her father's blessing.

The "out-of-the-blue" revelation, which seems at odds with Brom's characterization in both the opera and story, is the weakest aspect of Benét's libretto; the strongest is the dramatic structure and Benét's witty dialogue and lyrics, for example, the following scene in which Katrina explains her dilemma to a girlfriend early in the libretto:

> KATRINA: Poor Brom! He does love me, and oh, if it were only a question of tying Ichabod up in knots like a pretzel, or kicking him like a football, I'd call upon Brom at once. But, if he does *that*, you see, it still doesn't help about the ghost!
>
> 2ND GIRL: Couldn't he *try* to be a schoolmaster?
>
> KATRINA: I'm afraid not. You see, it took him three years to get through seventh grade. I *think* it was really Ichabod's fault. He always gave Brom zero—even when I did his lessons for him.
>
> 2ND GIRL: How mean!
>
> KATRINA: It was mean. But it discouraged Brom. Three years in the seventh grade would discourage anybody [4].

Benét's skill as a poet also enabled him to write comic lyrics for Moore's score, as in Katrina's father's solo:

VAN TASSEL: Cornelius Van Tassel's my name!
          And I state, without shyness or shame,
          That Van Rensselaers and such are extremely Low
            Dutch
          Compared to the name I proclaim!
          For I am Cornelius Van Tassel!
CHORUS: To family pride he's a vassal!
          And even his cows, as they peacefully browse.
VAN TASSEL: Rejoice in the name of Van Tassel! [7].

In fact, the major influence upon Benét and Moore's *The Headless Horseman* may very well have been the comic operas of Gilbert and Sullivan, such as *The Pirates of Penzance* and *H.M.S. Pinafore*.[6] In that context, the implausibility of Brom's taking a correspondence course to become a schoolmaster so that Katrina's father will withdraw his objections to Brom and Katrina being married is less an aesthetic weakness than a convention of romantic comedy and light comic opera. Thus, although *The Headless Horseman* is unsatisfying as an adaptation of Irving's brilliant tale, it at least partially succeeds on its own terms. Furthermore, it reveals Benét's grasp of drama, in that he recognized the story was inherently undramatic, being more than half exposition, and would require a fundamental reimagining to bring it to life on a stage.

In 1936 Benét had published his most famous short story in the *Saturday Evening Post*, America's best-selling weekly magazine. "The Devil and Daniel Webster" struck a chord with millions of readers. The story of the great lawyer and orator who saves a man who had sold his soul to Ol' Scratch resonated with readers who were just getting over the Depression but were now troubled by the fascism in Europe. Webster has to convince a judge and jury of scoundrels handpicked by the devil to acquit Jabez Stone. As a parable, Jabez represents the average American down on his luck; the judge and jury represent the fascists, Mr. Scratch the forces of evil, and Daniel Webster, as the United States, comes to the rescue. No short story has ever had the national impact of "The Devil and Daniel Webster." It was almost immediately reissued in book form complete with illustrations, and elevated Benét to the rare status of a literary American spokesman, as suggested by Fenton:

"The Devil and Daniel Webster" consolidated the national role which had been slowly materializing for Benét ever since the publications of the ballads in 1922 and 1923.... Americans responded in a way that astonished the *Post*.... After the publication of "The Devil and Daniel Webster" Benét became a story-teller to the nation. He could now write for the largest magazine in the United States stories about leprechauns and sea serpents, Nazi tyranny and American responsibilities [Fenton 293, 295].

It was inevitable that the story would find its way to the stage and then a film. (See Konkle's assessment of the stage and film adaptations earlier in this volume.)

Douglas Moore had wanted to do a longer opera with Benét after their collaboration on *The Headless Horsemen*. Benét's popularity opened doors and "The Devil and Daniel Webster" was the logical choice for a new opera. But adapting "The Devil and Daniel Webster" for the stage presented a formidable challenge, for much of its effect is dependent on the narrator's summation of speech and action. For example, Webster's closing speech to the judge and jury is described by its effect on the listeners:

> He painted a picture ... and to each one of that jury he spoke of things long forgotten. For his voice could search the heart, and that was his gift and his strength. And to one, his voice was like the forest and its secrecy, and to another like the sea and the storms of the sea; and one heard the cry of his lost nation in it, and another saw a little harmless scene he hadn't remembered for years. But each saw something. And when Dan'l Webster finished he didn't know whether or not he'd saved Jabez Stone. But he knew he'd done a miracle. For the glitter was gone from the eyes of judge and jury, and, for the moment, they were men again, and knew they were men [SVB: *D & DW* 1999, 26].

In the opera, Webster's oratorical genius would have to be conveyed through Webster himself. Benét's libretto rendition of Webster's speech is longer and must accommodate Moore's music, but it is no less effective as the closing lines show:

> WEBSTER: Do you know him? He is your brother. Will you take the law of the oppressor and bind him down? / It is not for him that I speak. It is for all of you. / There is a sadness in being a man, but it is a proud thing too. / There is failure and despair on the journey—the endless journey of mankind. / We are tricked and trapped—we stumble into the pit—but out of the pit we rise again. / No demon that was ever foaled can know the inward-

ness of that—only men, bewildered men. / They have broken freedom with their hands and cast her out from the nations—yet shall she live while man lives. / She shall live in the blood and the heart—she shall live in the earth of this country—she shall not be broken. / When the whips of the oppressors are broken and their names forgotten and destroyed. / I see you, mighty, shining, liberty, liberty! I see free men walking and talking under a star! / God save the United States and the men who have made her free! / The defense rests.

JURY: [*Exultantly*] / We were men—we were free—we were men—we have not forgotten—our children shall follow and be free [71–2].

Benét was quite aware that in 1939 Webster's words would also serve as a warning that fascism in Europe and Asia were threats to freedom everywhere. The opera was staged with the support of the American Lyric Theater under the direction of the legendary Mercury Theater's John Houseman. Benét's reputation and winning personality attracted famous names to work with Houseman, who later said in his autobiography, *Run-Through*,

> My collaborators were men whose work I admired: Fritz Reinder was our conductor; Eugene Loring, creator of Aaron Copland's *Billy the Kid*, was my choreographer. Even more important—and the main reason for doing the production in the first place—was the presence of [set designer] Robert Edmund Jones.... For years he had been an illustrious figure in the American theater; histories of the contemporary stage were filled with his designs... [430].

The Devil and Daniel Webster premiered 18 May 1939 in Broadway's Martin Beck Theater to great acclaim. Renowned *New York Times* theater critic Brooks Atkinson wrote on 6 May 1939 that "*The Devil and Daniel Webster* represents some of the finest and most painstaking work of the season" (qtd. in Fenton 352). The expense of the production prevented a long Broadway run, but the opera was done many times by USO troupes during World War II and was an annual feature for many years at the Old Sturbridge Festival in Massachusetts. Benét almost immediately revised the libretto as a straight play, which continues to be reprinted in anthologies of one-act plays, such as *Best Plays: Middle Level* (1998).

Two years later Benét would fashion another adaptation of the story for film and cowrite the screenplay. The film was released by RKO Pictures in 1941 and was also well received. Unfathomably, however, RKO changed the title. Instead of using the title of what was the most famous story ever written in America—insuring the film's instant recognition by the public—the film was called *All That Money Can Buy*. (In 1943, the screenplay would be included in *Twenty Great Film Plays* as one of the twenty best scripts since the "talkies" began in 1927. In the film, Walter Huston, previously cast as Benét's Lincoln in the Griffith epic, played the devil.)

During the late 1930s Benét, just as many other Americans, was alarmed at the tragedy of fascism in Asia and Europe. He took seriously his role as national spokesperson and began to write poems and stories as warnings to the American people. Among these were "The Blood of the Martyrs," "Into Egypt," "The Last of the Legions," "Nightmare at Noon," and "By the Waters of Babylon," the last of which is credited by science-fiction historians as establishing many of the conventions of stories about a future world of survivors after an apocalyptic war (*Science Fiction Encyclopedia* 66, 291). Benét wished to reach more Americans and realized radio was the way. In those pre-television days, radio had as devoted audiences as TV does now. Benét's poems and stories were read over the air and heard by millions. His good friend, the poet Archibald MacLeish, had written three plays just for radio, and encouraged Benét to do the same. What followed would be the most astonishing output of original works for radio by a literary author ever produced, and more importantly, ever listened to over a four-year period. Benét was a natural writer for radio. As Norman Rosten says in his foreword to the published radio scripts, "Steve Benét had that gather-ye-round quality, and the folks sure did gather when he spoke!" (vii). His mastery of poetry and the short story suited the need for compactness with a singular effect; his reputation as a man of conscience and a patriot who loved his country was exactly right for an America facing the threat of fascism that was already producing killing fields abroad. But, as Rosten points out, writing "[p]ropaganda was nothing new to [Benét]. He was always selling Americans the idea of America" (vi).

Benét wrote tirelessly for the American cause before and during the war and accepted no payment or directed that payment be sent to the USO. Benét's scripts were broadcast over national radio. The first was "We Stand United" (6 November 1940) and its impact was hailed in a front-page story nationwide, and the *New York Times* praised its "Lincoln-like words." His next script was "Listen to the People" broadcast over NBC radio on Independence Day, 4 July 1941. Three days later *Life* magazine published the text. Biographer Fenton notes, "The response was extraordinary. Letters and telegrams came to him [Benét], and to *Life* and

NBC, from every part of the nation: 'Your poems thrilled me,' Arthur Train wrote him, 'It is superb and inspiring and will have a tremendous effect throughout the nation. Congratulations!'" (qtd. in Fenton 364). More scripts followed: "Thanksgiving Day—1941," "A Time to Reap," "They Burned the Books," "A Child is Born," and "Dear Adolf."

Although Rosten, Fenton, and Stroud each refer to the radio scripts as drama and/or plays, only "A Child is Born" can be considered a play in the conventional sense of a work with plot, character, and setting conveyed through dialogue. It presents itself in part as a Christmas pageant; in the prologue Benét even alludes to medieval mystery plays or Corpus Christi plays, as they were also called, that dramatized episodes from both the Old and New testaments of the Bible. As the title suggests, "A Child is Born" retells the story of the Nativity, but it also functions on an allegorical level with King Herod as Hitler, the Innkeeper as those who would appease the enemy, and the Innkeeper's Wife as those who take a stand against occupation forces. Thus the major conflict is between the Innkeeper and his headstrong Wife. He has been ordered to host a party for the Roman prefect and his men, thus creating the "no room at the inn" scenario. When Joseph and Mary knock on the door, the Innkeeper tries to turn them away, as per the prefect's orders, but the Wife offers them shelter in the stable. The Innkeeper relents, but it takes the visitation of the shepherds and the magi to convert him to the ideal of brotherhood, and a moving speech by the Wife to give him the courage to live his life without fear of the occupiers:

> …. Life is not lost by dying! Life is lost
> Minute by minute, day by dragging day,
> In all the thousand, small, uncaring ways,
> The smooth appeasing compromises of time,
> Which are King Herod and King Herod's men,
> Always and always. Life can be
> Lost without vision but not lost by death,
> Lost by not caring, willing, going on
> Beyond the ragged edge of fortitude
> To something more—something no man has ever seen.
> You who love money, you who love yourself,
> You who love bitterness, and I, who loved
> And lost and thought I could not love again,
> And all the people of this little town,
> Rise up! The loves we had were not enough.
> Something is loosed to change the shaken world,
> And with it we must change! [176–77].

The amazing thing about "A Child is Born" is that, unlike the other propaganda pieces he wrote for radio, here Benét does not speak out directly against fascism and accommodation but creates a drama with similar issues of occupation and resistance and leaves it to the audience to see—or, rather, to hear—the connection between the situations of biblical Palestine occupied by the Romans and contemporary Europe occupied by the Nazis.[7]

"Dear Adolf," a series based on actual letters from a farmer, businessman, working man, housewife and mother, soldier, and foreign-born American, also enjoyed immense popularity. Although they do not add up to a play, the letters are, essentially, dramatic monologues all dealing with a historical conflict, which, ironically, brought Benét full circle back to his first book, *Five Men and Pompey.* Here Benét achieves the elegance of fervent conviction expressed simply and directly, such as this excerpt from the Working Man's letter:

> There's no Gestapo pushing us around. We've adjourned the big strikes for the duration. We're doing that freely. We're giving up extras and working overtime. We're doing that freely. We're back of the President and back of the government. And we're sending you a letter twenty million workers long. It's written in steel and flame—in the planes that fly the oceans and the bombs that drop from the planes—in the ships that slide down the ways and the plants that work night and day, day and night. It's written in brains and muscles and skilled hands moving fast on the assembly line—in war bonds and war stamps and the sweat and grind of the shift. It's written in plain American and it's signed "Yours to blow you sky high—American labor!" [38–9].

New York Times writer John K. Hutchens said this about "Dear Adolf" in an article of 5 July 1942:

> Mr. Benét could not have chosen a better time or a greater subject ... and it would seem that some of his colleagues among the first-rank writers might follow his lead—the "names" who wrote so passionately a little while ago, and should not be silent now.... [I]f they have their doubts about [radio's] value as an artistic medium, let them ponder on the success with which Mr. Benét, long established as a poet and short story writer before he turned to radio, adjusted himself to the new field. Not all of them are so well equipped as he, lacking the poet's gift of sharp, exact words and the singing phrase. But they might have a try at it [qtd. in Fenton 370].

Although frail health from a weak heart prevented Benét from active military service, he worked as a soldier of democracy through his words. On 13 March 1943 America's most beloved writer died of a heart attack in his wife Rosemary's arms. He was only forty-four years old. His work remained enormously popular in anthologies throughout the 1950s, and many of his poems and stories were adapted for stage and screen or set to music because of their inherent dramatic qualities.[8] Had he lived into the 1950s, 1960s and 1970s—a normal life span—a postwar Benét could have written in his maturity works that would have superseded his last patriotic writing that came to limit his reputation and obscure his other artistic successes.

As a dramatist Benét is chiefly remembered only for his film and opera versions of "The Devil and Daniel Webster." Yet, from 1940 to 1944, his dramatic writings for radio were listened to by millions of Americans. Stephen Vincent Benét chose to be a patriot at a time when patriotism was a virtue and this may have affected his standing in the academic world in the second half of the twentieth century, but it did not affect the impact of his words. His words remain an artist's words with all the drama and power that were then needed.

In a one-man play, *The American World of Stephen Vincent Benét*, written and performed for Benét's one-hundredth birthday celebration on 24 July 1998, Benét's ghost speaks to the audience and recites from his work. The audience (as well as others for later performances) enthusiastically responded to Benét's words. Cynthia Gordon of the Easton, Pa., *Express Times* wrote of the play on 25 July 1998,

> He read portions of his work, agonizing with people devastated by the Great Depression of the '30s.... In uncanny foresight, "Nightmare at Noon" ... warned of the horror to come of World War II. The high point of his readings was the portion from *John Brown's Body* describing Pickett's Charge in the battle of Gettysburg. [The play] has created a remarkably moving portrait of one of the literary greats of the century. The warm, well-balanced qualities of Benét shone [Region 1].

Ultimately, the audience responded to the life and especially the words of Stephen Vincent Benét, which are as resonant today as when they were first written. Everything he wrote is imbued with dramatic qualities meant to be seen and heard. These recent audiences, knowing little, if anything, about Benét, came to listen without prejudice and left wanting to know more about the man and his work. In 1999, Penguin classics published the first Benét anthology in thirty years: *The Devil and Daniel*

Webster and Other Writings. In time perhaps Benét's reputation will overcome the albatross of being thought only a "patriotic" writer, and he will just be known as a wonderful writer again. Certainly, as a dramatist and innovator in radio, he deserves more recognition.

NOTES

1. Stroud reads this first publication as Benét's attempt to convey through his monologues "a dramatic action that goes beyond anything Browning attempted—perhaps, indeed, too far for the form" (24).
2. Vachel Lindsay died in 1931. In 1935 Wilder based the hero of his novel *Heaven's My Destination* on Lindsay, and in 1936 Benét published his poetic ode to Lindsay, "Do You Remember Springfield?"
3. To our knowledge, the screenplay for *Abraham Lincoln* has never been published; all comments on the film are based on a viewing of the videotape.
4. According to Fenton (350, 359), in 1939 Benét worked on adapting a best-selling novel for the screen, *Miss Bishop*, and sometime in the period 1940-1943 worked on a documentary *Power and the Land*.
5. Technically, *The Headless Horseman* is an *operetta*, the term printed on the cover of the published libretto, which is only 19 pages long.
6. Further evidence of this is in Brom's childish dream of wanting to be a pirate and he and his gang singing a chorus of "Yo ho, yo ho, yo ho" similar to Gilbert and Sullivan's comic pirate chorus.
7. Like some of the other radio scripts, "A Child is Born" was, subsequent to its broadcast, published in a national magazine, in this case the *Saturday Review of Literature*, because of the tremendous positive response to its initial performance.
8. For example, in 1953 actor/director Charles Laughton adapted *John Brown's Body* for the stage where it had a successful Broadway run and a national tour, and in 1954 the popular stage and film musical *Seven Brides for Seven Brothers* was adapted from Benét's short story "The Sobbin' Women."

WORKS CITED

Books

Benét, Stephen Vincent. *Five Men and Pompey.* Boston: Four Seas Press, 1915.
_____. *The Devil and Daniel Webster.* Weston, Vt.: The Countryman Press, 1937; New York: Farrar & Rinehart, 1937; revised as a play, New York: Dramatists Play Service, 1939; revised as a libretto New York: Farrar & Rinehart, 1939.
The Headless Horseman: An Operetta in One Act, libretto by Benét; music by Douglas Moore Boston: Schirmer, 1937.
Nightmare at Noon. New York: Farrar & Rinehart, 1940; revised with nine lines added, New York: Council for Democracy, 1940.
We Stand United. New York: Council for Democracy, 1940.
Tuesday, November 5th, 1940. New York: House of Books, 1941.

Listen to the People, Independence Day, 1941. New York: Council for Democracy, 1941.

They Burned the Books. New York: Farrar & Rinehart, 1942.

Prayer for the United Nations, words by Benét; music by Douglas Moore. New York: The H. W. Gray Co., 1943.

We Stand United and Other Radio Scripts. New York: Farrar & Rinehart, 1945.

Stephen Vincent Benét: The Devil and Daniel Webster and Other Writings. New York: Penguin, 1999.

Motion Pictures

Abraham Lincoln, screenplay by Benét, directed by D. W. Griffith, United Artists, 1930.

Cheers for Miss Bishop, adaptation by Benét from the novel, *Miss Bishop*, by Bess Streeter Aldrich, United Artists, 1940.

All That Money Can Buy, screenplay by Benét and Dan Totheroh from Benét's adaptation of his story "The Devil and Daniel Webster," RKO Pictures, 1941; published in *Twenty Best Film Plays*, edited by John Gassner and Dudley Nichols (New York: Crown, 1943).

Play Productions

Nerves, written with John Farrar, The Comedy Theater, 1 September 1924.

That Awful Mrs. Eaton, written with John Farrar, Morosco Theater, 29 September 1924.

John Brown's Body, adapted and directed by Charles Laughton, The Century Theater, 14 February, 1953.

Operas

The Headless Horseman: An Operetta in One Act, libretto by Benét; music by Douglas Moore, Bronxville High School, 17 March 1937; broadcast on NBC Radio, 22 April 1937.

The Devil and Daniel Webster, libretto by Benét; music by Douglas Moore, under the direction of John Houseman for the American Lyric Theater, Martin Beck Theater, 18 May 1939.

Radio Scripts

We Stand United, read by Raymond Massey on CBS radio at an America United Rally in Carnegie Hall sponsored by the Council for Democracy, 6 November 1940.

The Undefended Border, broadcast on NBC Radio, 18 December 1940.

Listen to the People, broadcast on NBC Radio, 4 July 1941.

Thanksgiving Day—1941, broadcast on NBC Radio, 19 November 1941.

They Burned the Books, broadcast on NBC Radio 11 May 1942.

Dear Adolf, series of six scripts based on original letters written by Americans and broadcast on NBC Radio on successive Sunday afternoons from 21 June 1942 (with the exception of 19 July) to 2 August 1942: "Letter From a Farmer,"

"Letter From a Businessman," "Letter From a Working Man," "Letter From a Housewife and Mother," "Letter From an American Soldier," "Letter From a Foreign-Born American." Music composed by Tom Bennet for the NBC orchestra.

A Child is Born, broadcast on NBC Radio, 21 December 1942, 20 December 1943.

A Time to Reap, broadcast on WABC and CBS Radio, Thanksgiving night, 26 November 1942.

Your Army, a syndicated broadcast on more than six hundred radio stations in thirteen segments on successive Saturday evenings beginning 14 February 1944.

Farrar, John. "For The Record." New York: *Saturday Review of Literature* and Farrar & Rinehart, 1943.

Fenton, Charles. *Stephen Vincent Benét*. New Haven: Yale University Press, 1956.

Houseman, John. *Run-Through*. New York: Simon and Shuster, 1972.

Izzo, David Garrett. *The American World of Stephen Vincent Benét*, a biographical one-man play. Orem, Ut.: Encore Publishing, 1999.

_____. "Thornton Wilder and Vachel Lindsay," in *Thornton Wilder: New Essays*. Edited by Martin Blank, Dalma H. Brunauer, David Garrett Izzo. W. Cornwall, Ct: Locust Hill Press, 1998.

About the Contributors

David Garrett Izzo was a journalist-writer-editor in New York City for many years before becoming an educator in 1985. His books are: *The American World of Stephen Vincent Benét: A One-Man Play; Thornton Wilder: New Essays* (coeditor); *Christopher Isherwood: His Era, His Gang, and the Legacy of the Truly Strong Man; The Writings of Richard Stern: The Education of an Intellectual Everyman; Aldous Huxley & W. H. Auden: On Language; W.H. Auden: A Legacy; Advocates and Activists Between the Wars.* David has published essays on Benét, Wilder, Auden, Isherwood, Huxley, Gerald Heard, Archibald MacLeish, Carl Sandburg, Elinor Wylie, Conrad Aiken, Sara Teasdale, Genevieve Taggard, Zona Gale, Paul Rosenfeld, V. F. Calverton, Scott Nearing, and Lew Sarret.

Lincoln Konkle is a professor at the College of New Jersey where he teaches American drama, modern drama, and creative writing. He has published articles on Thornton Wilder, Edward Albee, Tenessee Williams, William Vaughan Moody, Edward Taylor, J. B. Priestley, and Christine Brooks Rose. Linclon has published stories and poems in various literary magazines. He is currently working on a book about Wilder's plays and novels.

Tom Benét moved to San Francisco in the mid 1950s and retired as the editorial page writer for the *San Francisco Chronicle*. He is now devoted to getting more recognition for his father and mother.

Nancy Bunge is a professor in the Department of American Thought and Language at Michigan State University; the editor and interviewer of *Finding the Words: Conversation with Writers Who Teach*; and the author of the book *Nathaniel Hawthorne: A Study of His Short Fiction*. Bunge has also written on Thornton Wilder and other American dramatists.

Robert Combs is the author of *Vision of the Voyage: Hart Crane and the Psychology of Romanticism* and articles on modern American dramatists including Israel Horovitz, David Mamet, and Wallace Shawn. He is an associate professor at George Washington University.

Gary Grieve-Carlson is a professor at Lebanon Valley College in Pennsylvania who received his Ph.D. from Boston University and has been a Fulbright lecturer in Germany. He teaches courses in grammar, linguistics, and American literature.

Edwin Clark (Toby) Johnson, Ph.D., is author of several nonfiction works about the ideas of Joseph Campbell and several gay-genre novels that demonstrate the *Twilight Zone* style of wisdom writing, including his Lambda Literary Award–winning *Secret Matter*.

Jared Lobdell has a B.A. from Yale (1961) where he spent many hours at the Elizabethan Club. One of his class fellows was the nephew of Thornton Wilder, Benét's Yale classmate and friend. He later received a Ph.D. from Carnegie-Mellon. He is the author of *England and Always*, and the editor of *A Tolkien Compass*.

Patricia McAndrew was born and raised in Bethlehem, Pennsylvania (Benét's birthplace), where she graduated with honors in history from Moravian College. A Fulbright-Hays fellowship to Denmark (1968) led to the publication of *My Theatre Life*, her highly acclaimed translation of the three-volume autobiography of nineteenth century Danish ballet master August Bournonville. She has written and lectured extensively on Bournonville and his world, and serves on the advisory board of the scholarly journal *Dance Chronicle*. In 1997, McAndrew was cofounder of the Stephen Vincent Benét Centennial Committee, for which she wrote an award-winning television documentary, *Out of American Earth: The Story of Stephen Vincent Benét*. She has also served as president of the S. V. Benét Society, and is currently working on a biography of the poet, and on several projects dealing with the American Civil War.

Laura Shea has a B.A. from Barnard College and a Ph.D. from Boston University. She is an associate professor of English at Iona College and specializes in drama. Her essays and reviews have appeared in the *Eugene O'Neill Review, Theatre Journal, Theatre Annual,* and the *Comparatist*.

Stephen Vincent Benét
Bibliography

BOOKS

Five Men and Pompey (Boston: Four Seas Press, 1915).

The Drug Shop, or, Endymion in Edmonstoun (New Haven: privately printed, 1917).

Young Adventure (New Haven: Yale University Press, 1918).

Heavens and Earth (New York: Henry Holt and Company, 1920).

The Beginning of Wisdom (New York: Henry Holt and Company, 1921).

Young People's Pride (New York: Henry Holt and Company, 1922).

The Ballad of William Sycamore (New York: The Brick Row Book Shop, 1923); with music by Halsey Stevens (New York: Highgate Press, 1961); with music by Douglas Moore (New York: King's Crown Music Press, 1974).

Jean Huguenot (New York: Henry Holt and Company, 1923).

King David (New York: Henry Holt and Company, 1923).

Tiger Joy (New York: George H. Doran, 1925).

The Bat, anonymous, a novel adapted from the stage play by Mary Roberts Rinehart (New York: George H. Doran, 1925).

Spanish Bayonet (New York: George H. Doran, 1926).

John Brown's Body (Garden City, N.Y.: Doubleday Doran, 1928; London: William Heinemann Ltd., 1928); with drawings by James Daugherty (New York: Doubleday Doran, 1930); edited and annotated by Mabel A. Bessey (New York: Farrar & Rinehart, 1941); with an introduction by Douglas Southall Freeman, illus. by John Steuart Curry (New York: Limited Editions Club, 1948); as sound recording adapted and directed by Charles Laughton, music and effects by Walter Shumann (New York: Columbia Records, 1953); with illustrations by Fritz Kredel and Warren Chappell (New York: Rinehart, 1954); as staged at the Yale Drama School and Off-Broadway under the direction of Curtis Canfield (New York: Dramatists

Play Service, 1961); with an introduction and notes by Jack L. Kapps and Robert Kemble (New York: Holt, Rinehart and Winston, 1968); with an introduction by Archibald MacLeish, drawings by Barry Moser (New York: Book-of-the-Month Club, 1980).

The Barefoot Saint (Garden City, N.Y.: Doubleday Doran, 1929).

The Litter of the Rose Leaves (New York: Random House, 1930).

Ballads and Poems: 1915–1930 (Garden City, N.Y.: Doubleday Doran, 1930).

A Book of Americans with Rosemary Benét (New York: Farrar & Rinehart, 1933); *Sing a Song of Americans: Fifteen Songs from a Book of Americans*; set to music by Arnold Shaw (New York: Musette Publishers, 1941); as cantata with music by Leo Snyder (New York: Leeds Music, 1962).

James Shore's Daughter (Garden City, N.Y.: Doubleday Doran, 1934).

Burning City (New York: Farrar & Rinehart, 1936).

The Magic of Poetry and the Poet's Art (Chicago: F. E. Compton & Company, 1936); reprinted from the Nineteenth Edition of Compton's Pictured Encyclopedia, 1936, for the Fifty-seventh Conference of the American Library Association, Richmond, Virginia, 11–16 May 1936.

Thirteen O'Clock (New York: Farrar & Rinehart, 1937).

The Devil and Daniel Webster (Weston, Vt.: The Countryman Press, 1937; New York: Farrar & Rinehart, 1937); revised as a play (New York: Dramatists Play Service, 1939); revised as a libretto (New York: Farrar & Rinehart, 1939).

The Headless Horseman: An Operetta in One Act, libretto by Benét; music by Douglas Moore (Boston: Schirmer, 1937).

Johnny Pie and the Fool Killer (New York: Farrar & Rinehart, 1938).

Sherlockiana: My Favorite Fiction Character (Ysalta, Texas: E. B. Hill, 1938).

Adam Was My Grandfather, words by Benét; music by Douglas Moore (New York: Galaxy Music Corporation, 1938).

Tales Before Midnight (New York: Farrar & Rinehart, 1939).

The Ballad of the Duke's Mercy (New York: House of Books, 1939).

Nightmare at Noon (New York: Farrar & Rinehart, 1940); revised with nine lines added (New York: Council for Democracy, 1940).

Daniel Drew, words by Benét; music by Gail T. Kubik (New York: Arrow Press Music, 1940).

A Summons to the Free (New York: Farrar & Rinehart; London: Oxford University Press, 1940).

We Stand United (New York: Council for Democracy, 1940).

Tuesday, November 5th, 1940 (New York: House of Books, 1941).

Listen to the People, Independence Day, 1941 (New York: Council for Democracy, 1941).

They Burned the Books (New York: Farrar & Rinehart, 1942).

Selected Works of Stephen Vincent Benét, 2 volumes (New York: Farrar & Rinehart, 1942).

American Muse, words by Benét; music by Henry Cowell (New York: Music Press, 1943).

Prayer for the United Nations, words by Benét; music by Douglas Moore (New York: The H. W. Gray Co., 1943).

Western Star (New York: Farrar & Rinehart, 1943).

America (New York: Farrar & Rinehart, 1944; London: Heinemann, 1945).

We Stand United and Other Radio Scripts (New York: Farrar & Rinehart, 1945).

The Last Circle (New York: Farrar & Rinehart, 1946).

The Stephen Vincent Benét Pocket Book (New York: Pocket Books, Inc., 1946).

From the Earth to the Moon, screenplay (New Haven: privately printed, 1958).

Christopher Columbus, choral profile, mixed chorus with piano, words by Benét, music by Gail T. Kubik (New York: Ricordi, 1960).

Stephen Vincent Benét on Writing, a Great Writer's Letters of Advice to a Young Beginner (Brattleboro, Vt.: S. Greene Press, 1964).

The Bishop's Beggar (Flemington, N.J.: St. Teresa's Press, 1968).

By the Waters of Babylon (Mankato, Minn.: Creative Education, 1990).

Stephen Vincent Benét: The Devil and Daniel Webster and Other Writings (New York: Penguin, 1999).

MOTION PICTURES

Abraham Lincoln, screenplay by Benét, directed by D. W. Griffith, United Artists, 1930.

Cheers for Miss Bishop, adaptation by Benét from the novel *Miss Bishop* by Bess Streeter Aldrich, United Artists, 1940.

All That Money Can Buy, screenplay by Benét and Dan Totheroh from Benét's adaptation of his story "The Devil and Daniel Webster," RKO Pictures, 1941; published in *Twenty Best Film Plays*, edited by John Gassner and Dudley Nichols (New York: Crown, 1943).

PLAY PRODUCTIONS

Nerves, written with John Farrar, The Comedy Theater, 1 September 1924.

That Awful Mrs. Eaton, written with John Farrar, Morosco Theater, 29 September 1924.

John Brown's Body, adapted and directd by Charles Laughton, The Century Theater, 14 February 1953.

OPERAS

The Headless Horseman: An Operetta in One Act, libretto by Benét; music by Douglas Moore, Bronxville High School, 17 March 1937; broadcast on NBC Radio, 22 April 1937.

The Devil and Daniel Webster, libretto by Benét; music by Douglas Moore; under the direction of John Houseman for the American Lyric Theater, Martin Beck Theater, 18 May 1939.

RADIO SCRIPTS

We Stand United, read by Raymond Massey on CBS radio at an America United Rally in Carnegie Hall sponsored by the Council for Democracy, 6 November 1940.

The Undefended Border, broadcast on NBC Radio, 18 December 1940.

Listen to the People, broadcast on NBC Radio, 4 July 1941.

Thanksgiving Day—1941, broadcast on NBC Radio, 19 November 1941.

They Burned the Books, broadcast on NBC Radio, 11 May 1942.

Dear Adolf, series of six scripts based on original letters written by Americans and broadcast on NBC Radio on successive Sunday afternoons from 21 June 1942 (with the exception of 19 July) to 2 August 1942: "Letter From a Farmer," "Letter From a Businessman," "Letter From a Working Man," "Letter From a Housewife and Mother," "Letter From an American Soldier," "Letter From a Foreign-Born American." Music composed by Tom Bennet for the NBC orchestra.

A Child is Born, broadcast on NBC Radio, 21 December 1942, 20 December 1943.

A Time to Reap, broadcast on WABC and CBS Radio, Thanksgiving night, 26 November 1942.

Your Army, a syndicated broadcast on more than six hundred radio stations in thirteen segments on successive Saturday evenings beginning 14 February 1944.

OTHER

The Yale Book of Student Verse, 1910–1919, edited by Benét, John Andrews, John C. Farrar, Pierson Underwood, with fourteen poems by Benét (New Haven: Yale University Press, 1919).

Christopher Marlowe, *Tamburlaine the Great*, acting version prepared under the direction of Benét and Edgar Montillion Woolley (New Haven: Yale University Press, 1919).

The History of the Class of 1919, essay by Benét (New Haven: Yale University Press, 1919).

The Yale Record Book of Verse, seven poems by Benét (New Haven: Yale University Press, 1922).

The Collected Prose of Elinor Wylie, introduction by Benét to the novel *The Orphan Angel* (New York: Knopf, 1933).

Shirley Barker, *The Dark Hills Under*, foreword by Benét (New Haven: Yale University Press, 1933).

William Rose Benét, editor, *Fifty Poets*, "The Hider's Song" (New York: Duffield & Green, 1934).

Burton Rascoe and Groff Conklin, editors, *The Smart Set Anthology*, "Summer Thunder" (New York: Reynal & Hitchcock, 1934).

Muriel Rukeyser, *Theory of Flight*, foreward by Benét (New Haven: Yale University Press, 1935).

Edward Weismuller, *The Deer Come Down*, foreword by Benét (New Haven: Yale University Press, 1936).

The Yale Literary Magazine: Centennial Number, special hardcover edition, "Ode to the Austrian Socialists" (New York: Coward-McCann, 1936).

Margaret Haley, *The Gardener Mind*, foreword by Benét (New Haven: Yale University Press, 1937).

Robert Nathan, *The Barley Fields*, introduction by Benét (New York: Knopf, 1938).

Joy Davidman, *Letter to a Comrade*, foreward by Benét (New Haven: Yale University Press, 1938).

R. Denny, *The Connecticut River and Other Poems*, foreward by Benét (New Haven: Yale University Press, 1939).

Norman Rosten, *Return Again Traveler*, foreward by Benét (New Haven: Yale University Press, 1940).

Jeremy Ingalls, *The Metaphysical Sword*, forward by Benét (New Haven: Yale University Press, 1941).

Margaret Walker, *For My People*, forward by Benét (New Haven: Yale University Press, 1942).

LETTERS

Selected Letters of Stephen Vincent Benét, edited by Charles Fenton (New Haven: Yale University Press, 1960).

BIBLIOGRAPHY

Gladys Louise Maddocks, "Stephen Vincent Benét: A Bibliography," *Bulletin of Bibliography and Dramatic Index* (September, 1951; April 1952) Part I, pp. 142–46; Part II, 158–60.

BIOGRAPHIES

Charles Fenton, *Stephen Vincent Benét* (New Haven: Yale University Press, 1956).

David Garrett Izzo, *The American World of Stephen Vincent Benét*, a biographical one-man play (Orem, Ut.: Encore Publishing, 1999).

REFERENCES

Bacon, Leonard. *Semi-Centennial* (New York: Harper & Brothers, 1939).

Benét, William Rose. *The Dust Which Is God* (New York: Dodd, Mead & Company, 1941) a Pulitzer Prize–winning autobiography in verse.

_____. "My Brother Steve" (New York: *Saturday Review of Literature* and Farrar & Rinehart, 1943).

Davenport, Basil. introduction, *Stephen Vincent Benét: Selected Poetry and Prose*, Volume I (New York: Farrar & Rinehart, 1942).

Farrar, John. "For The Record" (New York: *Saturday Review of Literature* and Farrar & Rinehart, 1943).

Houseman, John. *Run-Through* (New York: Simon and Shuster, 1972).

Izzo, David Garrett. "Thornton Wilder and Vachel Lindsay," in *Thornton Wilder: New Essays*. Edited by Martin Blank, Dalma H. Brunauer, David Garrett Izzo (W. Cornwall, Ct: Locust Hill Press, 1998).

Ludington, Townsend. Introduction, *Stephen Vincent Benét: The Devil and Daniel Webster and Other Writings* (New York: Penguin, 1999).

Olson, Stanley. *Elinor Wylie: A Biography* (New York: The Dial Press-James Wade, 1979).

Rosten, Norman. Foreword, *We Stand United and Other Radio Scripts* by Stephen Vincent Benét (New York: Farrar & Rinehart, 1945).

Stroud, Parry. *Stephen Vincent Benét* (New York: Twayne, 1962).

Van Gelder, Robert. Introduction, *The Stephen Vincent Benét Pocket Book* (New York: Pocket Books, 1946).

PAPERS

The Beinecke Library, Yale University, New Haven, Ct.

Index